What Your Colleagues

"If you care for kids in any capacity, pick up th... ...now. It's innovative, humane, solution oriented, and both powerful and incredibly practical."

Anya Kamenetz
Author of *The Stolen Year*

"*Whole Child, Whole Life* is a book that speaks to the 'wholeness' not just of children, but to those of us who love, care for, and educate them. Practical strategies, interwoven with moving personal narratives, make this a must-read for anyone looking to expand their compassion, competency, and knowledge about what it takes to positively impact a future generation."

Gina Warner
CEO, National Afterschool Association

"Momentum for expanding social, emotional, mental, and physical health and development has grown to an all-time high across the country. No one can argue that this is one of the most critical fields in public education. *Whole Child, Whole Life* is an excellent 'go-to' resource for school districts that are committed to creating and sustaining social emotional learning programs as part of their strategic plans on behalf of the students who are learning and growing in their communities."

Daniel A. Domenech
Executive Director, AASA, The School Superintendents Association

"*Whole Child, Whole Life* is a vivid and thoughtful recipe for adults interested in supporting children to realize their potential and achieve success. Krauss boldly describes the ways and means people and systems can utilize to personalize child development, meet children where they are and give them what they need to flourish, to become both resilient and accomplished. This is an incredibly useful manual for caring adults who want to help our children thrive in these challenging times."

Paul Reville
Professor, Harvard Graduate School of Education and Founding Director, EdRedesign
former Massachusetts Secretary of Education

WHOLE CHILD, WHOLE LIFE

WHOLE CHILD, WHOLE LIFE

10 WAYS TO HELP KIDS LIVE, LEARN, & THRIVE

STEPHANIE MALIA KRAUSS

ILLUSTRATIONS BY
MANUEL S. HERRERA

FOR INFORMATION:

Corwin

A SAGE Company

2455 Teller Road

Thousand Oaks, California 91320

(800) 233-9936

www.corwin.com

SAGE Publications Ltd.

1 Oliver's Yard

55 City Road

London EC1Y 1SP

United Kingdom

SAGE Publications India Pvt. Ltd.

Unit No 323-333, Third Floor, F-Block

International Trade Tower Nehru Place

New Delhi 110 019

India

SAGE Publications Asia-Pacific Pte. Ltd.

18 Cross Street #10-10/11/12

China Square Central

Singapore 048423

President: Mike Soules

Vice President and
  Editorial Director: Monica Eckman

Publisher: Jessica Allan

Content Development
  Editor: Mia Rodriguez

Editorial Assistant: Natalie Delpino

Editorial Intern: Lex Nunez

Production Editor: Tori Mirsadjadi

Copy Editor: Tammy Giesmann

Typesetter: C&M Digitals (P) Ltd.

Proofreader: Barbara Coster

Cover Designer: Gail Buschman

Marketing Manager: Olivia Bartlett

Printed in Canada

Paperback ISBN 978-1-0718-8442-3

This book is printed on acid-free paper.

MIX
Paper from
responsible sources
FSC® C103567

23 24 25 26 27 10 9 8 7 6 5 4 3 2 1

Contents

Visit
wholechildwholelife.com
for downloadable resources.

List of Tables and Figures

Tables

Preface

Written by Justice Hi'ilani Krauss (age 11) with contributions from Harrison Drew Koali'i Krauss (age 9)

JUSTICE AND KOA

Hi. My name is Justice Krauss and I'm a sixth-grade student. Most people would start a preface by talking about how long they've known the author of the book, but I've known Stephanie my entire life. Literally. She's my mom.

I've also known this world my entire life. I was born into it! This world is different from the one most adults grew up in. Kids have to deal with school shootings, a huge mental health crisis, changing weather like snow in Texas, and tons of war. And that's our normal! We need people who understand that. We need people who respect what we're going through. People who listen to kids and take us seriously. We have ideas and dreams, and we deserve to be heard and respected as much as adults.

The people in my life who have understood this the most are caring, want to know what I have to say, and they share my belief that things are hard and we can make them better. These people want me to feel great and be great.

One of the biggest examples of this is my former teacher, Mrs. Dawson, who I had for third and fifth grade (yes, she was my teacher twice). Mrs. Dawson is the type of teacher every kid should be able to have. She made me want to go to school, feel welcome, and like I belonged. With her, I knew I mattered, and I was wanted. Because of who she was and how she treated me, I became a better student and person.

Then there's Coach Mike, my counselor. He pulled me out of an emotional ditch, which you'll learn about in the chapter on the brain and body. He is someone I can talk to and trust to help me when I'm having a hard time with OCD, or with life in general.

I also have a church community. They've always been there for me, even when I didn't want to go to services. Now I look forward to going because they are like my family. I know they love me and I know they will be there for me no matter what.

Lastly, there's my mom. She's someone I can trust with anything because I know she won't judge me. If I have something on my mind, I go to her first. She makes sure I am healthy, happy, and safe. I know she loves and supports me always. She is the one who wrote this book, and she really does practice what she preaches.

Every night before we go to sleep, this is the prayer my mom prays over me and my brother:

> May the Lord bless you and keep you safe from all harm.
>
> May He cause His face to shine upon you.
>
> Blessing your physical development, spiritual development, emotional development, and cognitive development.

May He wake you up safe and sound, full of joy and good
health in the morning.

Amen.

I know this prayer is actually her promise. She's said it every night since
I was born. When I hear her pray, I also hear her saying she will do
whatever she can to make my life a good one.

I'm positive that it's hard to be a grown-up right now. The world is
weird for all of us, not just kids. I hope you can be a person who helps
everybody be well, and I hope you have people in your life who can help
you be your best self too.

My mom thought that a book about kids and what they need should
start with the perspective of a child. So you got me. Enjoy the book, and
please do what my mom suggests.

To the adults who love my kids—their teachers, coaches, counselors, faith leaders, neighbors, family, and friends. Every day you bring the principles and practices of this book to life. Thank you for everything.

—*Stephanie Malia Krauss*

To my two sons, Gray and Hudson. Thank you for always being true to who you are and accepting to those around you. You each inspire me to continue being my true self and to be empathetic toward others. I love you both.

—*Manuel S. Herrera*

Introduction

This is a challenging time to be young. Kids are growing up amid pandemics and other health scares, economic crises, extreme weather, divided politics, violence, extremism, and more. Global problems are personal and proximate. Fear for the future and worry for the present is palpable. Young people must keep living and learning during historic firsts at times when we are struggling to cope ourselves.

During this time, we continue to teach, coach, counsel, and care for kids. We try our best to protect their childhoods—to do whatever it takes for them to go to school, do sports, play music, create art, hang with friends, fall in and out of love, and become good humans.

The hope of this book is to help you in that work. This book is for people like me who care for and about children, from little ones to teens, across learning and life. Maybe you do this for free, out of love or obligation. Maybe you get paid. Perhaps both.

Think of this as an education book for more than educators and a youth development book for more than youth workers. It's a book that a whole team or an entire community can read and discuss together. Too often, I walk into a bookstore and go to the parenting section for a resource on substance abuse or spiritual development and to the education section for books about learning styles and disabilities. At conferences, professionals are separated by sessions and tracks. If I want to learn about mental health, I go to a session for counselors, but if I need help with social emotional learning, I attend one for teachers.

Then I look at my kids and their everyday experiences. For them, these distinctions are arbitrary. My older son relies on the collective support of his family, teachers, therapist, pediatrician, church leaders, coaches, and camp counselors. My younger son learns and grows during his 4 hours of afterschool programming, like he does during 6 hours at school. His teacher is also his YMCA summer camp director, and the teacher down the hall was his soccer coach. We should all be cross-trained in ways we can support the boys' health, learning, and development.

Reflecting this reality, I have written *Whole Child, Whole Life* with kids at the center, making sure that it is relevant for any adult who cares for them. The following chapters connect us with the questions and concerns we share: Will the kids be ok? What do they need? What can I do?

The genesis of this book is a long time coming. It braids together what I've learned as an educator, social worker, and parent. It has roots in my childhood with moments of feeling unknown and unable to imagine a life beyond the one I felt trapped in. It took the deep investment of a mighty group of adults to set me on a (very unconventional) course for the life I have today.

My childhood taught me that feeling *whole* and *well* were states of being I had to work for. At the same time, there were people and environments where that was easy, even effortless. These were the places where and people with whom I was safe, supported, and knew I belonged. Like magic, they could bring me to life and inspire me to learn no matter what else was going on.

I'm a lifelong student of that art, science, and mystery—what I think of as the *alchemy* of working with children. For years, I pursued and practiced it on the frontlines with kids. Then, when my kids were little, I left my work in schools and tried to implement it in policy, philanthropy, and program design. As I moved farther from the frontlines, my own children were getting older and starting school. As I worked to make education more student centered and policies more child friendly, I was also raising two very different humans in troubling times.

When the first terrifying wave of COVID-19 shut down society, my household—like so many others—suddenly became a homeschool. I was finishing my first book on what kids need to "make it" in the future. During my pandemic-forced book tour from my basement, I did virtual speaking engagements with educators and counselors across the United States. Every time, I saw my own fears reflected in their pixelated faces. When I would finish speaking, someone would ask a version of the same question: "Now that we know what kids need to be ready, can you tell us what they need to be well?"

I felt that question in my bones. As a mom, I would doomscroll the news and panic about what life would be like for my kids. I was desperate for practices to help them thrive now (well-being) and in the future (well-becoming). I needed these practices to be durable and able to weather whatever the world would throw at us next.

I started looking for a book with all that information in one place, knowing that if I found it, I would read it and give it to every adult spending time with my kids. All of us were doing our best, but most of us felt like we were missing the mark.

I couldn't find the book, so I wrote it. I reached out to more than 50 scholars and experts, asking if they would contribute their stories and wisdom. I dug into research and trends on learning, human development, resilience, thriving, longevity, mental health, and more.

I wrote as fast as I could because while I wrote, a youth mental health crisis went from a slow heat to a rolling boil. Before finishing the first chapter, America's pediatricians and the U.S. Surgeon General declared youth mental health a crisis of epidemic proportions.[1] My interviews backed that up. In 2022, I spoke to dozens of parents and mental health professionals who each expressed alarm. More kids were depressed, anxious, and suicidal. Emergency rooms were full and kids in crisis were being turned away. Child psychiatrists were refusing health insurance, and waiting lists were years long. There weren't enough therapists to meet demands. Educators saw it too. Problem behaviors in class were on the rise and students were struggling more intensely and frequently than before—quicker to anger, act out, or withdraw. Teachers couldn't tell what was due to the pandemic and what was a more serious problem.

This book attends to these mental health and behavioral concerns by focusing on prevention, protection, and preparation. I hope I've addressed many of your concerns, because this is information I have needed personally, as a parent and youth advocate.

Whole Child, Whole Life aims to be both timely and timeless. It's full of principles and practices that have always been good for kids but are urgently needed now. The book is organized to be read cover-to-cover or as a guidebook where you can focus on one chapter at a time. Many of the tables and figures utilize concepts from researchers, and I recommend checking out the original source materials, found in the endnotes. These studies and reports take on a level of depth and detail that isn't covered here.

This is a book about wholeness, which means it covers a lot of ground. In Part I, we learn who kids are, from the profiles of what they look like and where they live to the parts of their personality that bring them into high definition. In Part II, we explore the 10 practices to help kids thrive. These chapters take on what can help or hurt kids, grounding you in science, story, and strategies. Part III explores what thriving looks like in real time.

In writing this book, I have seen how the same practices that are good for kids are good for adults. To that end, I hope this book will be supportive to your own well-being. As you read, be open to what this means for you, and remember it's all connected. Young people will be better if the adults in their lives are taking care of themselves.

At the end of every chapter in Part I there are key takeaways and reflection questions you can use individually or in a group. The 10 whole life practices in Part II include "Try Now" sections with tips and tools to use right away. Many of these were suggested by field leaders, and as a result, I have found myself not only writing this book, but using these techniques with my own children.

If you are an expert in a particular practice, you might feel like my treatment is too light. Where experts get narrow, this book is intended to be expansive, offering a comprehensive look at what kids will experience and how we can support them. I have deliberately left out words and acronyms that might be confusing, divisive, or only meaningful for some professions. Kids' lives are at stake, and we don't have time to get caught up in jargon. As you'll see in the acknowledgments, a bunch of scholars generously reviewed some of the more complex concepts and trickier topics to make sure the language was accessible and actionable while remaining factual.

This is a book about the relationships we have with kids in the systems and settings where they spend time. It is not a book about how to make those systems work better for kids or how to get rid of systems that cause harm. Systems change can extend and enhance well-being and thriving beyond what happens in a single setting or with one person. It is a charge we must take on together. This book, however, attends to the immediate and interactional work we take on individually.

As you read, I hope you will highlight, dog-ear, and take notes in the margins. My favorite books have stains, folds, and annotations. Use Manuel's illustrations to remember and synthesize key points. As you'll read in "About the Illustrations," the three characters who journey with us across the book—Kai, Riley, and Marcos—were developed by Manuel and me, using the concepts from the chapters.

May this book provide you with whatever you need to bring your best self into the spaces and relationships you share with children. Today's young people are wonderfully wired and growing up in complicated times. They need us to put these practices into play every day so they can live their best lives.

About the Illustrations

KAI   RILEY   MARCOS

This book is a collaborative effort between the author, Stephanie Malia Krauss, and internationally recognized illustrator, Manuel S. Herrera. Together, Stephanie and Manuel used the *Whole Child, Whole Life* framework—the five parts of a whole child portrait, 10 whole life practices, and five dimensions of wholeness/thriving—to develop the stories of three fictional characters, Kai, Riley, and Marcos.

Throughout the chapters, illustrations of the kids are used to visualize key concepts. Illustrations at the beginning of each chapter serve as a visual summary, while figures illustrate specific concepts. At the end, Manuel—a renowned sketchnote artist—has provided a two-page spread of the entire *Whole Child, Whole Life* framework.

Kai, Riley, and Marcos are fictional kids from different backgrounds and life stages. They are meant to remind readers that thriving shoud be possible for any child, anywhere.

PART I

Whole Child Portrait

Demographics and Determinants 1

When I was in elementary school I lived with both parents. In middle school, it was just my mom. By freshman year, I was "couch surfing," moving between my parents' houses and various friends.

At 14, I was in a treatment program for eating disorders at our local hospital, and by 15, I had left New Jersey for a drug and alcohol rehab center in Florida. Growing up, I lived in a cash-strapped household in a wealthy town. Everyone knew our family. This was often a point of pride and sometimes a cause for embarrassment. As a kid, I thought we were poor but now I know better.

I look white but I am Native Hawaiian and Jewish. I am strongly rooted in both cultural identities, even though I don't look like either. My fair skin and little nose mean I avoid the disparaging remarks and treatment some family members experience.

Malia is my Hawaiian middle name, which I always use, and Kilstein is the Jewish maiden name I had until I married. My names never cost me a job, housing loan, or the chance to get accepted into a school I applied for. If anything, they have distinguished me enough for employers to consider me a "diversity" hire and colleges to offer me a scholarship.

I grew up speaking English. My family sprinkles it with Hawaiian at home, but we can easily stop in public. Most of the people in school, at work, and out in the community speak the same language I do. I don't have a different accent from my neighbors, and as my brothers would say, we sound like the people on TV.

I'm straight. I was born a girl and have known that was my gender ever since. I dated boys and eventually married one. I've never been conflicted about which bathroom to use or worried about how people will look at me in the one I choose.

I have excellent hearing and terrible eyesight. This requires that I always wear contact lenses or glasses, with emergency pairs stashed in my house, car, and bags. I move easily and don't require extra assistance or accommodations to get around.

All of this gives you a basic picture of my life, but it doesn't tell you who I am. It gives you insights into how I grew up, what categories I fit in, and how the world sees me. It doesn't tell you what I am good at, what I like, and what makes me, me. You might sense challenges (there were plenty) and privilege (also plenty). Though this listing of personal details is limited, these pieces of my background have had an outsized impact on my life.

In our work with children, the first picture we have of them is like this one, rudimentary and flawed. This is because we profile them. It is our unavoidable starting point.

This starter profile is a crude outline of a young person. It is drawn from data found on rosters and registration forms—age, race, disability, medications, health history, primary contact, and who not to contact. It is informed by what others tell you or you tell yourself. Perhaps a child's former teacher told you what to expect. Maybe you know the family, or the neighborhood where the family lives.

Profiles are drawn with data and colored by assumptions, personal biases, and other people's stories. We fill in blank spaces with speculations that come from not knowing as well as past experience. We assign details, deciding who kids are, and what their lives must be like. Profiles shape, texture, and limit how we see and understand children. Profiles are inescapable and incomplete.

Profile Parts

Profiles are the outlines or silhouettes of kids, based on whatever available, observable, and reportable data we have. They are constructed from different combinations of demographics and determinants, unique to every child. **Demographics** are personal characterizations and population-level categories such as race and gender. Demographics tell us the types of advantage kids have in school, other systems, and society. **Determinants** are the social, environmental, political, and historical conditions kids are born with and grow up in, including whether they have access to good healthcare and schools and how safe it is at home and in the neighborhood. Determinants give us a sense of young people's protections and vulnerabilities.

Less Societal Advantage	DEMOGRAPHICS personal characteristics and categories	More Societal Advantage
−	←——————————→	+
Fewer Protections and More Vulnerabilities	DETERMINANTS social, environmental, political, and historical living conditions	More Protections and Fewer Vulnerabilities

Table 1   Demographic and Determinant Profiles

Every child's profile is made up of their personal demographics and life determinants (see Table 1). As a kid, I was a white-passing female, who was straight, mostly healthy, low income, with divorced parents, who lived in a safe neighborhood. While I didn't live in poverty, I did experience economic inequality.[1] I am Hawaiian and Jewish, and while I didn't experience the marginalization of being brown, I did inherit historic trauma and political determinants that increase my risks of certain health issues and addiction.

Viewed together, my unique profile reveals the advantages and disadvantages I had and the protections and vulnerabilities I experienced. Some of my profile parts changed over time, but most stayed the same.

Profiles place kids at different starting points in life and learning. These pictures reveal the incredible influence and impacts of biology, background, and personal circumstances.

Demographics

Consider a census survey or school district report card. Demographics are the population-level data these surveys collect. Some demographics are observable, and others are self-reported. Common demographics include race and ethnicity, age, gender and sexual identity, income level, disability status, citizenship and immigration status, and how many people live in the home. Less common but still important are spoken languages and religious and/or cultural practices.

Demographics tell us how much societal advantage—sometimes called privilege—a young person has. Privileged groups hold more institutional and societal power. Life and learning are hardest for kids who belong to demographic groups with the least advantage because schools, systems, and society rarely prioritize their needs.

Table 2 shows a partial breakdown of demographics, so we can see which demographics hold more advantage. It's imperfect because there is a lot of variation within groups. For instance, kids can be wealthy but not as wealthy as others. They can be heterosexual but discriminated against because they are seen as too effeminate or masculine. A child can have a mild or less visible cognitive or physical difference, or several that are severe. Between races and genders, there are groups who have experienced more suffering and violence, even compared to those who also experience marginalization.

Table 2   Demographics and Relative Advantage

DEMOGRAPHICS personal characteristics and categorizations		
Less Societal Advantage (−)	⟷	More Societal Advantage (+)
Poor	SOCIOECONOMIC STATUS	Wealthy
Black, Indigenous, People of Color	RACE	White/Caucasian
Gender-Diverse or Transgender	GENDER	Cisgender
LGBTQ+	SEXUALITY	Heterosexual
Living with a disability, physical or cognitive difference(s)	DISABILITY + DIFFERENCES	No disability, physical or cognitive difference(s)
Undocumented, Immigrant, Evacuee	CITIZENSHIP + IMMIGRATION STATUS	U.S. Citizen

The less societal advantage a kid has, the more likely they are to suffer from structural and societal harm, as well as individual maltreatment. This can include harassment, discrimination, exclusion, persecution, and violence. Levels of marginalization are not equally distributed across places and people. They can be worse in certain parts of the country and at different times in history. Demographics are loaded with biases and judgments, some of which we know we have, and others that we might be unaware of.

Determinants[2]

While demographics characterize and categorize who kids are, determinants give us a sense of how they live. Determinants tell us about a child's home and community life, schools, and the bigger historic and global context they are growing up in. This part of their profile reveals the types of resources and opportunities they have, as well as how safe and stable their lives are.

Table 3 is another imperfect but helpful picture, this time showing different determinants kids grow up with. Determinants are the observable and reportable conditions that largely determine the life, health, and learning young people have available to them.

Table 3 Determinants and Relative Protection and Vulnerability		
DETERMINANTS **living and learning conditions**		
(−) Fewer Protections and more vulnerability	←——————→	(+) More Protections and less vulnerability
Poor air and water quality. Climate and extreme weather vulnerability.	ENVIRONMENTAL	Healthy air, drinkable water, climate and weather resilient home and community
Lacks access to critical opportunities and resources, including quality healthcare, schooling, basic services, and/or food. Lives in a house and/or community that is unsafe and/or violent.	SOCIAL	Ample access to opportunities and resources that support healthy development and learning. Lives in a house and/or community that is safe and free from violence.
Lives in a politically dangerous and divided place and/or time.	POLITICAL	Lives in a place and/or time when politics are either positive or don't harm families or children's learning and development.
Growing up in a time and context when opportunities, resources, safety, and stability are limited, lacking, and/or actively decreasing.	HISTORICAL	Growing up in a time and context when opportunities, resources, safety, and stability are present, available, and/or increasing.

Determinants are more changeable than demographics. It's possible you've seen this in your own life. When I moved and changed who I was living with, my social determinants shifted. Similarly, the political and environmental conditions of my life have adjusted across time and locations. Other determinants are historic and fixed. For example, I can't change who my biological family is or my ethnic and cultural history.

Profiles Show Cumulative Challenges

Kids don't have just one determinant or demographic. It's their full set that gives us a picture of how easy or hard their lives are now and may be in the future. Profiling is largely harmful, but profiles can be helpful. We can better serve and support kids when we are clearheaded about the risks and realities they face.

Sometimes young people have cumulative disadvantages and marginalization, which means they are burdened by multiple demographics and determinants that bring disadvantage and vulnerability, including high levels of stress and trauma.[3]

Consider a Black child who recently immigrated to the United States who has a severe learning disability, limited English, and lives in poverty with his single parent. Because of his family's financial and transportation situations, he can't get the healthcare he needs. His language and learning needs are unmet because his neighborhood school is underfunded and short-staffed. As a young Black immigrant with special needs, he faces heightened risks. He's among the most likely to be suspended, expelled, arrested,[4] and to spend time in jail or prison.

Many children experience **cumulative disadvantage** and **marginalization**. They are born and live with characteristics and conditions that elevate their risks of hardship, harm, and adversity. The more accumulation, the deeper the disparities, and the greater detriment to life, learning, and life expectancy. There are many reasons why, and all require more time and study than this book provides. Historic policies of exclusion, suppression, and oppression are often to blame. Disadvantage begets disadvantage. Cumulative disadvantage and marginalization were best described by author and reporter Jonathan Kozol as producing "savage inequalities."

Here are four examples, from many more:

- Kids of color and native youth have higher levels of chronic inflammation and health problems. They experience unequal treatment by healthcare providers.[5] This stresses caregivers and can make things harder at home. Poor healthcare and household stress can negatively impact young people's ability to learn, develop,[6] and stay healthy.

- Living in poverty saps mental resources, making it harder to learn and retain new information. Poverty and being poor are chronic stressors, which contribute to and often drive developmental disparities, delays, and mental health conditions.[7]

- Before COVID-19, nearly half of U.S. families of color lived in poverty.[8] The combination of being a person of color and living in poverty impacts everything from future education and employment outcomes to overall life expectancy. For example, tribal members of the Pine Ridge reservation in South Dakota die up to 2 decades earlier than white neighbors who live a few hundred miles away.[9] Residents in St. Louis City who live several miles apart have nearly a 20-year life expectancy difference based on income and race.[10] Early data from the COVID-19 pandemic indicates that these life disparities were made worse by the pandemic.[11]

- During the COVID-19 pandemic, kids with disabilities and cognitive or physical differences faced disproportionate marginalization and disadvantage. Without major prevention and intervention strategies, this trend could reoccur in the face of another disruption. Many of these young people were cut off from vital therapies, medical supplies, and care.[12] This was worst for children who already experienced cumulative disadvantage and marginalization, including those living in poverty, attending under-resourced schools, and/or living with a single parent.

From Profiles to Portraits

Let's draw these demographic and determinant profiles in pencil so we can remove the parts we get wrong and add in important details about children as we learn them. While profiles only tell part of a young person's story, they carry profound power and often lifetime problems.

Our job is to consider the characteristics, categories, and life conditions assigned to kids and use that information to inform and improve how we support them. We must commit to a lifetime of our own learning, action, and reflection, seeking to understand what it means to live with different demographics and determinants, and doing what we can to make things better, not worse.

At its worst, profiling dehumanizes children. It depicts them without dimensions and details, leaving us to sort, group, assume, and judge. At its best, profiles are a jumping-off point—a collection of data and insights that begin to tell us who a kid is and what they need to thrive.

We must push ahead and commit ourselves to gather our materials and expand the picture we have of each child from *basic profile* to *holistic portrait,* understanding that this initial information will stay with kids and inform their life experience. We can use profiles as the outline for higher-definition portraits that respect and represent the fullness of who young people are.

CHAPTER TAKEAWAYS

- The first picture we have of a young person is rudimentary and flawed because we profile them. This is an unavoidable starting point. Profiles can be helpful and harmful.

- Profiles are the starting picture of who a young person is, based on whatever available, observable, and reportable data we have. Profiles are made up of different demographics and determinants, unique to every child.

- Demographics are personal characterizations and population-level categories, such as race and gender. Demographics give us a sense of how advantaged kids are in school, systems, and society.

- Determinants are the social, environmental, political, and historical conditions kids are born with and grow up in, including whether they have access to good healthcare and schools, and how safe it is at home and in the neighborhood. Determinants tell us the types of protections and vulnerabilities kids experience in learning and life.

Many young people experience cumulative disadvantage and marginalization. They are born and live with characteristics and conditions that make adversity far more likely. The more accumulation, the deeper the disparities. The deeper the disparities, the greater the risks to life, learning, and life expectancy.

REFLECTION QUESTIONS

- Consider your own profile and how it impacted you as you grew up. How does it impact you today?

- What profile parts do you understand the least and why do you think that is? Which ones—if any—make you uncomfortable?

- In what ways have you profiled kids? How has that changed the way you treated them?

- What do you plan to do with the information you read in this chapter?

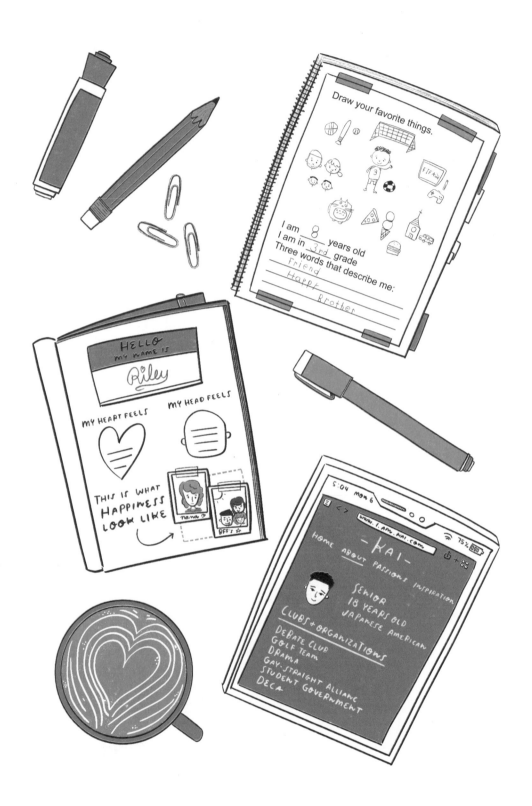

Age and Stage 2

My kids stayed home the entire 2020–2021 school year. My mom moved in, my husband and I worked remotely, and our family hunkered down and tried to ride out the COVID-19 pandemic. Time moved forward and my boys kept learning and growing from home. The following fall, the boys returned to school without us knowing if they were academically and developmentally ahead, behind, or on track with their peers.

On the first day back, we waited an hour in a long line of cars to drop the kids off. There were big posters with instructions on who to drop off where: little kids—kindergarten and first graders—got dropped off at the first door; older kids at the second and third. When it was our turn, my husband pulled up to the first door. I look at him confused. "Why are we stopped?" I asked. Looking equally confused he said, "To let Harrison out. First graders go in this door."

The thing was, Harrison was not in first grade. He was a third grader. My husband's slip showed how frozen in time our boys' in-person schooling was during the 18 months they were home. That morning was our first time back to the building since Harrison *was* in first grade. All time and no time had passed in between.

We found the right door, dropped the boys off, and had a good laugh over the mix-up. Still, I was unsettled. I worried about what it meant that the boys had gone for so long without the relationships and experiences that fuel healthy childhood development, and that happen at school and during afterschool activities. We were lucky to stay home with the boys, but our love and interactions could not make up for everything that was lost when shutdowns and public health restrictions were in place.

A Pandemic Pause

The COVID-19 pandemic shows what happens when learning and development changes for all kids at once. The effects were most profound for kids in a period of significant developmental growth— little ones who missed preschool and spent kindergarten online; high schoolers who missed the socially stormy and forming middle school years; college students who entered adult learning spaces without having fully experienced the last 2 years of high school in person.

Early into the pandemic, the Social Policy Institute (SPI) at Washington University in St. Louis began surveying about 5,000 families on pandemic impacts, including how their children's education and social-emotional development were affected. Participants were surveyed five times between April 2020 and May 2021.

The research team found that kids who struggled the most during the pandemic were those with *profiles* (determinants + demographics) that made life hard before the pandemic started.[1]

As soon as schools and the world shutdown, here is what happened:

- Children living in poverty lost the consistent, healthy meals provided to them at school. These same kids may have struggled with virtual learning because they lacked digital devices, internet access, and/or a dedicated space to focus.[2] If they also lived in a financially poor household, they were likely to stay in *virtual* learning longer than wealthier peers.[3]

- Children everywhere had to stop their in-person extracurricular and enrichment activities, as well as time with friends and family outside of the home. These activities and connections were vital for learning, health, and development.

- Children with disabilities were suddenly cut off from critical services, supports, and supplies.[4] Many lost needed accommodations because they didn't convert to an online format, and it was too risky to deliver services in person.

- Children who experienced abuse and neglect found themselves trapped in unhealthy and dangerous living and learning environments, without the protective factors provided by school, afterschool programs, and from other adults. For many, maltreatment worsened because of the pressures and confinement brought on by the pandemic and economic crises.[5]

Dramatic shifts and restrictions in life, learning, and relationships—regardless of reason—always impact learning and development.[6] Although some kids did better at home and online, most struggled. Across stories, studies, and articles, it's clear that young people who struggled the most were those who were already in vulnerable situations.

The COVID-19 pandemic was also hard for kids who experienced grief and loss. The SPI team found that nearly one in four adults lost their jobs or income during the pandemic. This destabilized and made family life more stressful. Additionally, more than 140,000 kids lost a caregiver to the COVID-19 virus and many more lost loved ones for different reasons, but with the added complexity of it happening during a pandemic.[7]

There were also kids who were burdened with household and family responsibilities in addition to school. Many older kids had to take care of siblings so parents or caregivers could work. These were often the same kids whose families struggled with other hardships that were brought on or made worse by the pandemic.

Overall, COVID-19 accelerated and intensified problems at home and in families. Historic firsts and complex challenges have meant that today's kids are growing up fast and slow. Based on what's happening to them environmentally and experientially, their development is simultaneously speeding up and slowing down. The impacts will be felt for years to come.

Growing Up Fast and Slow

Life-changing circumstances like a pandemic illuminate how important environments and experiences are for learning and development, because kids' brains are wired and rewired by them.[8] **Development** is a highly dynamic, fluid process that is shaped, sped up, or slowed down by what's happening—from everyday situations and interactions[9] to broader changes in the world at large.[10]

Research suggests that when kids experience prolonged adversity, it interferes with their abilities to learn and thrive.[11] Prolonged stress and toxic circumstances can lead to developmental delays and future issues.[12] These challenges can cause children to become wise beyond their years and keep them younger longer.

As we consider who a young person is, we must consider the circumstances and challenges they face. This requires knowing their demands and stresses as well as their protective factors like coping skills and whether they have supportive family members. These **protective factors** can minimize or even prevent the damaging effects adversity has on development, allowing kids to do well even when times are tough.

Wise Beyond Their Years

The young people we view as "wise" beyond their years are often kids going through difficult circumstances, who have been forced to assume adult responsibilities. While they may not be mature in every way, these young people have been aged by suffering, sacrifice, and struggle. They may have survived a disaster, suffered a tragedy, or experienced living with or loving someone with a chronic illness. These can be kids who have lost someone or something dear to them or who live with that fear every day. Often, they are kids who experience a combination of intensely stressful and challenging situations.

Life challenges change kids, speeding up aspects of development while slowing down or stalling others. A child might be ultra-responsible to survive and support family members while still missing out on developmentally rich experiences and being behind in school.

When this happens, kids get stretched between two life stages: the one they are in chronologically (e.g., teenager) and the one they are in circumstantially (e.g., adult). We cannot mistake demonstrated maturity for developmental maturity. When we do, we miss seeing kids for who they are and what they need.

In extreme cases, young people end up in adult roles that cause them to fall extremely behind in school. I used to run a school for youth who were older (ages 17–21) but far behind academically. Many of my students had caregiving responsibilities and worked. These demands made it hard and sometimes impossible to attend school and engage in class, sports, or extracurricular activities.

"Adultification" of Children

Some kids are treated as adults because of how they look or where they live (their *profiles*). This is especially true for Black and brown children. Adultification has roots in racism and sexism, and in the worst-case scenarios it can be a cause of violence or death. Adultification can lead to improper care or treatment by healthcare providers, police, teachers, and other authority figures. When children are seen as more adult than they are, they may not receive the age- and stage-appropriate care, compassion, attention, and resources they need.

Adultification is at play when kids are treated as their parent's partner, hypersexualized, or perceived as dangerous and capable of adult crimes.[13] It is why families of Black boys worry about teenage growth spurts, because getting physically bigger means the risk of being perceived as a dangerous grown-up instead of an innocent child. Adultification intensifies the chances of anti-Black violence, which has led to the killings of Black boys for doing normal activities, like walking home or playing with toys at the store. Black girls, starting as early as kindergarten, are seen as less innocent and older than their classmates, leading to exclusionary discipline at school and disproportionately high rates of arrest and incarceration.[14] Adultification is also why Asian parents worry about their daughters being victims of sexual violence—a risk that has increased in recent years.[15]

While this book is about how to help young people thrive, it requires we understand what prevents that from happening. We must examine our own actions, behaviors, and power to stop adultification. If you see it, try to intervene, and offer support and protection to minimize damaging effects.

Whenever young people's ages and stages of life are rejected or denied, it jeopardizes their learning, health, and development. In the same way we would never want to dehumanize someone, we should never watch their childhoods taken from them.

ADVERSE CHILDHOOD EXPERIENCES

Adverse Childhood Experiences ("ACEs") is a common term used to describe traumatic experiences that happen in childhood and adolescence. ACEs can disrupt young people's learning and development.

The original Adverse Childhood Experiences Study was led by two doctors, Vincente Felitti and Robert Anda. They analyzed the medical records of 17,000 patients and found 10 common stressors and traumas associated with future health and life challenges.

The original study was made up of mostly white and upper-class patients, but it inspired extensive and related research, which is far more diverse and focuses on the developmental consequences and long-term effects of childhood trauma, toxic stress, and adversity across various populations.

(Continued)

(Continued)

Today there is ample evidence to suggest that the more adversity young people experience, the more they will struggle to learn and develop, and the more likely it will be they experience physical and mental illnesses and disorders, as well as risky behaviors like addiction.

These are five of the most common ACEs:

- Physical, emotional, or sexual abuse

- Physical or emotional neglect

- Witnessing violence

- Loss of a parent or caretaker

- Systemic oppression

While ACEs can occur at any time, the earlier something happens the harder it is for children to make sense of it.

There are a few things we can do to support children who have experienced ACEs: (1) Respond to current circumstances in age- and stage-appropriate ways; this can include supporting the family and child in whatever ways are appropriate. (2) Offer supports and accommodations that enable learning and development to continue; this can include providing a low-stress and healing-centered environment. (3) Keep future risk factors in mind and work to build up a child's resilience and resourcefulness.

Younger Longer

Developmental differences go beyond the impacts of a child's environment and experiences. Kids develop differently because of biology, culture, and even generational trends. Kids also inherit genetic predispositions that cause development to go faster, slower, or happen in unique ways.

Collectively, we are in the middle of a historic shift in understanding young people. Before the 20th century, *adolescence* (the tween and teen years) wasn't a universally recognized stage of development. This was probably because people didn't live as long, and many kids transitioned straight from childhood into adult responsibilities.[16] Over the past 200 years, this incredibly vibrant developmental period has become more recognized and valued.

Today, adolescence begins with the onset of puberty (usually 11 or 12 years old) and lasts into the mid-20s (through age 25), collectively representing more than half of the "growing up" years. Adolescence is as intense a period of change and exploration as early childhood.[17] This stage is summed up nicely by clinical psychologist Robert Sherman: "Adolescence is a time in life when the core tasks are navigating a changing brain and body, new relationships, and identity formation."

Developmental Protective Factors

While global shake-ups like COVID-19 and ACEs may jeopardize development, researchers have found protective factors that nurture young people and protect them from the risks of adversity. Protective factors like strong self-esteem and safety are characteristics that lower the chances that a child's development will be negatively impacted by hardship.

Table 4 Developmental Protective Factors[18]	
TYPE	**PROTECTIVE FACTOR**
Individual	• Coping skills • Positive physical development • Strong self-esteem • Problem-solving skills • Self-regulation
Family	• Supportive relationships • Strong values • Parents and caretakers who set limits and provide structure • Clear behavioral expectations
Community	• Safety • Supportive community relationships • Programs and people who support passions and interests • Positive norms and interactions • Opportunities to engage and belong

Source: Adapted from *Risk and Protective Factors for Youth* table at https://youth.gov/youth-topics/youth-mental-health/risk-and-protective-factors-youth

Protective factors provide benefits at every age and stage of life. We can encourage and strengthen the protective factors kids have by integrating them into our daily interactions with them.

Developmental Growth Charts

No two kids are the same. Kids' developmental journeys have to do with their living and learning conditions, individual characteristics, and broader context. Development happens across different domains, the main ones being physical, cognitive, spiritual, social, and emotional. Often, kids are developmentally *older* in one domain and *younger* in another. As a result, developmental stage is much more complex than chronological age.

Whenever I take my kids to their annual check-ups, I think about how helpful it would be to get a personalized developmental growth chart from my children's pediatrician or teachers. I value the physical growth chart because it shows me my boys' weight, height, and body mass over time. I can see what is normal or "on track" for them.

A few years ago, my older son told his pediatrician he was worried about being too big. He was taller and heavier than his friends and feeling insecure. His doctor pulled out my son's growth chart and showed him where most kids his age were—below his height and weight—and explained that he was tracking "beautifully" for his unique body. He was born in the 90th percentile and has been there ever since. She used the chart to describe how and when his friends might catch up, and what would need to happen for her to be concerned.

Imagine if we could work with kids to chart their development over time, generating a dynamic and comprehensive picture of their unique development (see Figure 1). We could use developmental milestones to measure and track growth, showing developmental stage and domains against chronological age and academic grade. This would help us visualize areas of strength and concern, variation, and differences with same-aged peers. It could be a valuable tool to gauge how young people are doing and project a more accurate developmental journey for each individual child.

Figure 1   Developmental Growth Charts

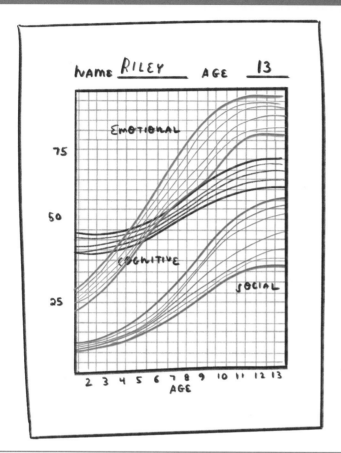

The American Academy of Pediatrics (AAP) and the Centers for Disease Control and Prevention (CDC) each have developmental milestone charts and accompanying adult recommendations that offer a solid base for this type of charting work. In 2022, the AAP updated its developmental milestones for the first time, making it easier to identify signs of neurodivergence (e.g., autism) and various disabilities and disorders. We can use these resources, along with system- and program-specific milestones and requirements, to chart and discuss growth across the ages and stages of childhood and adolescence.

Developmental Milestones

Let's consider some of the major milestones from childhood to adulthood (see Table 5). A broad sense of what happens in the first

25 years will make it easier to determine where kids are developmentally and what they need to live, learn, and thrive.

From birth to 25, kids move from infancy and early childhood (babies and toddlers) through childhood (little and older kids), into adolescence (tweens, teens, and young adults), and eventually transition into adulthood. Each developmental stage has stage-specific tasks, demands, and opportunities.

All kids have variation within their developmental stage. If a 15-year-old is emotionally older than their chronological age, maybe closer to a 17- or 18-year-old, her "emotional age" still falls within the same stage as her chronological age—adolescence. However, if this same 15-year-old lives with severe developmental delays, she may have functioning that is closer to a young child. Kids who live with large developmental gaps require specialized services and supports.

Table 5 Developmental Milestones		
	STAGE	**MAJOR MILESTONES**
Infancy	Babies and Toddlers (Ages 0–3)	• Full reliance on and attachment to caregivers and family • Recognize and respond to familiar people • Development of gross motor skills and increased body control • Initial social interactions and give-and-takes (smiles, giggling) • Initial development of language and communications, often by copying • First evidence of major health concerns and physical differences
Childhood	Little Kids (Ages 3–7)	• Discovery and learning through imaginative play, games, and role playing • Development of fine motor skills, such as holding a pencil or tying shoelaces • Fluency over whatever language is spoken at home • Progress from side-by-side play to easy play and fast friendships • Reliance on caregivers for safety, security, and permission to take risks • First evidence of certain physical limitations, such as hearing or vision

	STAGE	MAJOR MILESTONES
	Older Kids (Ages 8–11)	• Learning through active engagement, experiences, and reflection • Establishment of significant friendships that could last for years • Reliance on caregivers for safety, structure, and limits on risk taking • First evidence of certain cognitive differences and disabilities • Initial onset of certain mental illnesses, like anxiety and obsessive-compulsive disorder • Development of more complex thinking and independent decision making • Heightened awareness of self and social pressures
Adolescence	Tweens (Ages 11–14)	• Onset of puberty • Greater capacity for abstract thinking and executive functioning • Begin to see self in the context of relationships and a bigger world • Start of an intense period of personal identity formation, including gender and sexual identity • Awareness of marginalization, discrimination, and harassment • Increased sensitivity around image, peer perspectives, and pressure • Start of regular independent risk taking • Increased reliance on peers over family • Possible start of certain behavioral health risks, such as eating disorders and addictions
	Teens (Ages 14–18)	• Puberty progresses with hormonal and mood fluctuations • Puberty initiates significant physical and cognitive growth • Reliance on peers over family and other adults • Hypersocial with a need to be socially connected • Push for independence and autonomy • Increased independent risk taking

(Continued)

(Continued)

STAGE	MAJOR MILESTONES
	• Possible start or acceleration of certain behavioral health risks, such as eating disorders and addictions • Initiation of romantic relationships and sexual exploration • Pregnancy and parenting are possible
Young Adults (Ages 18–25)	• Move to independence and autonomy • Strengthened sense of self and identity • More fully aware of the impacts of demographics and determinants, including oppression, harassment, and discrimination • Stabilization of body and hormonal changes caused by puberty • Experience of longer-term romantic relationships and friendships • Most can live independently and launch into adulthood

Individual variation is why charting kids' unique developmental journey is so important. It can be harmful to chart the development of a child who is neurodivergent against the projected journey of someone who isn't, or to expect children who experienced a pandemic to track with previous generations who did not. Developmental journeys, projections, and recommendations must account for the many factors influencing a child's life.

CHAPTER TAKEAWAYS

- Dramatic shifts or restrictions in life, learning, and relationships—regardless of reason—always impact learning and development.

- The COVID-19 pandemic is an example of a generational event that impacted all children's learning and development. The pandemic made learning and school easier for some, but harder for most. It was most harmful for young people who already experienced challenges, and/or whose special services and supports were limited or stopped.

- Young people's brains are wired and rewired by environments, experiences, and interactions.

- Development is a highly dynamic, fluid process that is shaped, sped up, or slowed down by what's happening around us—from everyday situations and interactions to broader changes in society and the world at large.

- Prolonged adversity can prohibit or prevent kids from being able to thrive and lead to developmental delays and future issues.

- Whenever children's age and stage of life is rejected or denied, it jeopardizes their learning, health, and development.

- Children develop differently because of biology, culture, context, and historic events/generational trends.

- Protective factors are internal and external resources that lower the risk of adversity negatively impacting a child. (See Table 4 for examples.)

- Children develop across different domains, the main ones being physical, cognitive, social, spiritual, and emotional. Kids can be developmentally *older* in one domain and *younger* in another.

- From birth to 25, kids move from infancy (babies and toddlers) to childhood (little and older kids), into adolescence (tweens, teens, and young adults) with the eventual transition into adulthood. Each major developmental stage comes with stage-specific tasks, demands, and opportunities.

REFLECTION QUESTIONS

- Consider the children in your life. How do you see their environments, experiences, and interactions changing or challenging how they are growing up?

- How have you seen kids' development change because of historic events (e.g., COVID-19 pandemic)?

- Look at the protective factors listed in Table 4. Which are you able to provide and which—if any—can you not to provide? Think back to Chapter 1 when you reflected on your demographic and determinant *profile*. Which protective factors did you have growing up and what difference did they make?

- Consider developmental growth charts. How could you make this idea work, and what difference would it make?

Brain and Body 3

Right before Halloween of 2020, my son started spending more time than usual in the bathroom. He would flush and take forever washing his hands. Within days, his morning routine was upended. It was taking him twice as long to get changed, and sometimes he would try on more than one outfit, frustrated with the first. By the next week, his hands were red and raw, chapped from too much washing. When I asked if he was ok, he told me he was afraid of getting sick. This made sense. We were in the middle of a global pandemic, and I was still wiping down grocery bags with Clorox bleach. I was afraid of getting sick too. Then one day he asked me to check the stove. Then check it again. A fear of fire gripped him and soon my son was not only obsessing over cleanliness but also convinced our house would go up in flames.

That's when I knew something was wrong. I reached out to a family member for advice, and he encouraged me to find a therapist trained to work with kids with anxiety and obsessive-compulsive disorder (OCD). Based on his own experience, he felt strongly that something was happening neurologically, and my son needed to see a specialist right away.

After a lot of searching, my husband and I found someone who seemed like a good fit. During the initial intake call, he listened to us recount how many big changes we had seen over a short period of time. When we finished, he asked if our son was sick. I didn't understand the question and asked him to clarify. He said, "Sick. Like a cold or strep throat. Is he complaining of not feeling well?" I said he seemed fine, but the therapist responded with a strange recommendation: "I think you need to get your son tested for strep. Sometimes, kids with strep develop a rapid onset of obsessive-compulsive behaviors. This might be what's happening to your son."

The next day, I took my son to the pediatrician and joked with the nurses about this therapist's recommendation. I thanked them for doing the test and left the office before the rapid results came back. Minutes later, my phone rang. My son had strep throat. I was stunned.

Since then, our family has learned a lot about the connection between the brain and body, namely, the strong connection between physical and mental health. It turns out my son's symptoms were an autoimmune response to untreated strep. He'll probably always struggle with the condition he developed, but the acute and life-challenging issues he experienced were addressed by a combination of physical and mental health care, and medication. We treated the infection with antibiotics, lowered the body's inflammation with anti-inflammatory drugs, and engaged in counseling to address the neuropsychological symptoms (namely, the onset of OCD). The decisions we made during that time required coordinated involvement and decision-making between me, my husband, my son's pediatrician, his therapist, his teacher, and an infectious disease specialist.

We were lucky to catch the condition quickly and to have trained professionals who believed us and did the research to figure out what was going on. If it had continued unaddressed, my son could have experienced steep developmental and neurological declines. His life, learning, and well-being would have been severely compromised from a common childhood infection we didn't know he had.[1]

It's All Connected

Over the past few decades, our scientific understanding of the relationships between health, living, and learning has grown a lot. Advances in brain and body imaging, along with the scholarship of many researchers, have built a sizable evidence base that suggests that many childhood learning and behavioral challenges have roots in simple or complex health issues. Sometimes, a change in attitude or energy is due to a vitamin deficiency or lack of sleep. Other times, academic challenges or developmental delays might be symptoms of an autoimmune disorder or some other condition. By attending to the body's needs, we can keep kids healthy, improve their cognitive functioning, and help them experience optimal energy and joy.

Health is foundational for kids to live, learn, and thrive. When health is good, everything is easier. Physical health and mental health *are both health*, and who kids are and how they are doing relates to what's going on in their brains and bodies.

When kids are struggling behaviorally, we have to figure out why they are acting a certain way and make a judgment call—deciding whether the behavior warrants intervention or a consequence. If we want to make sound judgment calls, we must be cross-trained in the basics of physical and mental health. Otherwise, we could cause inadvertent harm to kids we care about. I am so thankful my son's counselor was trained in the connection between childhood infections, inflammation, and mental illness. Otherwise, we never would have thought to test our son for strep.

This type of cross-training opens us up to important insights into childhood health, behavior, and development. Knowledge will improve the support we can provide, experiences we offer, environments we build, and the interactions we have.

The "BBB" of Childhood Health and Wellness

My first home was gorgeous and historic. For all its beauty, it required upkeep beyond what I could provide. I needed people I could trust to do repairs and I often looked for the Better Business Bureau seal of approval to know if the contractor I was hiring was reputable and reliable.

We can use the same "BBB" idea and convert it into a concept that helps us choose activities for kids that will reliably support their health and wellness. For our purposes, "BBB" stands for *Brain, Body, and Belly*. The BBB standard should be people and programs that take care of children's brains, bodies, and bellies. For us to be those people, we must understand the basics of how the "Bs" operate, affect each other, and contribute to young people's well-being.

- **Brain:** Ultimately weighing in at 1 to 3 pounds, the brain is the body organ that makes us human and controls our body.[2] The brain enables us to think, be, do, respond, and relate. Doing this requires one quarter of the body's blood and food energy, and one fifth of our oxygen intake.[3] When someone is hungry for food or air, the brain doesn't have the energy it needs to function properly. This is like a person with asthma and the feeling of spaciness or mental exhaustion after an asthma attack, or how hard it is to focus when you're hungry. Early childhood and adolescence are the two times in life when the brain grows and changes the most.

- **Body:** Our bodies are made of highly interconnected and interdependent systems, including the brain and belly. These body systems make sure our lungs breathe, hearts pump, temperature heats up and cools down, and more. The body is designed to move, protect itself, and follow instructions set by DNA. Bodies need good nutrition, physical fitness, and effective treatment for health issues and illness.[4] The intersections between the body and kids' learning and development extends from the cellular level[5] out to society and the environment.

- **Belly:** Sometimes called the *second brain*, the belly includes the stomach and colon and is made up of trillions of microorganisms, including bacteria, viruses, and fungi—collectively called the gut microbiome. The belly is where food goes, and energy is made. There's a strong brain-belly connection that most of us intuitively understand—think about our use of the phrases *food-coma*, *sugar-high*, or *gut feeling*. The brain and belly are physically connected by the vagus nerve—the superhighway of our nervous system that sends signals throughout the body for physical and emotional regulation.[6] Emerging evidence suggests that some neurological conditions, including autism, could be linked to the belly's microbiome.[7]

Wherever you spend time with kids, you should strive toward BBB healthfulness. To do this, focus on incorporating or encouraging essential activities for health and address situations or structures that keep these activities from happening.

Big Six "BBB" Essential Health Activities

To understand what kids need healthwise to learn and thrive, I turned to one of my mentors, Elliot Washor. In 1995, Elliot cofounded Big Picture Learning (BPL), an international network of schools committed to students being at the center of their own learning. For years, Elliot advised me on how kids should learn, and schools should run. In recent years, I have looked to him for advice on how kids should live. This is because he and his colleagues have a partnership with the American College of Lifestyle Medicine (ACLM) to run Big Picture Living, a resource for schools and youth development organizations that promotes young people's health and well-being as key to their learning and futures.

Big Picture and ACLM promote six *life-changing* health activities for any kid in any context or culture. Each activity is backed by research as being essential for learning and development. Table 6 provides an adapted version of these big six activities.

Table 6	Essential Health Activities That Support Kids' Health and Wellness[8]
ACTIVITY	**YOUNG PERSON**
Nourishment	• Eats healthy food, including plenty of plant-based options • Obtains a variety of healthy food options • Drinks toxin-free water
Sleep	• Gets enough sleep • Gets restful, quality sleep with limited disruptions • Uses naps in the early part of the day, if needed
Movement	• Exercises the brain and body regularly • Limits sedentary activities
Relationships	• Engages in positive and supportive social interactions • Has healthy relationships with friends and family • Limits social isolation
Stress Management	• Copes with life's challenges • Has positive ways to calm down after stressful events • Uses mindfulness as a way to reduce stress and relax
Sobriety	• Avoids harmful drugs and illegal substances • Avoids harmful consumption of legal mood-changing or addictive substances • Avoids addictive and negatively mood-altering activities

Source: Adapted from Big Picture Living and the American College of Lifestyle Medicine. https://www.bpliving.org

Nourishment

Food is fuel and medicine. For kids to function, they need to eat, eat enough, and eat enough nutritious foods to experience BBB health. According to Save the Children, one in five U.S. families don't have enough food, let alone healthy food options. As of 2022, that was more than 17 million kids (equivalent to the population of the Netherlands), with families of color 2 to 4 times more likely to experience hunger than white families.

Childhood hunger is always worse in the face of macro issues like poverty, political conflict, climate change, and large disruptions like schools shutting down or economic crises.[9] It is harder for families to overcome hunger if they live in a "food desert,"[10] which is a place with limited healthy and affordable food options.

Nourishing kids starts with making sure they're fed and full. Being hungry is distracting and being hungry for long periods of time stunts learning. This is true no matter why a kid is hungry, whether from poverty, illness, an eating disorder, or some other reason.

Kids need to eat foods that power their BBB. These are foods that are nutrient-rich and high in antioxidants and fiber (fruits and vegetables), high in good fats (nuts and seafood), complex carbohydrates (whole wheat, beans, and oatmeal), and full of good bacteria (yogurt and fermented foods). The healthiest foods are the least processed.[11]

The food pyramid many of us learned in school doesn't reflect what kids need. In fact, *Scientific American* called it "grossly flawed."[12] The iconic pyramid taught us to limit fats and eat plenty of complex carbs, but our BBB need fat (the brain is 60 percent fat!)[13] and complex carbs should be balanced by other healthy options.

Kids also need to eat foods that are safe for them. One of my kids is gluten-intolerant, which we learned after he stopped growing and gaining weight. Food intolerances, allergies, sensitivities, and vitamin or mineral deficiencies can cause alarming physical, psychological, and behavioral changes and challenges in kids. Always investigate nutritional deficiencies and food allergies/sensitivities if you think it might be a problem.

Many kids don't have access to the healthy and safe foods they need. Others don't want to eat those foods, even if they are available. Anyone with picky eaters or who grew up with limited food options knows that kids can still turn out fine even if they have periods of poor eating. That said, not having enough nourishment for long periods is risky and unhealthy.

As much as possible, we must give children healthy food exposure and options. When resources are the issue, look for community gardens, or consider growing your own produce. Ask local restaurants if they'll donate leftovers or see what grocery stores accept public benefits or offer discounted goods. Know where nearby food pantries are. If you can, keep healthy snacks on hand and let kids take them when they need them.

Sleep

We need sleep to survive and thrive. According to parenting journalist and author of *The Sleep-Deprived Teen*, Lisa L. Lewis, many kids (especially teens) don't get enough. Sleep is when the brain processes new experiences and information and when our body repairs itself.[14] Sleep is foundational for health, learning, and development.

There's plenty of evidence that shows that sleepy kids are more likely to make impulsive choices, be irritable, and even have an increased risk of suicide, Lisa notes. Sleep deprivation makes it harder for kids to learn, retain information, and retrieve that information later. Some studies demonstrate that the symptoms of sleep deprivation are like ADHD, leaving questions about whether certain behavioral diagnoses could be due to lack of sleep.[15]

Brains and bodies need a certain amount of quality sleep to do important regeneration work that can only happen while we snooze. This is jeopardized when kids go to bed too late or wake up too early. Often schools and schedules are to blame. Many kids and parents have told me how high school homework, sports schedules, and "early bird" classes make it hard, if not impossible, to get enough sleep. This is even more difficult for students who work or have long rides to and from school.

Sleep quality is also impacted when kids wake up or are woken up during the night. This could be from safety and noise issues, health issues like restless legs or anxiety, or the lights and dings of digital devices. The blue light from smartphones makes it harder to fall asleep, and notifications make it harder to stay sleep.

Table 7 shows how much sleep the National Sleep Foundation recommends kids get according to their age and developmental stage:

Table 7	Sleep Recommendations From the National Sleep Foundation	
	AGES	**RECOMMENDED SLEEP**
Infancy	Ages 0–3	• Newborns: 14–17 hours • Infants: 12–15 hours • Toddlers: 11–14 hours
Childhood	Ages 3–6	• 10–13 hours
	Ages 6–10	• 9–11 hours
Adolescence	Ages 11–14	• 9–11 hours
	Ages 14–18	• 8–10 hours
	Ages 18–25	• 7–9 hours

These recommendations must be personalized based on young people's individual needs. Some kids need more or less than the recommended range. Developmentally, young people's sleep "clock" (circadian rhythm) changes as they get older. A shift in circadian rhythm initiated by the onset of puberty means that tweens and teens don't get tired until later in the evening. The problem is most middle and high schools start early in the morning, making it unlikely that these kids get the sleep they need. Fortunately, some schools and states are listening to the science and establishing later start times for middle and high school students, ensuring they have the chance to get enough rest.[16]

The National Sleep Foundation found that 3 out of 5 middle schoolers and nearly 9 out of 10 high schoolers don't get enough sleep. With numbers this high, we can assume most tweens and teens are chronically tired. While our options might be limited, we can help them navigate or skip early and late commitments, encourage them to sleep without their phone nearby, and provide education on sleep like why it matters, and what happens when they don't get enough of it.

Additionally, while rest is not a substitute for sleep, it is an important part of overall wellness and—ironically—productivity and performance. Young people have a lot vying for their time and attention, and it's easy to get mentally fatigued and exhausted. Research shows that *downtime*—which can include short naps, leisurely walks, quiet and relaxing activities—improves learning and overall achievement.[17]

Movement

I feel good when I exercise. Doing it regularly makes me a better parent, person, and worker. I see the same thing happen with my own children and science backs it up. Regular brain and body fitness supports physical health, as well as mental and social health. Short-term and long-term benefits of movement include reduced stress, increased learning, longer lifespans, and a better quality of life.[18]

For children, healthy movement means having ways to stay physically and cognitively fit.

Once kids are school aged, they are supposed to get at least 1 hour of moderate to intense exercise every day. This is this kind of exercise that makes kids sweat and gets the blood pumping. Think running, swimming, jumping, and hard play. This can happen in structured ways—like gym class or playing sports—or in unstructured ways, like running around at a park or during an afterschool program. This is even more important in adolescence, when the brain and body undergo rapid growth and maturation.[19]

With my own children, I think about their movement in four daily shifts: (1) morning, (2) school or camp, (3) after school or after camp, and (4) evening. In elementary school, their 1 hour of exercise happened during the second and third shifts. I could count on recess and their afterschool program. Now my older son is in middle school and there is no recess or afterschool option. Movement requires creativity, advanced planning, or his own initiative to make sure he gets the exercise he needs.

According to the Centers for Disease Control and Prevention, physical exercise strengthens young people's body systems, muscles, and bones. It also improves their ability to pay attention, remember information, and sleep. Beyond immediate benefits, exercise reduces chronic inflammation and stress, helping young people recharge, and experience deeper healing.[20] It is possible for kids (and adults) to have too little or too much movement, so finding balance is key.

Cognitive Fitness

An equally important but less talked about form of exercise is cognitive fitness. Cognitive fitness can include mindful movement like yoga or walking in nature. While it's usually less sweaty, it has important benefits for the brain and body, including stress management, staying limber, and relaxation. Cognitive fitness includes brain games that support executive functioning skills. Executive functioning—which includes the ability to focus, organize, remember things, pay attention, and complete tasks—operates from the front part of the brain and doesn't fully develop until our mid-twenties. In childhood and adolescence, brain games and other cognitive exercises can be a fun way to help develop and strengthen those emerging skills.[21]

Cognitive fitness is even more important when kids' technology use increases, making them more susceptible to digital distractions like phone notifications and social media. Growing up in a digital world requires a level of mental strength to be able to power down and turn away from tech and devices. Some kids cannot do it on their own, which makes parental and teacher controls and screen limits extremely useful. Over time, kids must learn to identify what it feels like when tech negatively impacts their BBB and how to reduce the risk. This can include knowing when to get up and get moving or when to stop playing addictive apps and games on their devices.[22]

For kids who are differently wired—because of neurodivergence, mental health, or attention differences—cognitive fitness might include targeted or more therapeutic exercises, as recommended by a trained professional. My older son has several cognitive behavioral exercises that help him manage obsessive-compulsive thoughts and behaviors. They are a part of a toolbox he can use to stay cognitively and physically fit throughout his life.

Relationships

This book includes an entire chapter on the importance of nurturing healthy relationships, so for now I'll keep this short and simple. I have studied child and youth well-being for more than 2 decades, and across all the research I've read, the most common reason why kids thrive is the presence of nurturing and healthy relationships. Healthy relationships are a protective factor against adversity, they help us learn, they are where we experience and process life, and often they are the spaces where we derive purpose and meaning. The research shows—unequivocally—that the best way to live a long and healthy life is to have strong friendships and social connections that feed your spirit and fuel your brain and body.[23]

Stress Management

For as many times as I've read about relationships being good, I've read about too much stress being bad. Stress is an unavoidable part of life, and it can be beneficial in small bursts. As Robert M. Sapolsky describes in *Why Zebras Don't Get Ulcers: The Acclaimed Guide to Stress, Stress-Related Diseases, and Coping,* stressors are things that throw us out of balance, and the stress response ("stress") is our body's way of trying to reestablish balance. Stress becomes harmful when it accumulates.

Too much stress, called *toxic stress,* messes with kids' ability to regulate their BBB. The amygdala, which is the primitive "stay alive" part of the brain, goes into hyperdrive and treats everything as a possible threat. On high alert, the brain uses up energy and reduces executive functioning. This is so the brain and body can apply all energy and attention to surviving. The part of the brain responsible for aggressive behaviors—the locus coeruleus—ramps up so it can help the amygdala combat the enemy, real or perceived. The nervous system carries messages and signals across the BBB, hormones go haywire, and everything from appetite to physical growth is affected.[24]

When kids experience toxic stress, it becomes harder to learn and self-regulate. It is more difficult to retain information and easier to engage in risky behaviors. In her groundbreaking book on childhood trauma, *The Deepest Well*, Dr. Nadine Burke recounts how pediatric patients with four or more **adverse childhood experiences** (ACEs)[25] were 32.6 times more likely to have been diagnosed with learning and behavioral problems and disorders. She also found that children with four or more ACEs ended up being 5 and one half times more likely to get addicted to alcohol and 10 times more likely to use hard drugs than those children with no ACEs.

Toxic stress makes kids sick, inflaming their bodies and putting them at risk of many health and life issues, including premature death.[26] Stressed-out kids use their energy to stay alive, sometimes burning out or giving up before they grow up.

Toxic stress can chronically dysregulate the body and create long-term changes in brain wiring, body mechanics, and behavior.[27] To further complicate things, the stress kids experience can be personal or inherited from parents or grandparents. Trauma imprints itself on our bodies and gets passed down across generations, through epigenetics. Scientists have discovered that the **epigenome** is a set of chemical markers that decide which parts of our genes get activated, and to what degree. Imagine our DNA as the orchestra, and the epigenome as the conductor. The epigenome responds to the environment, especially stress. Children inherit their parents' epigenetic changes, potentially becoming genetically predisposed to unhealthy ways of responding to the world, like being wary or overly anxious.[28] Too often, the kids who experience toxic stress because of life circumstances are also the ones fighting an invisible monster, which is inherited trauma and trauma responses.[29]

Beyond the individual impacts of toxic stress is the inescapable fact that kids are growing up in stressful times. Even kids with relatively low levels of stress will absorb and feel the impacts of global, social, and economic disruptions. They might be protected from certain adversities like abuse and neglect, but they will be impacted when global events become personal.

Stress is unavoidable and kids will bring it with them wherever they go. To help them, we must understand the science of stress and its role in our lives, helping kids to do the same. Then we can work with kids to find strategies that reduce it, heal from it, or live with it.

We can counter stress by providing young people with opportunities to build self-efficacy and see their successes and strengths. Stress can feel like something being done to us. Being strengths-based is something kids can do for themselves—it is an internal protective factor.

Every kid experiences stress and an increasing number suffer from prolonged and toxic stress. Stress management should be a prioritized area of support, and stress management strategies should be unique to each kid, because what works for some will not work for others.

Effective stress management techniques include the following:

- Movement

- Nourishing connections and conversations in the context of nurturing relationships

- Reaching out for social support

- Doing something that inspires awe and wonder, like going into nature, attending a concert, or visiting a museum

- Moving the body in a safe, culturally, and identity-affirming way[30]

- Other coping skills like making art, writing gratitude lists, or journaling

Sobriety

The final BBB essential activity is sobriety. Sobriety is avoiding the use of harmful substances and activities and supporting kids who are recovering from addictions. While substance abuse usually shows up in the teen and young adult years, addictive tendencies can emerge earlier, and substance abuse can happen with younger kids. For young people with family histories of addiction and other risk factors, early education and awareness are key.

In my house, I talk openly to my children about our family history of addiction, including my own recovery. When my children were little, I talked about alcoholism as an allergy. My kids both have allergies, and it was easy to explain that I can't have alcohol like my younger son can't have gluten. The boys immediately understood that alcohol would make me sick no matter how much I wanted it. Now that they are older, our discussions are evolving. At this point, they understand alcoholism runs in our family, which means they are more likely than others to develop it. We talk about what they might say if someone offered them alcohol or drugs, a conversation I hope we continue as they get older. When a family member relapsed, I talked openly about it. We talked about the difference between who that person is as a loving family member, and what alcoholism and being drunk causes them to say and do.

I consider open and honest communication about substances, addiction, and sobriety a life-saving practice for my children and nonnegotiable parenting responsibility. Education on substance abuse and addictions should be a required part of supporting their health and wellness.

Part of sobriety is prevention, which means helping young people understand why they would choose to engage in activities or substances in unhealthy or addictive ways. Intervention is stepping in and offering a better alternative that meets young people's needs. These needs tend to be physical, emotional, hormonal, and chemical. Some of the best prevention and intervention strategies are the "big six" essential activities, including sleep and exercise, healthy relationships, and positive ways to manage stress.

We can support young people's sobriety by understanding what addiction is, what kids can get addicted to, who is at risk of it, and how their BBB will be impacted. Risk taking and sensation-seeking are at an all-time high during adolescence, but substance use and addiction do not have to be a part of that.[31]

For kids who become addicted, sobriety is possible early in life. I know because I got sober at 15. If you care for tweens and teens, educate yourself on addiction and recovery options *before* you need the information and resources. Substance abuse and other addictions can be obvious or a well-kept secret. If a kid reaches out for help, you'll want reliable information and resources to respond.[32]

Four Health Hazards for Learning and Development

Issues in the brain, body, and belly (BBB) show up when the "big six" essential activities aren't happening or when underlying health issues or changes are at play. To support kids, we need a baseline understanding of common health hazards that make it harder to live and learn.

I am not a medical professional, but I have done lots of research on childhood health and well-being. To the best of my understanding, the four biggest health hazards kids experience are inflammation, illness, injury, and imbalances. These health hazards happen for many reasons, often in connection with kids' immune systems. In his book *Brain Inflamed,* Dr. Kenneth Bock describes this as an "immune kettle" that gets filled up with genetic predispositions, diet, allergies, hormones, environment, relationships, lifestyle, and infections.[33] Once the kettle overflows, things get hazardous. Hazards tend to coexist and make each other worse.

Inflammation

The more I learn about inflammation, the more I think it's responsible for most of the body's healing and suffering. Inflammation is how the body fights illness, infection, or injury. Chronic inflammation is when the brain and body can't stop fighting because of ongoing damage or threat due to sickness, or from historic, environmental, or systemic issues, including trauma. Inflammation is behind many mental illnesses, and most physical ones.[34] Kids with profiles (demographics + determinants) associated with disadvantage tend to suffer from chronic inflammation—or will later in life.[35] In their book *Inflamed,* Dr. Rupa Marya and journalist Raj Patel say that "racial violence, economic precarity, industrial pollution, poor diet, and even the water you drink can inflame you."

Illness

Kids can get physically and/or mentally ill. Illness impacts the "big six" essential activities, especially sleep and movement. If an illness is bad enough, it causes kids to miss school and other activities, including time with family and friends. Illnesses that are recurrent and long-lasting can seriously disrupt life, learning, and relationships. When kids are hospitalized—depending on reason and length of stay—they might be able to keep up with schoolwork or receive educational services at the hospital,[36] but that's not always the case. Kids returning to school and activities after a hospital stay need transition support and extra care and understanding. In terms of mental illness, rates of anxiety and depression have been rising steadily for the past 20 years,[37] and numbers have risen dramatically since the start of COVID-19. In 2021, the American Academy of Pediatrics and the U.S. Surgeon General declared youth mental health a national emergency.[38] More on mental illness is covered in Chapter 7, "Prioritize Mental Health."

Injury

Injuries also interfere with life, learning, and thriving. An orthopedic injury such as a broken bone or sprain can mean the end of a sports season, a missed chance to be in the school play, a summer spent indoors, or exhaustion from the extra time it takes to navigate on crutches or in a wheelchair. If a kid injures a dominant hand or arm, it can make writing, eating, and other basic tasks hard to do. Physical injuries can also be visible and embarrassing, sometimes putting young people at risk of peer rejection, unwanted attention, or bullying. Injuries can send a kid to the hospital for emergency care, specialty care, or surgery. Some young people experience traumatic brain injuries (TBIs), often due to an accident or sports injury. Studies show that teachers (I suspect most of us) don't know a lot about TBIs and need training on how to help students recover.[39] Kids with TBIs often need more school-based services than those with orthopedic or other physical injuries because the injury causes serious academic and developmental challenges.[40]

Imbalances

In our everyday interactions with kids, we might experience them suddenly acting out, behaving differently, or struggling to learn. These sudden swings could be due to medical, nutritional, or chemical imbalances. When these imbalances are severe and long-lasting, they cause or contribute to illnesses. When they are acute, there are often ways we can help or even fix the problem—we just need to know what to look for and do.

Here are common imbalances children experience:

- Dehydration and a spike or drop in blood sugar can cause kids to become tired, emotional, and confused. For children with certain medical conditions, these changes can be life threatening.

- A vitamin or mineral deficiency, like vitamin B-12 or iron, can cause children to have a hard time remembering and processing information, concentrating, and completing tasks or assignments.[41]

- A medication change or starting a new medicine can trigger changes in mood, behavior, cognitive functioning, and overall feelings of health and wellness.

- Certain activities like parties or movies can cause imbalances in kids' brain chemicals, causing them to get overly happy, hyped, sad, or agitated.

- With older kids, imbalances can be caused by substance use or abuse.

We don't have to be healthcare providers to discern (or ask) whether an imbalance might be causing a change in a child's behavior. We also don't have to be a child's parent or caregiver to be attentive and responsive. If you notice something is "off," try to get to the root causes.

Once we are aware of these four health hazards, we can evaluate concerning behaviors or learning difficulties with a health lens and better diagnose and address whatever is going on. Instead of discipline, kids might need to change a medication. Instead of being reprimanded, they may need a drink or snack.

Health information is often confidential and not always shared. We want to protect our children's privacy and not have them stigmatized or treated unfairly. We also want to make sure they get the help and support they need when they need it. If you are a parent who is on the fence about sharing a health hazard with the other adults who care for your kid(s), consider this: Those adults might observe and react to your child's health hazard, misperceiving and treating it as something it's not, like a behavior problem. If you work with children—this is also your responsibility. You are with young people during prime awake time. You might see things their parents and caregivers will not. By educating ourselves on these hazards and being on the lookout for them, we can work together to identify and address health-related causes behind young people's barriers to thriving.

Charting Kids' Health Profiles

Let's take a tip from medical professionals and start charting what we know and observe about young people's health and wellness. It is extremely useful to document observations and write down what young people share about their experiences. When we see things over time and in context, it leads to new insights, strategies, and solutions.

When we assess kids according to the *big six BBB essential health activities* with the *four health hazards,* we end up with a real-time personalized health profile (see Table 8). This gives us important information we can use to figure out what's going on with young people and what they may need. Essential health activities are kids' prevention and protection measures. Health hazards are areas where kids need services and supports.

Table 8	Health Activities and Hazards That Impact Kids' Well-Being	
HEALTH PROFILE	**EXAMPLES**	**QUESTIONS TO ASK YOURSELF**
Six Essential Health Activities	1. Nourishment (diet and nutrition) 2. Sleep 3. Movement (physical and cognitive) 4. Relationships 5. Stress Management 6. Sobriety	• To what degree are these happening or not happening in this child's life? • What needs to be prioritized and addressed? • What can I do to support this child's health and wellness? • What additional services and supports might this child need, beyond what I can provide?
Four Health Hazards	1. Inflammation 2. Illness (physical and mental) 3. Injury 4. Imbalance	

Charting can become a continuous practice and one that we get better at with time. Eventually, these essential health activities and hazards will become a part of our vocabulary and what we use to help care for children. This kind of cross-training can only improve our care for kids, providing new context and considerations for what might be going on and what else or who else is needed. We can monitor these essential activities and health hazards for kids by ourselves and in partnership with them. As young people get older, we must help them learn to monitor and manage their health profile on their own.

CHAPTER TAKEAWAYS

- Kids' learning and behavioral challenges may have roots in simple or complex health issues that can be corrected by medical intervention and/or medication.

- Physical health and mental health are *both health*, and are foundational for kids to live, learn, and thrive.

- Optimal learning and development happen when kids have healthy brains, bodies, and bellies (the BBB). Even if we have no background in healthcare, we must cross-train on the basics of how the "Bs" operate, affect each other, and contribute to kids' well-being.

- The BBB: the *brain* enables us to think, be, do, respond, and relate; the *body* is what moves and protects us, and it follows instructions set by DNA and genetics; the *belly* is sometimes called the "second brain" and it is where food goes, and energy is made.

- The six essential health activities that support kids' learning and development are nourishment, sleep, movement, relationships, stress management, and sobriety.

- The four health hazards that can hinder learning and development are inflammation, illness, injury, and imbalance.

REFLECTION QUESTIONS

- How do you see health impacting and influencing the young people you care for and about?

- Look at the essential health activities and health hazards and consider your personal health profile. What do you need to prioritize and address yourself? How do these activities and hazards impact your well-being?

- Consider an individual child. What does that young person's personal health profile look like? What impact does that profile have on life, learning, and thriving?

People and Places 4

A few years ago, I visited two former students while I was in Phoenix for a conference. The last time we had been together, they were 10 and I was 20. At that time, I was single, with no kids, and proudly Ms. Kilstein—their fifth-grade teacher. Now they were older than I had been, both moms, and each bringing their babies to a pancake house to catch up on our years apart.

I'll never forget that morning. I got there early and grabbed a booth in the back. It had ripped red plastic cushioning wrapped around three walls. The kind you stick to when you stand up. As I waited, I thought back to the year we spent together. Back then, Maria was quiet and the kindest child I had ever met. She was brilliant and diligent. One time, her fidgety classmate ripped the arm off one of our stuffed animals. Maria snuck it home that night and the next day proudly delivered a kid-sewn-and-repaired "Mr. Reindeer." I still proudly display him every single Christmas. Brooklynn, on the other hand, was loud and precocious. She was lovable and instantly likable. She was new to our school that year, and while I knew things were tough at home, she always showed up with her signature spunk and smile.

The two women who met me at the pancake house were grown up but still felt like those young girls. That morning I held their babies and listened to their stories. They shared twists and turns I never expected. Their lives after fifth grade were both broken and beautiful.

We had all been shaped and changed by our time together. As they moved on from my classroom, they continued to shape and be shaped by the experiences, environments, and relationships that came next. That dynamic push and pull had led them to this moment, to being the people they were, to sharing their stories with me of their lives so far.

Kids in Context

American psychologist Urie Bronfenbrenner understood how much kids are shaped by—and shape—the world around them. Bronfenbrenner was arguably the world's greatest developmental scientist. He's famous in social work and psychology circles for his ecosystem theory of human development,[1] which started to form when he was a young child.

Bronfenbrenner was raised on a 3,000-acre state-run institution where his father worked as a neuropathologist. In Bronfenbrenner's book *The Ecology of Human Development,* he recounts long walks with his father—who held degrees in zoology and medicine—around the institution property. His father always talked to him about the ways animals needed the land and the land needed the animals.

This observation of interdependence became the cornerstone of Bronfenbrenner's scholarship.[2] Today, his ecology of human development theory is used by many to make sense of how the conditions and circumstances of our lives depend on the people we grow up with, the places we grow up in, and the dynamic interplay between us and "them."

Maria and Brooklynn's lives reflected experiences with many different people and places across years—including me, our fifth-grade class, our elementary school, their friends and family, and the community we lived in. But also, their sixth-grade teachers and classes, the next schools they attended, and so on. These women shared with me their core selves and the chiseling effect of what happens to us as we go through the events, experiences, environments, and relationships that shape our lives and selves.

Kids are not cogs, but when we view them without the background details, we tend to treat them that way. At school, we call them learners—or more narrowly, students in a certain grade or class. In sports, they are athletes—or players of a particular sport, playing one position, and seated in a specific rank. On the job, they are workers. In the doctor's office, patients. In human services, clients. In youth development settings, participants.

It is likely that the people who most profoundly impacted your life saw you as much more than someone in a single system or setting. These were the adults who took time to get to know you and your world. You were more than a student in their class or a player on their team. You felt seen and known, likely because they understood important parts of your story and circumstances.

Kids come with a complex map of connections to many people and places—those they are in direct contact with, like family, friends, classrooms, and clubs, and those indirectly impacting their lives, like superintendents, school boards, and healthcare providers. Knowing and supporting young people means learning their connections and context, the forces impacting their lives and our interactions with them, and the ways our words and actions impact them now and could impact them in the future.

We must become cartographers of children's contexts and connections. Mapping is taking time to learn about and plot the people and places young people interact with. As we map, we put kids at the center of their lives, and we learn their landscape by moving outward until we have drawn a constellation of the people and places who make up the ecosystem they live and learn in (see Figure 2).[3]

Figure 2   Kids in Context–A Human Ecology Model

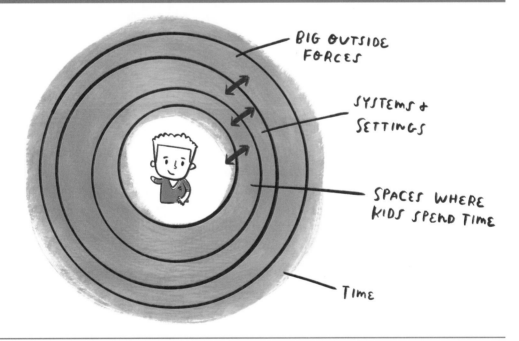

BIG OUTSIDE FORCES

SYSTEMS & SETTINGS

SPACES WHERE KIDS SPEND TIME

TIME

Mapping the Spaces Where Kids Spend Time

Children exist in their own human ecologies. If we know an animal that lives in the desert or near water, then we know some things about how they live and what their life is like. The same is true for kids. A lot can be revealed just by learning where kids spend time, what those spaces are like, and who's there with them.

Working with young people to map their lives and relationships is an effective way to get to know who they are, what matters to them, and what their everyday lives are like. Additionally, kids can act differently depending on where they are and who they are with. We may only see one part, but a map will illuminate the others. Maps can open the door to conversations about the roles, relationships, and responsibilities young people have as well as the things they like to do and the people they prefer to spend time with.

Here are questions you can ask young people to get them started with this mapping process:

- Where do you spend time when you aren't at school?
- What people do you most enjoy spending time with?
- What are your favorite activities at school and outside of school?
- What are your responsibilities at school and with your family?
- What does a typical week in your life look like, starting with Monday morning?

Then have kids draw or describe a map—literal or figurative—of their world.

We form a picture of an individual child when we learn their demographics and determinants, age and stage, and brain and body. Mapping places that picture onto the backdrop of their lives. Suddenly, we see kids in context. A wider lens and bigger picture illuminates who and what kids interact with, including which people and places are most in focus, and why. Like a search-and-find picture, these maps give us clues about where kids belong or struggle to fit in. Since young people are digital natives, make sure these maps include where they spend time online and who they spend time online with.

Mapping Youth-Serving Systems and Settings

The next part of mapping draws out the complexity and connectivity of a kid's life by identifying and flagging the systems, groups, and organizations they are a part of. This provides insights into the quality of their lives and learning and the types of resources and opportunities they have available to them. This illuminates spaces of abundance or scarcity, advantage or disadvantage.

Table 9 shows how you might map a child's connections to various systems and settings.

SPACE WHERE A CHILD SPENDS TIME	WHICH IS A PART OF	SETTING	WHICH IS A PART OF	SYSTEM
Classroom	>>>>>>	Elementary School	>>>>>>	Public Education
Soccer Team	>>>>>>	YMCA	>>>>>>	Out-of-School Time
Bedroom	>>>>>>	Foster Home	>>>>>>	Child Welfare
Brookhaven	>>>>>>	Roblox	>>>>>>	Online Gaming/ Internet

Table 9   Mapping to Youth-Serving Systems and Settings

Once we have an expanded map that includes the spaces, systems, and settings a child is connected to, we can start to see points of interconnection—what Bronfenbrenner called mesosystems. A **mesosystem** is created when two or more settings and systems come together. If you look at Table 9, one possible mesosystem is a partnership between the elementary school and YMCA. These connections show how people and places are linked together—with or without the child's involvement.

Here are questions to ask when trying to determine what systems and settings a child is connected to:

- Where does this child live and who do they live with?

- Do they live at more than one household, and if so, who do they stay with and what is each place like?

- Do they spend long periods of time with extended family or other adults (e.g., grandparents, godparents)?

- Is this child involved in systems like foster care or the youth justice system?

- Does this child move around a lot? For instance, could they be homeless, living with caregivers who are migrant workers or active in the military?

- What kinds of school-based clubs, sports, or activities do they participate in?

- What kinds of before school, afterschool, or summer programs and activities do they participate in?

- How do they spend their time online?

- What do they do on the weekends?

Once you have the answers to these questions, consider what you know about the child, the systems and settings they are engaged in, and the possible impacts those connections could have on their life and learning.

The Stigma and Strain of Being Involved in Certain Public Systems

Every day, millions of kids are both helped and harmed by public systems. Systems involvement can be obvious or less visible, and it can be a part of any kid's experience, regardless of background or income level. All children are at risk of experiencing a natural disaster, losing housing, getting sick, or experiencing an economic crisis.

A child in foster care is a part of the child welfare system. Young people who are homeless or facing housing instability may stay at emergency shelters, or in temporary public housing. Youth who are arrested and go to a juvenile detention facility, or whose family members are incarcerated, are involved with the justice system. Young people with chronic health conditions might qualify for Medicaid and spend time in a hospital system. There are other systems too: for example, young people who are old enough to work might participate in youth employment programs, which are a part of the workforce development system, and older youth with disabilities might engage in vocational rehabilitation programs or live in residential care facilities.

These public systems are behemoths and difficult to navigate. A part of caring for kids is learning about what their "systems involvement" looks like and means. Young people have told me that navigating these systems can be lonely, confusing, embarrassing, frustrating, and stigmatizing. When I ask what the adults in their lives could do to be more supportive, their answer is always the same: They want adults who care enough to learn about these systems and the types of situations young people face when they are in them.

Many kids tell me their systems involvement makes it hard to stay and succeed in school, sports, and other extracurriculars. Unfortunately, the data shows that systems involvement can lead to more and different systems involvement. Kids in foster care are more likely to become homeless or get arrested.[4] Similarly, kids in the justice system are more likely to end up homeless or in foster care.

Systems-involved young people want to feel less alone, and they need adults who provide unconditional and ongoing support, guidance, understanding, and answers. You don't have to become a systems expert, but you do need to learn what these public systems are, what they mean for kids who are in them, and what you can and should do to help.

Populating Maps With People

To understand kids-in-context we must recognize them as kids-in-community. A map of kids' worlds comes alive when we understand the *who*, as much as the *what* and *where*. *Who* they spend time with. *Who* they see most often. *Who* they are influenced by.

Many of us have heard or used the saying, "It's about the people." We say it to describe why we decide to stay at a job or in our neighborhood. We use it to describe where we worship or the activities we sign up for. For those of us raising kids, it can be the deciding factor when choosing between sports teams, clubs, or classes. So often, people matter most.

We must populate the map of children's spaces and places with their people. As Susan Pinker describes it in *The Village Effect: Why Face-to-Face Contact Matters,* our social interactions and relationships are what lead us to decisions and actions. Even when conditions in one place are crushing, the right people can offer a lifeline[5] that keep kids afloat until they can get someplace safer. Those people can also drag children down because of how conditions impact them. People have a profound impact on how kids live and whether they thrive.[6] Similarly, kids have a profound impact on other people's lives.

When I think about this impact, it helps to consider my own children. My kids have their steadies, the people who are constantly in their lives (like me!). They have seasonal people (e.g., teachers, bus drivers, camp counselors, coaches). Then they have situational people (e.g., doctors, therapists, distant relatives). In my experience, the people who are most proximate to my kids are the ones who have the most influence over them. It helps to assemble an internal file on each child, with a list of their "proximate people" and observations you have about the nature and quality of those relationships.

Here are questions you can ask young people as you populate their maps of places with people—especially those who are most influential and impactful:

- Who do you spend the most time with in school and out of school?

- Who do you most enjoy spending time with?

- Who do you regularly connect with online (e.g., social media, games)?

- Who makes you feel safe and supported in school and out of school?

- Who are people you miss and don't see anymore?

Beyond these questions, there is another layer of people-mapping that can help you learn about a young person's world: mapping the indirect relationships in their lives that may have an outsized impact *on* their lives. Indirect relationships include people who parents and caregivers work for and other decision-makers who influence everyday experiences like school. For example, we live in a community with a large military base. Teachers in my town should know which students have family members employed at the base. If something happened there, they would know which kids and families were impacted.

Understanding and Using Maps of People and Places

Becoming a cartographer of children's worlds happens in different ways depending on your relationship with kids and the time you spend with them. For example, if you are a school counselor, mapping could be a part of your one-on-one conversations. If you're a coach, mapping could happen during "water cooler" conversations or preseason meetings with kids and their families. For teachers, mapping can be built into classroom activities, especially at the start of a school year. For parents and mentors, mapping should be ongoing. This *kid cartography* can be used or refreshed during any conversations with kids or the adults in their lives. A teacher I know makes mapping a student-driven project. He gives students a camera and a deadline and provides them with a chance to map their own world and present it to the class.

Once a map is made, there are three steps to put it into use: (1) learn the landscape, (2) consider the conditions, and (3) regularly revisit and revise.

- **Learn the Landscape** - When kids give you a picture of their world, you are being invited to learn and remember it. A map provides incredible insight into the people and places that are most important and influential in their lives. It's powerful to see kids light up when you remember something they told you that doesn't have to do with your relationship with them, or to see how a kid's entire ecosystem mobilizes to offer support during a crisis.

- **Consider the Conditions -** No one person or place gives kids everything they need—but the entire ecosystem should. In 2002, the National Research Council and Institute of Medicine released *Community Programs to Promote Youth Development.* This field-defining report described six features of positive developmental settings that help kids thrive in their environments and experiences. These characteristics are forecasting features that we can overlay on a map. Finding where these characteristics are present helps us predict whether kids have what they need to be healthy and well. According to the report, these six positive developmental features are the following:
  - Physical and psychological safety
  - Appropriate structure
  - Supportive relationships
  - Opportunities to belong
  - Positive social norms
  - Support for efficacy and mattering

- **Revisit and Revise Regularly** - Make your cartography work as an active part of the interactions and conversations you have with kids, and a data source you always consider. Look for changes in where they spend time and who they spend time with. Understand that changes can quickly shift circumstances and levels of well-being.

Through the mapping process, children share a great deal of information about who they are and the interior of their worlds, maybe even more than they understand themselves. Treat these maps with care; like the kids they reflect, they are precious and one of a kind.

CHAPTER TAKEAWAYS

- The conditions and circumstances of kids' lives depend on who they spend time with, where they spend time, and the dynamic interplay between them and those people and places. Kids are influenced by and influence the people and places in their lives.

- To learn and support children, we need to learn about their connections and context, understand the forces impacting their lives and our relationships with them, and reflect on the ways our words and actions can impact them now and later in life.

- Mapping is a process to get to know young people, including who they spend time with, what matters to them, and what their worlds include.

- Millions of kids and their families are involved in public systems, including the child welfare and justice/carceral systems. These systems are large and hard to understand and navigate. Kids need us to learn about these systems and understand what it means to be connected to them and how we can help.

- Once you have a map of the people and places that make up a kid's world, you should (1) study and learn their relational landscape, (2) consider the conditions they are living and learning in, and (3) revisit and revise the map as needed.

REFLECTION QUESTIONS

- Consider your relationships with kids. How could you incorporate and use this mapping process with them?

- Where would you find yourself in various children's maps? What responsibilities come with those placements?

- What does your "cartography" practice look like and how do you want to adjust or add to it?

- What is something you can start doing that will help you strengthen your knowledge and understanding of young people and the people and places in their lives?

Strengths and Struggles 5

I've heard it said that no two children are the same. As a parent of two, I agree.

To know my older son is to know his love of baseball. Born in St. Louis, Justice is a die-hard Cardinals fan. He wears baseball gear, is a phenom of sports trivia, and loves to play the game. He can rattle off baseball facts from obvious to obscure and is always up for driving down the road to play ball at the local parks.

On the other hand, his younger brother prefers to stay home and create. He is always thinking, tinkering, and working on new inventions and contraptions. While Justice wants to play baseball, Harrison wants to become a LEGO master, money maker, and cartoonist.

To really know my children is to know who is extroverted and who is introverted; who prefers touch, and who needs quality time; which one persuades with charm and humor, and which one goes at it with logic and persistence. To deeply know them is to be well acquainted with their quirks and struggles, to know what they have been through, and to pick up on when something is wrong.

As their mom, I want my kids surrounded by adults who deeply know them; who take time to learn their interests and idiosyncrasies, strengths and struggles; who meet them where they're at and see them in high definition; who want to see them living and learning vibrantly.

This deep knowing takes time and talent. It requires getting to know their internal and external worlds—who they are, where they come from, how they're doing, who their people are, and then taking it one step further, paying attention to what makes them come alive. These are the fine details, colors, and texture on our whole child portraits. We know we've done it right when kids tell us we really see them. This is a powerful compliment and sacred responsibility. We know this is true because we desire it too.

Learning Children's Strengths

In social work school, they teach you to always find and amplify the strengths a person has and to find ways to strengthen and build on them. In education and youth development, we call this a strengths- or assets-based approach. It's the opposite of being deficit based, which is what happens when adults hyperfocus on a kid's mistakes, shortcomings, and what they don't have.

By learning children's strengths, we see where they shine. We get an insiders' view into their personalities and abilities, what they are good at, and what sparks their interests. Strengths reveal kids' character and competencies, how they learn and lead, and what they do when given the choice. Young people can be unaware of their strengths, and it's our job to help them find them. Other times, strengths are overused—by choice, subconsciously, or because adults demand it.

A beautiful part of working with kids is helping them identify, embrace, and embody what they are good at, understand how they are wired, and explore what brings them purpose and joy. Through this, we help young people become the best version of themselves.

Character

Marvin Berkowitz is one of my favorite scholars. I met him in graduate school when I was evaluating my university's social entrepreneurship competition. During our first meeting he talked about education and innovation with arms flying, eyes dancing, and synapses firing at super speed. I was hooked. I've been asking for his advice and those conversations ever since, and this book is no exception.

When Marvin's not judging academic competitions, he is leading the *Center for Character and Citizenship* at University of Missouri-St Louis's College of Education. He's a prolific writer and researcher on children, character, and education. He's my go-to for understanding why character counts and how it develops in young people. Marvin taught me that character is about values and moral identity. It is what helps kids decide who they are and want to be.

Strength of character is about being a good person—in an ethical sense. It's about tapping into a moral compass that guides you toward doing what's right. For a time, I questioned who gets to decide what "good character" and the "right thing" are. Then I found a resource compiled by two of Marvin's colleagues that classify 24 character traits.[1] Once I saw the traits, which are listed in Table 10, I realized they were everything I wanted my own children to have and experience.

Table 10 Classification of 24 Character Traits[2]					
WISDOM & KNOWLEDGE	**COURAGE**	**HUMANITY**	**JUSTICE**	**TEMPERANCE**	**TRANSCENDENCE**
Creativity	Bravery	Love	Citizenship	Forgiveness and Mercy	Appreciation of Beauty and Excellence
Curiosity	Persistence	Kindness	Fairness	Humility and Modesty	Gratitude
Open-Mindedness	Integrity	Social Intelligence	Leadership	Prudence	Hope
Love of Learning	Vitality			Self-Regulation	Humor
Perspective					Spirituality

Source: Peterson, C., & Seligman, M. E. P. (2004). Character Strengths and Virtues: A Handbook and Classification. Oxford University Press.

This classification was developed in the early 2000s by Martin Seligman and Christopher Peterson, with contributions from many other social scientists. Today, *Character Strengths and Virtues: A Handbook and Classification* sits on my shelf as an often-used resource.

Between Marvin's wisdom and this book, I can see how kids' character is an invaluable strength, worth our attention and cultivation. Some character traits feel instinctive—like curiosity, humor, and persistence. Others don't—like forgiveness and self-regulation. All can be learned and strengthened over time, benefitting from specific instruction, skill building, and practice. Years ago, researchers believed you were born with these traits and they were fixed. Today, we have much more research that shows these traits are teachable and able to be strengthened over time.[3]

Competencies

While character strengths reveal what kids value and how they orient toward the world, competencies show us what kids can do. Competencies are different clusters of knowledge, skills, habits, and mindsets. You may have heard of or even experienced competency-based learning or career competencies. Across settings, competencies are talked about and organized in different ways, but fundamentally they are about how kids function in life and learning.

For years, I have studied competencies. It started when I launched a competency-based school for older youth on a technical college campus. We designed a curriculum called "21 by 21"—based around 21 competencies we believed students needed to master before their 21st birthdays. When I left the education frontlines, I continued to help schools, districts, colleges, and universities become competency-based. During that time, I ran a national effort called *The Readiness Project* with my colleagues Karen Pittman and Caitlin Johnson. The three of us spent more than 2 years studying and synthesizing the range of competencies kids need to be ready for adulthood.

Over time, my thinking on competencies has simplified. Across various lists and terms—employability skills, social emotional learning skills, 21st century learning skills, developmental milestones, work-ethic traits, and more—I found 10 core competencies that kids need to be ready and well, that appear in list after list, study after study. These ten "readiness competencies" are listed in Table 11.

Table 11   Ten Readiness Competencies
1. Focus and get things done
2. Think and create in ways that help to navigate, experience, and contribute to a rapidly changing world
3. Apply learning in the real world
4. Solve problems and make decisions
5. Get and stay physically, emotionally, and cognitively fit
6. Feel and express emotions appropriately
7. Persist through struggles and maintain hope
8. Relate to others and the world by forming, managing, and sustaining positive relationships
9. Be present and engage in meaningful, authentic, and appropriate ways
10. Use insights to grow and develop

Source: Krauss, S. M. (2021). *Making It: What Today's Kids Need for Tomorrow's World.* Jossey-Bass/Wiley.

Like character, some competencies feel innate, but all can be taught and strengthened. Kids might be naturally strong in one or have strength in specific skills or habits that help them get there. Gallup's popular resource, *StrengthsFinder 2.0,* talks about a "strengths equation." This is the idea of taking dominant talents—or in our case, competencies—and making those competencies stronger by investing time, practice, and knowledge.[4] In a follow-up book for parents, Gallup gives advice on four things to look for when trying to identify kids' budding talents and strengths: (1) *yearning* for certain activities and experiences; (2) *rapid learning* of skills and knowledge; (3) *satisfaction* when they do the competency or engage the talent; and (4) *timelessness,* or being able to become fully engrossed in doing the competency or engaging the talent.[5]

There are also technical competencies related to different activities, occupations, and specializations. For these, the same principles apply: help young people find and recognize what they are good at, invest in those strengths to make those skills even better, and help them develop new skills too.

Quirks

My brother Nick says, "Quirks are essential." He is a teacher and lawyer, who was smart enough to make it onto *Jeopardy*. He's also super quirky. It's endearing, and it makes him who he is. I can't imagine my brother without his idiosyncrasies—the way he fidgets when he's thinking, his style of questioning, his penchant for trivia (hence, *Jeopardy*), how he's polished in a courtroom or classroom, while also being a professional fighter.

When it comes to working with kids, and showing you care, understanding quirks and idiosyncrasies is as important as recognizing strengths of character and competencies. That's because quirks are key to a child's signature style. Quirks are the universe's way of making sure each child is truly one of a kind.

Quirks might include any of the following:

- habits and hobbies
- how someone speaks and communicates
- body language and behavior
- how someone gets energy (e.g., introvert, extravert, ambivert)
- emotional response
- personal style

Quirks should be embraced and celebrated, but when kids are in unsafe or toxic environments, quirks can make them vulnerable to mean or bullying behavior. Strive to create a culture in your classroom, on your team, in your home, and in your interactions, where kids feel safe to be their full, quirky selves. Embrace and share your own quirks openly and invite others to do the same. Have kids write or create something that showcases their personality and unique attributes. For younger kids, read or offer books with characters who are especially quirky, and then talk about it, asking kids to reflect on themselves. A friend told me about a teacher who had her students write stories where their quirks were superpowers. Kids in that class were excited to share and showcase their powers. It's harmful when young people feel like they need to suppress or stop parts of themselves. We must appreciate rather than diminish those special parts of who kids are.

Learning Strengths and Styles

New City School in St. Louis exemplifies what schooling can be when learning is built around kids' strengths and styles. Tom Hoerr is New City's retired school leader and has mentored me for years. He used to invite me to his school, and we'd walk through hallways teeming with students, their creations, and sounds and then settle in his back office, with books on all sides, to discuss ways to design school based on the science of learning. For everything Marvin taught me about character, Tom taught me about the different ways kids learn.

When Tom was at New City, his goal was to empower every kid with knowing which types of learning and multiple intelligences they gravitated toward, and how to find balance, joy, and areas of growth as learners. Some kids prefer the sciences, and others the arts (others like them equally). Some kids learn best with visual, tactile, or auditory supports. In Tom's experience, the best learning happens when kids engage and enjoy their learning preferences and strengths, while knowing they can shift and stretch when needed.

As we design learning experiences for children, we should consider various ways they might prefer to learn. Provide opportunities and experiences that cater to multiple styles and strengths. As you do, ensure you can also offer direct coaching and support to kids when they are engaged in a type of learning that may be more difficult or feel less natural.

Leadership Strengths and Styles

When I wasn't meeting with Marvin at coffeeshops or Tom at his school, I was driving across the Missouri River to learn from Jim Braun. Jim ran one of St. Louis's largest social service agencies, with programs ranging from Head Start preschools to emergency shelters for youth who were homeless. Jim was an inspiring leader who understood the importance of helping young people develop their own leadership styles and skills from an early age.

One of Jim's favorite leadership resources, which I used extensively, was Korn Ferry's *FYI: For Your Improvement Competencies Development Guide.* This guide is built around a leadership architecture that is competency-based and focused on the leadership skills needed to be effective in today's work context and across the globe.

I have taken Korn Ferry's 21st-century leadership competencies and adapted them for young leaders who will likely live and work in the 21st *and* 22nd centuries (see Table 12).

Table 12   Lifetime Leadership Strengths
Understands the world and what is at stake
Handles and manages complexity and polarities
Disruptive thinker and doer
Takes initiative and responsibility
Gets things done
Network weaver and systems thinker
Focuses and works toward the bigger picture
Builds collaborative relationships and alliances
Optimizes and supports others' strengths
Force for good
Authentic and trustworthy
Nimble and adaptable

Today's kids are growing up in a world that demands strong and evolving leadership, and many of them will lead before they feel or are ready. As we saw with COVID-19, global problems can become personal. When today's kids enter adulthood and become tomorrow's workers, they will face incredibly complex and life-changing problems.[6] Throughout childhood and adolescence, they must develop a strong sense of their leadership strengths as well as their skills and strategies to put those strengths into action.

Sharing in Children's Struggles

In the same way we shine a light on kids' strengths, we must share in their struggles. A core part of working with young people is making it clear that we care. Struggles show up when kids over- or underuse their strengths; when their character is questioned or compromised because of something they do, think, or see; when they can't do something they wish they could, or know they need to; when quirks get called out, made fun of, or become hard to manage and negatively impact their quality of life.

This is when we become diagnosticians. We gather data by watching and listening, asking good questions, interacting, and considering everything we know about kids to identify the underlying source of their struggles. Then we offer support and solidarity.

We can share in kids' struggles, meeting them in their places of pain, without having them bear the burden of our own. Showing concern and sharing your own similar experiences is different from calling on kids to carry or care about your challenges. Our work is to help them carry theirs.

Seeing Children for
Who They Are and Want to Be

Our portrait of a whole child is complete when we take our working knowledge of who kids are, where they come from, how they are doing, and the stage of life they're in, and blend those features with an authentic understanding of their real-time strengths and struggles.

Strengths and struggles color and texture the canvas. Now we see if a kid is captivated by joy or in trouble. We appreciate kids for who they are and want to be—quirks and all. When that knowledge is reflected through your relationship and the portrait you paint, children will feel known and know they matter. This is one of the most critical ingredients for their well-being and well-becoming.

CHAPTER TAKEAWAYS

- Take a strengths-based approach with kids. This gives you an inside view into their personalities and abilities, including what young people are good at and what sparks their interests.

- Strength of character is about values and moral identity. For kids, this is learning who they are and deciding who they want to be.

- Strength of skills is found in competencies. There are 10 core competencies kids need to be ready and well in the world. These competencies can be called different names (e.g., employability skills, social emotional learning skills). They are teachable, measurable, and interdependent.

- Quirks are strengths because they are a part of kids' signature identity. Quirks include habits, hobbies, body language, behavior, and personal style. Quirks should be celebrated and appreciated, but in unsafe situations they make kids vulnerable to mean or bullying behavior.

- Kids learn in different ways and have their own learning preferences. To cultivate a joy in learning, give ample opportunities for kids to explore those learning strengths and styles. To cultivate balance, provide direct support and coaching for the types of learning kids are less inclined toward, but that are equally important.

- Kids lead in different ways. In an increasingly complex and challenging world, we must attend to kids' leadership strengths and styles as much as their learning strengths and styles. Many of today's kids will live and work into the 22nd century and we must strengthen their lifetime leadership strengths.

REFLECTION QUESTIONS

- How do you already take a strengths-based approach with kids, and what could you do to help them strengthen their character, competencies, and quirks? What about their learning and leadership styles?

- Looking through the various tables in this chapter, where do you see yourself and your own strengths and struggles?

- How are you when a kid you care about is struggling? What is your approach to offering support, and what—if anything—do you want to change or keep doing?

"Whole Child" Interview Template

PORTRAIT PIECE	DETAILS	DETAILS ABOUT [CHILD'S NAME]
	Table 13 Template for Creating a Whole Child Portrait	
Demographics and Determinants	*What are this child's demographics?* (e.g., race, gender, sexuality, disability, and citizenship/immigration status) *What are this child's determinants?* (e.g., environment, social, political, and historical living conditions)	
Age and Stage	*What are this child's age and grade?* *Are they at age- or grade-level, and if not, where do you think they are?* *How are they doing developmentally?* • Socially • Emotionally • Cognitively • Spiritually	
Brain and Body	*What is the state of their six health essentials?* • Nourishment • Sleep • Movement • Relationships • Stress management • Sobriety *What is the state of the four health hazards?* • Inflammation • Illness • Injury • Imbalance	

PORTRAIT PIECE	DETAILS	DETAILS ABOUT [CHILD'S NAME]
People and Places	*What roles and responsibilities does this child have?* (e.g., brother, son, teammate, student) *What activities does this child participate in?* (e.g., school, afterschool program, baseball) *Where does this child spend time in person and online?* (e.g., clubs, cohorts, teams, groups, online) *What systems and settings is this child involved in?* (e.g., education, out-of-school time, child welfare, home) *Where does this child live and what is that place like?* (e.g., neighborhood, community, geographic region)	
Strengths and Struggles	*What are this child's strengths of character?* (e.g., curiosity, kindness) *What are this child's strongest competencies?* (e.g., engaging with people, staying fit, persisting through struggles) *What are this child's quirks?* *What are this child's learning and leadership styles?* *Where and how does this child struggle?*	

 Available for download at **www.wholechildwholelife.com**

10 Whole Life Practices

THE ART AND SCIENCE OF HELPING
KIDS LIVE, LEARN, AND THRIVE

"The soul is healed by being with children."

—Fyodor Dostoevsky

Caring for children requires science, art, and some magic. It is exhausting and exhilarating. This work is as unpredictable as it is predictable, as frustrating as it is freeing. When you reach that sweet place where connection sizzles, it feels like nothing else matters. When you've tried everything and still can't connect with a kid, it feels like nothing you do matters.

This work can be a call, a choice, and a chore. It spans caregiving, teaching, coaching, counseling, mentoring, advising, and more. Through it all, we journey alongside humans who are growing up and into themselves. Getting to play a role in their great creation story is sacred and a privilege.

What is good for kids is often good for us. Their needs speak to the deepest parts of ourselves, echoing our own desires for love, care, understanding, patience, connection, novelty, and opportunity. We too want to belong and have community to turn to. We yearn to know where we come from and why we are the way we are. We need ways to heal and have a healthy life. We also seek to serve and see the world in its splendor.

The art of this work is doing what is best for kids and having it also be good for us. It is the everyday actions that contribute to our collective well-being and in nurturing relationships, environments, and experiences that enrich everyone in them.

If we want kids to live, learn, and thrive, we must strive to do the same. As we seek to meet their needs, we must attend to our own. In some cases, this means putting principles into practice that should have been there when we were children ourselves. In other cases, this means passing on lessons we got from a healthy childhood to the children in our care.

The science of this work lives in child, youth, and lifespan development, which helps us to know what kids need at every age; it is in the science of learning which shows how the brain fires up and makes connections that become new knowledge and skills; it's in the science of health and longevity, and what our brains and bodies need for fuel, and what fulfilling lives look like and require.

This is work that asks us to commit to the care of children. To protect young people and make sure they know they are safe and welcome. It is doing whatever it takes to ensure young people have agency and autonomy over their own lives and learning. This work is prioritizing social health because relationships, relationships, relationships.

The magic emerges when we practice time-tested traditions that have worked across cultures, contexts, and generations. These include rituals, recognitions, ceremonies, and celebrations. We find ways to honor children's courage and mark their milestones and victories.

Our connection to children means they are more likely to thrive when we are doing well. Their welfare is bound up in our welfare, and ours in theirs. We live and function in ways that are highly interdependent, and often, thriving begets thriving. Even so, thriving is a state of being that is situational and seasonal. We must support kids when they are thriving, barely surviving, and everything in between. Our job is to show up with unwavering guidance, love, and support.

This is intergenerational work. This world we are working in will be the world they continue living in long after we're gone. It will become the world they'll do this care for children in, and so on.

Part II explores the 10 practices children need to live, learn, and thrive. As "whole life" practices, they work across the *wide* of life—anywhere young people spend time, and the *long* of life—being as critical for adults as for kids.

10 Whole Life Practices

1. Meet basic needs
2. Prioritize mental health
3. Invest in personal interests
4. Nurture healthy relationships
5. Build community and belonging
6. Embrace identities and cultures
7. Attend to the past and present
8. Act with a 100-year mindset
9. Be a force for good
10. Seek awe and wonder

These practices are powerful and perpetually important. They matter at each stage of life, even as the world shifts and context changes. Learn them, teach them, make them personal, and embrace them fully. They will support you and your children now and in the future.

Meet Basic Needs 6

"Everybody needs beauty as well as bread, places to play in and pray in, where Nature may heal and cheer and give strength to body and soul alike."

—John Muir

In 1943, humanist psychologist Abraham Maslow published "A Theory of Human Motivation" as an article in *Psychological Review*. In the piece, Maslow proposed five goals driving human motivation.[1] Later, this became known as "Maslow's Hierarchy of Needs," a popular framework used to describe basic needs.

Maslow's hierarchy is typically shown as a triangle or set of stairs. At the bottom are physiological needs—like clean air, water, and food. According to the theory, these must be met before you can experience higher levels, which—in the order they appear—are safety, love, esteem, and self-actualization. The theory suggests that if a person has unmet physiological needs, they cannot experience safety, love, and self-actualization.

While Maslow and his hierarchy are familiar to many, the theory is not a proven one. Some researchers even argue it's wrong.[2] For example, people can feel love and belonging without having food or housing, just like they can feel purpose while living in an unsafe environment. A mentee once told me how being homeless was one of the hardest, happiest times in their life. They worried about where they would sleep and get food, but they also experienced love and belonging at the shelter and among the young people they stayed with.

It is time to flatten Maslow's pyramid. Children need what he described and more. Accessing one level is not dependent on satisfying another, and each level is necessary to survive and thrive.

In this time of rapid change, there are new threats to basic needs and innovative ways to meet them. As you read, think about you and the kids you care about. Are your basic needs met? Meeting basic needs is a constant practice that must be a prioritized part of your relationships with kids.

Essentials

To survive, we need basic biological needs met. We must breathe, eat, drink, sleep, and relieve ourselves. We need places to shelter and sleep, clothes to wear, and a place to cool off or warm up, depending on the weather.

Young people can have unmet essential needs for many reasons. Sometimes their families can't afford essentials, or they don't have access to them. Sometimes they are denied essentials or given resources that are unhealthy and dangerous, like contaminated water. Sometimes essentials are cut off due to disaster or an emergency. There are young people whose essential needs hinge on medical treatments and medications, like a breathing machine or trach. In these cases, meeting essential needs requires ongoing access to specific medical treatments and supplies.

In the United States, people who can't meet basic needs can apply for public benefits. Benefits take many forms, including direct cash assistance, vouchers, discounts, training, referrals, and free services. This assistance is crucial, but the process can be grueling. Sometimes eligibility for one benefit makes you ineligible for another. You can be rejected because a form wasn't filled out properly. Applying can be cumbersome, frustrating, and hard to navigate. Once benefits are in hand, routine compliance checks and eligibility verifications can make it feel like you are in trouble. The process of getting benefits often feels more like surveillance or an investigation rather than assistance. This can be embarrassing and even dehumanizing.

For kids and families, this process is easier if they have navigational support and understanding. Being without essentials is hard enough. Seeking help shouldn't bring more hardship. Table 14 provides a breakdown of common U.S. benefits programs that children and their families may be eligible for.

BASIC NEED	PUBLIC BENEFIT	DESCRIPTION
		Table 14 Common U.S. Public Benefits Programs for Kids and Families[3]
Food	SNAP and EBT	The Supplemental Nutrition Assistance Program (SNAP) provides financial assistance to qualifying families based on meeting a low-income threshold. Benefits are received through an Electronic Benefit Transfer "EBT" card, which recipients use like a debit card to buy groceries. Each month, cash gets automatically deposited onto the EBT card. EBT cards are accepted at many grocery stores, convenience stores, and some farmers markets. SNAP EBT cards are a modern version of food stamps.
Food and healthcare	WIC	The Special Supplemental Nutrition Program for Women, Infants, and Children (WIC) is a benefits program for pregnant and new moms, babies, and children under five with nutritional risks. WIC provides food (e.g., formula), healthcare referrals, and no-cost social services to eligible moms and their young children.
Financial assistance and job training	TANF	The Temporary Assistance for Needy Families (TANF) is a benefits program to help eligible families reach economic self-sufficiency. TANF recipients receive direct cash assistance for basic needs, access to education and employment services, and certain health or social service referrals and services.
Health and human services	Medicaid	Medicaid is a federal and state program that provides eligible families and kids with free or low-cost health and human service care. Medicaid varies by state and serves as the largest funder of long-term care, including institutional and other residential care for kids with disabilities. Some states run Medicaid as managed care, others as fee for service, and some a combination for different populations and programs. Kids have special status under Early and Periodic Screening Diagnostic and Treatment (EPSDT) and Medicaid dollars, which can cover costs for many of their service and support needs.[4]
Healthcare	"Obamacare"	The Affordable Care Act created the Healthcare Marketplace, which provides affordable healthcare coverage for individuals and families from different income levels, including those living at or below the poverty line.

(Continued)

(Continued)

BASIC NEED	PUBLIC BENEFIT	DESCRIPTION
Financial assistance and human services	SSI	Supplemental Security Income (SSI) provides monthly cash assistance to families who are low income and have children with a disability. These cash benefits are meant to offset the costs of basic needs and services related to the disability. Children who have lost a parent may also be eligible to receive SSI survivor's benefits; to be eligible, their parent must have died after the age of eligibility for Social Security retirement benefits to start.
Childcare	Child Care Subsidies	The Child Care and Development Fund provides subsidies to families who qualify as low income to put toward stable, high-quality childcare services.
Housing for unaccompanied youth	Temporary Shelter; TLP and ILP programs	The Runaway and Homeless Youth Act provides qualifying community organizations with federal funds to offer housing and services to older youth who have run away, are homeless, and/or are in foster care. There are three types of programs: temporary shelters, transitional living programs (TLP), and independent living programs (ILP). Qualifying services include street outreach, counseling, and case management services.
Housing for families	Public Housing	The U.S. Department of Housing and Urban Development (HUD) provides housing assistance to qualifying families. These programs are meant to help families secure decent and safe rentals. Housing assistance includes housing vouchers or subsidized or free housing in the form of single-family homes, condominiums, or apartments. There are planned public housing communities and apartment buildings, as well as mixed-use or scattered site supportive housing options.
Transportation and education stabilizing services for youth who are homeless	McKinney-Vento	The U.S. Department of Education via the McKinney-Vento Act provides money to states and schools to pay for transportation, education services, and designated staff to identify and support students who meet the department's definition of homeless. McKinney-Vento ensures that students who are homeless can enroll in school immediately, even if they lack records; stay at school, even if they move out of boundaries, if it's in their best interest; and receive the supports they need to experience stability and success in school. Every state has a McKinney-Vento coordinator, and every district has a local homeless education liaison in charge of identifying students and coordinating services.

BASIC NEED	PUBLIC BENEFIT	DESCRIPTION
Transitional support services for older youth in or aging out of foster care	Chafee	The John H. Chafee Foster Care for Successful Transition to Adulthood (Chafee Program) provides direct cash assistance to older youth who have been or are in foster care to use toward education and employment training and supports, and the transition out of foster care and into adulthood. Funds can pay for tuition, job training, or related costs like childcare, transportation, or rent. There are also nongovernmental services and scholarships available for youth who are Chafee-eligible.
Emergency internet	Emergency Broadband Benefit	The USAC Affordable Connectivity Program provides qualifying low-income households with a $30 monthly discount for broadband services. For households on tribal lands, the discount is $75 per month. The program also provides a one-time discount of $100 toward the purchase of a computer or tablet.
In-school food services	Free and Reduced Lunch/Summer Meals Program	The U.S. Department of Agriculture (USDA) administers the National School Breakfast and Lunch Program and School Breakfast Program—two federal programs that waive or reduce costs of school breakfast and lunch for students living in households that meet a certain low-income threshold. The USDA's Summer Food Service Program (SFSP) ensures those same students can continue to access fresh, healthy meals during the summer months. This direct reimbursement program enables schools and community centers to become approved SFSP sites and provide meals to qualifying students when school is not in session.
Education and developmental intervention services for children with possible and diagnosed disabilities	Early Intervention	Early intervention is a free state-run program that helps families obtain screenings, services, and supports if they are concerned or know their child has a developmental delay and/or disability. At a minimum, states provide no-cost evaluations and assessment services, and the development of an Individualized Family Service Plan (IFSP).
Intervention services for children with diagnosed disabilities or other limiting conditions	IEP/504	The U.S. Department of Education via the Individuals with Disabilities Education Act (IDEA) administers funds and mandates to states and schools to ensure that the educational and developmental needs of students with disabilities, developmental delays, and other conditions are met in school.

(Continued)

(Continued)

BASIC NEED	PUBLIC BENEFIT	DESCRIPTION
		An Individualized Education Program (IEP) is a plan jointly developed by school staff, family, student, and relevant specialists. IEPs are for students who qualify for special education services and supports. An IEP articulates the unique needs a student has, and any specialized services and instructions needed to make their learning and school experience successful.
		A 504 plan is for students who may not need specialized instruction but do need special accommodations and accessibilities at school (and/or in getting to and from school). A 504 plan is important for students with certain physical and mental health challenges, or with disabilities that require non-instructional supports during the day or during specific times of year.
Workforce training and re-entry supports	WIOA youth programs	The U.S. Department of Labor via the Workforce Innovation and Opportunity Act (WIOA) provides funding to local workforce boards to distribute to qualifying programs and schools to support young people who aren't in school or working—sometimes referred to as "opportunity youth." Through WIOA, eligible young people can receive free education and employment programs and services, including YouthBuild, job training, counseling, case management, summer jobs, mentorship, tutoring, and re-entry supports if they are justice involved.
Financial assistance for higher education	FAFSA and Federal Student Aid	The FAFSA is an application young people and families use to determine eligibility for tuition assistance and need-based scholarships in college and other postsecondary credentialing programs. Individual higher education institutions may offer additional need- and merit-based financial assistance.
Cash and savings assistance	IDAs and other matched savings programs	Assets for Independence (AFI) is a community-based approach that assists children and families who struggle financially to save and build toward economic security. AFI uses Individual Development Accounts (IDAs) and similar matched-savings accounts to grow wealth. Often, IDA programs will match participants dollar for dollar up to a 3:1 match. Matched dollars can then be accessed and used to pay for assets, including housing or a car.

online
resources   Available for download at **www.wholechildwholelife.com**

When Kids Need Essentials

Essentials are about provision and sufficiency. There tend to be visible signs when essential needs are unmet. A kid who needs clothing might wear the same shirt multiple days in a row or have outfits that are dirty or don't fit. A kid who needs sleep might fall asleep when they are with you or act overtired. A child who is hungry might complain about a stomachache or ask for food. While these can be signs of unmet needs, they also may not be. Instead of jumping to conclusions, observe with an open mind and act when you're sure it is warranted.

There are many children with unmet essential needs who don't act or look like anything is wrong. Tune in to what is less visible or obvious. Maybe a child shows up late or infrequently, or a kid keeps "forgetting" their lunch or snack. You might notice gradual changes in mood or increased tiredness. If you know young people and have a "whole child" picture of who they are and how they are doing, then you will pick up on changes and know when basic needs aren't being met.

TRY THIS

- **Provide the essentials you can.** Do this in a way that upholds dignity and maintains privacy. If a family is in need, ask for donations of gift cards for food or clothing. Gift cards provide families with choice, autonomy, and flexibility. If you notice a child needs sleep, find them a safe and comfortable place to nap. Keep clean, reusable water bottles and snacks on hand for anyone who needs them. If you are a teacher or run a youth program, invite families to contribute to an emergency snack stash and regularly ask for new donations, providing suggestions of healthy and satisfying options.

- **Connect kids and families to resources.** When a child's essential needs fall outside of what you can provide, make connections to those who can help. Not knowing where to get help is a common reason why essential needs remain unmet. When I taught, I had no idea what local resources were available to my students and their families. See if your community has a resource hotline you can call and talk with trained professionals or look online for local organizations who can provide free essentials that they need.

(Continued)

(Continued)

- **Learn to navigate systems and services.** Young people who
  have experienced homelessness, foster care, and other vulnerable
  situations say they needed a navigator at school or in their
  community to rely on. Become that person. Be a caring and
  knowledgeable adult who knows about the process and paperwork
  they're faced with. If you can, take them to the benefits office
  and stay with them (and their families) while they are there. Work
  proactively to understand what they might need and where to find it.

- **Show authentic care and empathy.** Kids experience so much stigma
  and shame when essential needs are unmet, especially if outward
  signs, like dirty clothes, are evident. Showing you care and extending
  empathy for the experiences they are going through is a critical part
  of supporting children with these challenges.

Safety

We have had more than 20 years of continuous wars, political
division, racial violence, extreme rhetoric, intensifying storms, mass
shootings, economic crises, global pandemics, and more. There seems to
be no shortage of safety issues without an end in sight. Today's kids are
"disruption natives," living and learning in constant instability, knowing
something is off because they see adults' fear and anxiety. Additionally,
young people who are disadvantaged and vulnerable because of their
demographics and determinants regularly feel unsafe because of how
systems were designed and how people in those spaces treat them. Too
few spaces are designed to prioritize diverse and less dominant needs,
abilities, cultures, and contexts.

Today's kids face constant stress and threat and say they want nothing
more than to know they are safe—even though they know it's unlikely.[5]
Children crave certainty and stability, but many feel regularly unsafe. It
is an everyday worry[6] and a burden to bear.[7]

Safety is both physical and psychological. There is safety from
immediate harm and ongoing risks. There is systemic and structural
safety (I am safe in this place and with these people), environmental
safety (I am safe from toxins), school and neighborhood safety (I am
safe where I learn, live, and play), and personal safety (I am safe to
be who I am).

Kids must feel safe with us and in the spaces we share with them. We may not be able to solve all safety concerns, but we can do what we can to prioritize physical and psychological safety in the relationships, environments, and experiences we offer them.

When Kids Need Safety

Safety is about security and stability. Kids who feel physically unsafe often feel and express it in their bodies. Early signs relate to our "fight or flight" stress response—a faster heartbeat, butterflies, a tingling feeling, vision changes. These are physical ways our body prepares to respond to danger. Kids in this state can appear reactive, angry, skittish, anxious, scared, or panicked. Research on trauma and stress shows that kids who live and learn in threatening environments can easily turn on their stress response, but sometimes struggle to turn it off. These kids may respond to not-dangerous things as though they were a threat, or not respond to situations that are actually unsafe.[8]

Kids who feel psychologically and emotionally unsafe may be afraid to feel or express emotions, take risks, or try new things.[9] They might suppress parts of themselves to be less emotional or obvious. This is a survival tactic, to protect themselves from something bad happening. Signs kids might feel psychologically and emotionally unsafe include withdrawal, not wanting to participate in activities, lack of interest, becoming more aggressive or outspoken, stress, or difficulty focusing.[10] When severe, kids can become anxious, depressed, and even suicidal.[11] In these situations, young people become a threat to themselves.

When kids know they are safe, they describe the world as brighter and more beautiful. Safety frees them from the exhaustion of having to constantly assess surroundings and situations and from the need to self-protect or protect others. Being safe gives kids room to explore, take risks, enjoy themselves, and live and learn more freely.[12]

- **Assess risk and eliminate danger.** Your job is to do no harm and protect kids from harm. This requires observation and investigation. If you notice kids feel physically or psychologically unsafe, ask them about it. Pay attention to how they interact, react, and behave. If you can do so safely, directly address safety concerns. If it is unsafe, ask for help.

TRY THIS

(Continued)

(Continued)

- **Create and offer safe spaces.** Ensure your spaces are safe ones. Focus on building respectful and supportive relationships. Value social and emotional health above performance. Do not tolerate bullying, harassment, or meanness. Establish clear structures and rules that kids know, understand, and can follow.[13]

- **Develop safety plans.** Some kids benefit from having a safety plan or contract, especially when they might hurt themselves. A safety plan—sometimes called a crisis plan or safety contract—includes a child's commitment to specific actions that will keep them safe. It can list preferred coping skills (e.g., deep breathing, taking a shower), and sources of support (who to go to when things get bad). It might include activities or distractions kids enjoy. If you feel comfortable and capable of making a safety plan with a kid who needs one, do it. If you're not sure about it, but think it could be beneficial, reach out to a mental health professional for help.

- **Know when to get help.** Some safety concerns are out of your control and need outside intervention and expertise. Know your personal limits and triggers related to safety issues kids might face. Figure out when you would need to call family members, other adults, first responders (e.g., police, EMTs), or mental health professionals. You don't want to sit on a safety issue and not act because you don't know what to do. You also don't want to find yourself unprepared in a true emergency. Forecasting scenarios and planning may help mitigate risks.[14]

Belonging

Young people are biologically wired for love, connection, and attachment—key ingredients for belonging. We need connection to other people to survive, and our health and development are strengthened and propelled by nurture, comfort, touch, and affection.

In the 1950s, behavioral scientist Harry Harlow conducted a landmark study with baby monkeys to demonstrate the importance of attachment. He removed baby monkeys from their mothers and socially isolated them. Before long, the monkeys began to exhibit disturbing behaviors, including self-harm and refusing food. Some even died. Next, Harlow split a group of baby monkeys into two groups and gave them all wire-made, inanimate "mothers." Some got bare-wired surrogates while others got surrogates covered in a soft cloth. Harlow discovered that the monkeys with cloth surrogates fared better than those without. These monkeys nuzzled their cloth wire monkey moms for comfort and clung to it when frightened.[15] While I don't endorse Harlow's methods, his research was the first of its kind and it initiated a body of research that showed how important attachment and comfort are for a child's development and well-being.

Today, we have more humane research to look to. In recent years, leading scholars and thought leaders like Shawn Ginwright, Arnold Chandler, and Mia Birdsong have illuminated the crucial role belonging plays in health, healing, relationships, learning, development, and justice—especially for young people of color and other marginalized groups. Belonging is a critical part of physical and psychological safety, and it strengthens young people's self-acceptance and self-worth. Belonging is collective care that is beautifully carried out in cultural and community contexts.[16] It is a fundamental human need to stay alive and thrive in life.[17]

When Kids Need Belonging

Belonging is about love, connection, and care. It is tied to kids' being attached to and accepted by others. It is key to feeling welcome and wanted in communities and cultures. While it is socially steeped, belonging is an important part of developing a sense of self and personal identities. When children feel like they don't belong, they might self-isolate, withdraw, and experience intense loneliness. Children can appear connected on the outside but be privately insecure. Loss or lack of belonging can contribute to anxiety and depression.

In the worst cases, kids respond like Harlow's monkeys. Their lack of attachment and feelings of not belonging lead to social isolation, and potentially damaging and dangerous behaviors. This can make kids susceptible to political tribalism, gangs, radicalization, lone shootings, and other violent behaviors. Because we are wired for belonging, kids will gravitate to whoever offers it to them.

TRY THIS

- **Act with compassion and radical acceptance.** Like us, kids need love and connection, and suffer when they don't have it. Use this shared need to activate empathy and extend your capacity for love and connection to any child you interact with.[18]

- **Be reflective and responsive.** Be aware of the identities and power you carry in your relationships and interactions with kids. In group settings, try not to give more validity to certain kids if you agree with their opinions or beliefs. Steer clear of responses like "I agree" or "Good job." Instead, go for more reflective responses that center what you have heard, repeating it back for clarity or confirmation, rather than of validating (or invalidating) its correctness.[19]

- **Build beloved community.** Live out the belief that belonging is necessary for well-being. Prioritize culture building and fostering a healthy and welcoming environment. Engage kids in relationship- and community-building activities. Get training in how to facilitate healing circles, mediation, inner-group dialogue, and other strategies that foster love, acceptance, and connection with and among young people.

Purpose

Children need to know they matter and that their lives have meaning.[20] This is even more important during challenging times. A foundational human survival tactic is to find meaning in hardship, to cling to a bigger purpose and narrative, and use it for motivation to keep going.[21] We can look to ancient times and see how stories were used to press on through incredible suffering and into the wild unknown. Meaning-making and mattering is core to what keeps us alive and makes us human.

For Maslow, purpose was split between two levels—esteem and self-actualization. I believe they go together and can be thought of as meaning and mattering. According to Heather Malin, author of *Teaching for Purpose,* meaning is about having purpose, and purpose is different from passion. Every kid needs purpose but only some have specific passions. When I interviewed Malin, she told me that purpose and meaning clarify what matters to you and enables you to envision a future that includes and protects those things. Living a life of meaning is about understanding and living your purpose in the world and knowing you and your efforts matter. Purpose activates agency and fuels a desire to be a part of something bigger than ourselves.

Research shows that meaning and mattering are extra important in the tween and teen years. A core developmental task of adolescence is making meaning and finding purpose from life events and experiences. This basic need supports positive development and strengthens personal resiliency.[22] Research also shows that meaning and mattering are strengthened when kids have a sense of spirituality, which is explored in Chapter 15, "Seek Awe and Wonder." Regardless of whether spirituality attaches to religion, kids benefit from feeling connected to a higher power and calling, as well as being in a community of fellow believers. Children are naturally spiritual, and faith community and spiritual practices can be a way to tap into purpose.[23]

When Kids Need Purpose

Purpose is about meaning and mattering. These needs build fortitude that keeps kids going in a chaotic world. When children don't feel like they matter, or struggle to find meaning, they despair. In Maslow's pyramid, essentials ("physiological needs") are at the bottom while purpose is at the top ("esteem" and "self-actualization"). In life, losing purpose is like having your life force ripped from your body. It is as foundational to surviving and thriving as breathing.

Young people who struggle with purpose may experience sadness, despondency, and a sense of giving up or not wanting to go on. They might seem checked out, exhausted, or unmotivated. This can be because kids feel disrespected or unseen. Some may feel like their ideas

TRY THIS

- **Respect kids and what matters to them.** The best way to support young people's need for purpose is to show respect and make sure they know their ideas and contributions count. Practice active listening and give young people room to explore what matters to them.

- **Offer opportunities that support meaning-making.** Teach kids storytelling and reflection techniques, like journaling, creative writing, dance, and photography. Give them different ways to put those practices in place, allowing for plenty of creative freedom.

- **Explore your own purpose.** One of the best ways to honor this need in kids is to honor it in yourself. Purpose will be better prioritized with kids if it is present and prioritized in your own life.

(Continued)

(Continued)

- **Consider your feelings on spirituality.** Many of us work in spaces that are not religious and may not be appropriate places to talk with kids about faith or spirituality. Some people don't feel comfortable having those conversations. Think creatively about how you might support those who want to explore their spirituality. For example, if you work with older kids, consider conversations about what they think their life's purpose is, or what activities give them the most pride and satisfaction.

and opinions don't matter, or that their purpose isn't something they can pursue.

More Than Maslow

While essentials, safety, belonging, and purpose map to Maslow's theory of human motivation, there are four additional needs children have:[24]

- Play
- Downtime
- Exploration
- Community

These are what kids need to thrive, not just survive. Children need to develop and connect through unstructured play. They deserve and require time to rest, relax, and recharge. They delight in novelty and the chance to explore and experience nature. They benefit from our mutual need for each other, a flagship of living in relationship and community.

Rights Worth Fighting For

There are needs to meet and there are rights to defend (see Figure 3). Kids deserve to be treated with dignity and worth, and their bodies must be protected from harm. While that might seem obvious, it hasn't always been viewed that way. It wasn't until 1938 that the United States outlawed child labor. Back then, many kids left school to work and make money for their families.[25]

In 1948, a decade after the United States declared child labor illegal, international leaders established the Universal Declaration of Human

Rights, which described childhood as a time that requires extra care and assistance. Eleven years later, the General Assembly of the United Nations adopted the first-ever *Declaration of the Rights of the Child.* This declaration signaled a shift in the international community to recognize the specific and unique needs of children, and their entitlement to certain rights.

By 1989, the UN General Assembly unanimously adopted the *Convention on the Rights of the Child*, which included 54 articles outlining child rights with minimum standards for protecting those rights.[26] Like a "Kids' Constitution," the Convention is still in place, and it can be revisited and amended by the General Assembly.

Here are some of the child rights found in the 54 articles, paraphrased, which we must uphold:

- Right to fair treatment

- Right to personal identity

- Right to personal agency

- Right to family connections and a home

- Right to personal expression

- Right to privacy

- Right to information

- Right to protection from harm

- Right to get help that's needed

- Right to healthcare and education

We must do everything we can to ensure these rights are protected. Ideally, they will be firmly in place. Sometimes kids are denied rights because of where they live, who they are, or the situations they are in. Consider children trapped in abusive households, children in foster care, young people exploited by peers or predators, young people rejected by family and faith community because of who they are attracted to, young people denied healthcare or education because they are incarcerated, or young people falsely accused of crimes because of how they look. And so on. The less advantage and more vulnerability kids have (see Tables 2 and 3 for a refresh), the more likely they are to have their rights diminished or denied.

Figure 3   Children's Basic Needs and Rights

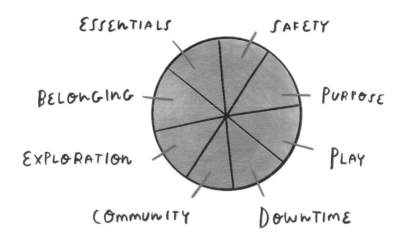

NEEDS

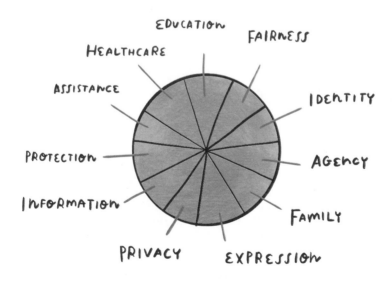

RIGHTS

Meeting Basic Needs in Times of Crisis

Care for kids long enough and you will walk with them through crisis. Crises can be global, local, or personal. Often, a crisis will cut across levels because there's a downslope effect: global disasters become local and personal, and local crises impact us personally.

Crises are a hard and inevitable part of life. They also seem to be happening more often. While we can't stop them, we can support kids as they experience them, working hard to ensure they have their basic needs met throughout.

Times of crisis are also times to pull together. This is when we can help organize and participate in food drives, fundraisers, meal trains, and donation requests. We can protest and petition if help isn't available to those who need it. We are called to be there and stand up for kids who are hurting and facing unfair treatment.

Crises can be times when basic needs are most pronounced and at risk. Amazingly, beautifully, the ripping away of one need (e.g., essentials or safety) sometimes leads to an exponential increase of another (e.g., love, belonging, purpose). This offsetting helps children *and* adults survive and recover. Think about stories of people coming together, sometimes spontaneously, to respond, grieve, and make sense of a tragedy or disaster. It happened in my community after Ferguson, and again after a school shooting. In the days and weeks that followed, people gathered in parks for prayer vigils, and in living rooms to cry, process, and plan action. While the news shined the camera on protests, those of us living locally saw many different pockets of people gathering to share grief and support one another. Crisis can bring out the worst *and* best parts of the human experience.[27]

I have a dear friend who counsels the dying at our city hospital. She is my neighbor, and we spent hours during the COVID-19 pandemic walking our trails and processing what was happening. During those walks, I confessed how worried I was about our children. She shared that a part of supporting kids' well-being is letting them know that bad things happen and that when they do, it is appropriate to grieve loss and feel pain. We don't want to think about and prepare for these moments because we don't want kids to hurt or disasters to happen. Yet, we take first aid and CPR classes in case kids need emergency medical attention. We have fire drills and active shooter drills in case disaster comes to our building. We must also prepare for how to help kids meet their basic needs during and after crisis.

Partnering With Others

In my first year of teaching, a student's home burned down. Overnight, she and her family lost everything. Her parents were in a tight financial position, and they didn't own their home or have insurance. There was no money saved to replenish what was lost. My student showed up the next day, sooty and in shock. I had no clue what to do. I was trained to develop and deliver lesson plans and curriculum and I lacked know-how and skills to show up for my student in a crisis.

When I think about why I left the classroom to become a social worker, this is the memory that comes to mind. I wish I had known what to do: how to offer effective assistance to her and her family, what to say, and what connections to make. I wish I had known how to help in practical and tangible ways.

Too often, we engage with kids without understanding their needs and rights or what we can and should do to meet them. We are their trusted teachers, counselors, coaches, caregivers, and mentors. We are the people they look to for support and answers and the ones they turn to in tough times. We owe it to them to educate and equip ourselves on how to meet their most basic, human needs.

Meeting basic needs is something you don't have to do alone. Connect with others who have experience and expertise in areas you do not. This whole life practice should be approached with humility, honesty, and a willingness to reach out for help yourself.

WHOLE LIFE PRACTICE

Meet Basic Needs

Learn

- Children have four basic needs to survive: essentials, safety, belonging, and purpose. These needs can be pursued and experienced together, and each need can be experienced in the absence of others.

- Children have four additional needs to thrive: play, downtime, exploration, and community.

- Children have rights that must be upheld and defended. These rights include fair treatment, family, protection, privacy, personal expression, healthcare, and education.

- Crises are happening more frequently. Get trained in how to help kids through disasters and other traumatic events. Learn about local and professional resources for kids and families; that way, you can make connections when they are needed.

Reflect

We all need our basic needs met. It's like oil for a car—necessary fuel to live and grow. Our needs can be depleted and filled, and if we run on empty for too long, we can't run at all.

Use the basic needs inventory chart to take stock of how you and your kids are doing.

Basic Needs Inventory for You

RATING 0-UNMET; 5-FULLY MET							REFLECTIONS
Essentials	0	1	2	3	4	5	
Safety	0	1	2	3	4	5	
Belonging	0	1	2	3	4	5	
Purpose	0	1	2	3	4	5	

(Continued)

(Continued)

Basic Needs Inventory for a Child

RATING 0-UNMET; 5-FULLY MET							REFLECTIONS
Essentials	0	1	2	3	4	5	
Safety	0	1	2	3	4	5	
Belonging	0	1	2	3	4	5	
Purpose	0	1	2	3	4	5	
Play	0	1	2	3	4	5	
Downtime	0	1	2	3	4	5	
Exploration	0	1	2	3	4	5	
Community	0	1	2	3	4	5	

 Available for download at **www.wholechildwholelife.com**

Once you've completed the inventories, reflect on these questions:

- How am I doing?

- How are the children?

- Where am I struggling?

- What do I need to do?

This is an informal inventory that can be used as an observational and reflection tool; it is not an empirical instrument. Use it to magnify basic needs and figure out what you need to prioritize.

Act

As you absorb what you read and reflected on, consider how you can put insights into action. Take time to set a few commitments and intentions on how to *Meet Basic Needs:*

- What is one small action you can take *today* to put this practice into action?

- What is one larger action you can take *this month* to put this practice into action?

- What is one big action you can work toward *this year* to put this practice into action?

Prioritize Mental Health 7

> "Wellness, I came to realize, will not happen by accident. It must be a daily practice, especially for those of us who are more susceptible to the oppressiveness of the world."
>
> —Jenna Wortham

In October 2021, more than a year and a half into the COVID-19 pandemic, America's pediatricians declared child and teen mental health a national emergency. In a press release, the American Academy of Pediatrics (AAP), American Academy of Child & Adolescent Psychiatry (AACAP), and the Children's Hospital Association described a mental health crisis that had been building for more than a decade. The pandemic and increased racial violence, plus persistent inequities, had created a maelstrom that brought mental health challenges among young people to all-time emergency levels.[1]

Three months later, the U.S. Surgeon General released an advisory and report, *Protecting Youth Mental Health*. He called the challenges today's kids face "unprecedented and uniquely hard to navigate." He wrote that the "effect these challenges have had on their mental health is devastating."[2]

The Surgeon General's report offered these sobering statistics:

- From 2009 to 2019, the number of high schoolers reporting sadness or hopelessness increased by 40 percent. In those same years, youth suicide attempts increased by 36 percent.
- In 2021, during the first year of the COVID-19 pandemic,
  - Global rates of young people experiencing mental illness more than doubled, with one in four experiencing symptoms of depression and one in five experiencing anxiety.

- ○ Girls requiring emergency room care because of attempted suicide went up by 50 percent.
- ○ Black children younger than 13 were more than twice as likely to commit suicide than white children, which was a rapid rise from previous years.
- ○ Children in poverty were 3 times more likely to develop mental health conditions than wealthier peers.

My conversations with educators, counselors, and caregivers back these numbers up. School counselors tell me they create more student safety contracts each week than they used to in a school year. Teachers insist most high schoolers have diagnosable depression or anxiety. Parents share stories of taking their suicidal teens to emergency rooms and being turned away because there are no available beds or psychiatrists.

Everyone I know who cares about kids worries about their mental health. They report that young people who struggle the most are those with other challenges—often because of their demographics and determinants (see Chapter 1).[3]

Since 2022, kids have been trying to recover from the collective and individual traumas they faced during the COVID-19 pandemic, in addition to overlapping economic crises, natural disasters, and high-profile acts of racial and political violence. This reminds me of something Anya Kamenetz said in her book about children's learning and lives during the first year of the COVID-19 pandemic:

> We are living in an era where human-induced disasters rain fresh blows on already-bruised skin. We need to get a lot better at education in emergencies.[4]

If we are going to prioritize kids' mental health, we must recognize and accept their realities. This requires ruthless honesty and compassion along with consideration of how complex and chaotic things are for young people and the adults around them. We must equip kids to take charge of their own mental health, so they can take care of themselves and each other now and in the future.

Responding to Mental Health Challenges

My son developed OCD at the same time America's pediatricians and the U.S. Surgeon General declared youth mental health an emergency. By then, one in six school-aged kids were experiencing identifiable mental health conditions.[5]

Even though I met my husband in graduate school for social work, we still missed signs of our child's mental health challenges. It was a global pandemic and he was afraid of getting sick and dying; so were we. I figured his elevated anxiety and changed behaviors were circumstantial, not clinical. They were, in part. Mental health conditions are shaped by family history, genetics, environmental circumstances, brain and body chemistry, and larger forces.[6] Circumstances caused by the pandemic probably activated OCD in my son early, but his predispositions already made him a likely candidate for the condition.

Red Flags for Mental Health Challenges and Conditions

Mental health is reflected in a young person's positive and productive relationships, responsibilities, and activities (e.g., school and family), while **mental illness** is reflected in disturbing thoughts, emotions, and behaviors that interfere with or impede that positive engagement.[7]

All kids have times when they are upset, stressed, or anxious. These strong feelings can last an hour, day, week, or more. Sometimes a physical illness, grief, or trauma looks like mental illness. We must do the work and take time to identify various factors that might be causing a child's suffering.

Like physical illness or injury, mental illness may require professional care. Professionals can evaluate symptoms and consider a child's living situation, culture, and circumstances. Proper diagnosis is a precondition for an effective treatment plan, and diagnosing a mental health condition is complicated. Sometimes, as with medical doctors, professionals might misdiagnose or recommend interventions or medications that don't work.[8] Kids need professionals who are responsive to concerns in treatment choice and willing to adjust as necessary.

Young people should not go through these types of professional evaluations and treatment decisions by themselves. They need adults who know and care about them, and who have enough knowledge about mental health to be a discerning and active presence throughout the process.

COMMON SIGNS OF YOUTH MENTAL HEALTH CHALLENGES

There are red flags that can alert us to children struggling with their mental health. If you see any of the following, seek more information and be prepared to offer support and assistance:[9]

- Any time a young person tells you they need help, or that something is wrong

(Continued)

(Continued)

- Any time a young person tells you they feel "off" and not themselves

- Slipping grades or performance on schoolwork

- Isolation, reluctance, or refusal to go to school, and/or withdrawing from activities

- Sudden changes in relationships, friendships, and social interactions

- Surprising changes in clothing, like long sleeves in warm weather, which could hide self-harm behaviors like cutting or weight loss

- Out-of-character or disturbing behaviors

- Sudden changes in personal hygiene

- Disrupted sleep, including insomnia, nightmares, or sleeping during the day

- Emotional volatility, including getting easily upset, sad, or angry; having a hard time controlling emotions or calming down

- Excessive worry and expressed feelings of anxiety, dread, or panic that don't get better with reassurance or logic

- Temporary relief from fear or anxiety after doing a repetitive action, like saying the same word or phrase or following a particular rule or routine

- Excessive social media and internet use, or suddenly stopping online activity

- Overly secretive and sneaky behaviors

- Use of violent or hateful language toward self or others

- Distinctly flat affect

- Perfectionism or hypervigilance about what others think

- Negative self-talk

These signs may mean a young person is struggling with their mental health, or they could be a red flag for some other issue, like bullying, harassment, or physical illness. There are also young people who suffer silently and have no visible signs of distress. Any child can have a mental health challenge or condition, no matter how "together" or "normal" they seem to be.

 This list is available for download at **www.wholechildwholelife.com**

In your relationships with kids, try to be someone they feel safe talking to about their challenges and concerns. Talk about mental health and normalize conversations about it. Maintain open lines of communication and let them know you are available to talk.

Grief and Loss

Grief wounds young people emotionally. When a child is grieving, they need space to do it their own way. That means we need to know what grief looks like. Grief can include many of the red flags, including a change in appetite, restlessness, trouble focusing and paying attention, anger, and deep sadness. When we see these symptoms and know a child has lost someone or something, we can help them name what they are feeling as grief. When young people don't have language for their feelings, they might misinterpret what is happening and think they have a mental illness. If grief makes it hard for a young person to function and impairs their psychological well-being, they might benefit from professional support and care.

Grief counselors, like my friend Katie Gholson, have realized the stages of grief aren't set or sequential—kids can be in denial and angry at the same time; they can seem to be accepting a loss and then shift to anger. Young people should be able to feel whatever they need to feel for however long they need to feel it. For example, anger is an appropriate response for a child who has lost someone or something they love. Don't try to stop or suppress it. Support kids while they are in it. As Katie taught me, grief that isn't allowed out becomes trauma.

Young people grieve all kinds of losses: the loss of a person or experience, the loss of a family because of divorce, or the loss of a home because of a move. They might grieve the ending of a school, team, or relationship. By naming the feelings connected to these losses as grief, we normalize what kids are experiencing and help them heal.

Stigma and Shame

Even if you are open to talking about mental health, children might not be. Young people may resist or reject mental health care because of stigma and shame, or because of a bad experience with treatment or therapy. These feelings can be situational, cultural, or historic.[10]

As my son wisely says, telling someone he fights OCD is one thing. It makes him feel brave and strong. Being told he has a "disorder" is another. It makes him feel sick and insecure. Be careful with the words you use when talking with young people about their mental health.

As a social worker, I learned to use person-first language to decouple diagnoses from the person. This strategy leads with the person, followed by the situation or experience. Be careful not to use a clinical diagnosis to describe a nonclinical situation (e.g., "I need things clean, it's my OCD" or "She's acting like she has ADD"). Never disclose a young person's mental health status or diagnoses without permission and a good reason.

Table 15 demonstrates how person-first language works.

Table 15 Using Person-First Language to Reduce Stigma and Shame	
INSTEAD OF SAYING	TRY THIS
"My depressed student"	"My student has symptoms of depression"
"That anxious kid"	"That child seems/is anxious"
"Her alcoholic parent"	"Her parent has alcoholism"
"My behavioral disorder student"	"My student has a behavior disorder"

Many kids are eager to discuss mental health and may be more open about it than adults. The young people I know seem to realize mental health is a serious problem for their generation, and most have personal stories and struggles. This openness is admirable, and it can be uncomfortable for people who grew up keeping mental illness a secret. If that's you, you're not alone. That's also not a reason to dismiss children's struggles, which can perpetuate stigma and shame.

Mental Health First Aid

In 2000, Betty Kitchener wanted to make it easier to respond effectively to mental health red flags. She used her background in education, counseling, and nursing and worked with her husband Professor Tony Form to codevelop and launch "Mental Health First Aid." MHFA is taught by trained instructors, with a set curriculum and coursework, like CPR and first aid. It is a way for teens and adults to become mental health first responders. Today, MHFA is an international model, adapted and promoted in the United States by the National Council for Mental Wellbeing and the Missouri Department of Mental Health.

When I was a kid, my mom taught CPR and first aid classes, and over the years I listened to hundreds of hours of instruction on how to respond to a medical emergency. First, you survey the scene for danger; then, you call or direct someone to call 911; next, you assess the victim(s) for injuries; if needed, you initiate first aid or CPR until help arrives. MHFA teaches a similar action plan, called ALGEE, which we should all learn and practice:

- **A - Approach and assess for risk of suicide and harm.** Find a safe, appropriate place to talk to a child you are worried about. If they don't want to talk, encourage them to share with someone they trust and make sure they know you are always available to listen.

- **L - Listen nonjudgmentally.** If a child chooses to share, allow them to talk without interrupting. When they finish, express empathy and show acceptance even if you don't fully understand or agree.

- **G - Give reassurance and information.** Offer hope, care, and useful information and resources. Before a crisis, learn what in-person and online resources are available and who to contact if a challenging situation or crisis occurs.

- **E - Encourage appropriate professional help.** Offer to assist in finding help. This could mean connecting a child with a school counselor, social worker, therapist, or therapeutic program. To learn more about different types of therapy, see the insert in this chapter, *A Starter Guide to Child and Youth Therapy*.

- **E - Encourage self-help and other support strategies.** Work with the child to brainstorm immediate self-care strategies and coping skills, which can include any of the emotional care and hygiene strategies described later in this chapter. Strategies also include support groups, family engagement, or changing personal habits like getting more sleep.

If you can, get trained in MHFA.[11] Also research in-personal and virtual resources that you feel comfortable recommending. My go-to resource is the National Alliance on Mental Illness (NAMI) website, which includes information for you and kids. It breaks down different types of mental illness, provides resources for working with and raising kids, and offers useful guidance for different identities and cultural backgrounds.

TRY THIS
- If you live in the United States, commit 988 to memory. It is the 911 for mental health emergencies. If you live outside the United States, find the mental health and crisis hotlines in your area. If those phone numbers are hard to memorize, add them to your phone contacts.

- Find someone who you can learn and practice mental health first aid with. Get together and come up with a few scenarios. For example, a high school teacher might find a suicidal message or picture written in a student notebook; a coach might have an athlete suddenly withdraw from the team; a parent might notice dramatic changes in a child's behavior or hygiene.
  - Once you have your scenario, follow these three steps:
    - Look through the red flags and talk about any signs you might observe, and how you'd respond.
    - Run the scenario through the ALGEE five-step Action Plan.
    - Reflect on what you'd need if this scenario happened in real life. Plan a way to get that information or training.

A STARTER GUIDE TO CHILD AND YOUTH THERAPY

Professional mental health care is like physical care. There are generalists, specialists, and various treatments to consider. Approaches and effectiveness range by condition, circumstances, and child. Mental health care can happen in person, online, or a combination. Some therapists even check in with young clients by text or meet in a virtual platform using avatars. Young people are digital natives and may prefer tech and text options. Be sure to follow a young person's lead and preferences when considering and choosing care.

The different types of therapy can be overwhelming, but there are common ones that are good to be aware of. Before referring a child to an individual therapist, you can ask for an interview. Here are some questions you might ask and discuss:

- What are your specialties?

- What's your professional training and experience?

- What types of therapeutic techniques do you use most often?

- Have you worked with children like [describe the child and situation], and can you tell me about how you would approach this child and situation?

- How have you seen your strategies and training work with children like [again describe the situation]?

If a child is dealing with a specific issue, they might need multiple mental health specialists and therapeutic options. Children can also benefit from having a therapist with a similar background (e.g., faith, race, gender). Sometimes this is hard to find, but it is appropriate to share that desire with a prospective therapist as a way of discerning whether they are a good fit.

Here is a breakdown of common types of specialized therapy. Most require professional training and certification beyond a general counseling or social work degree:

- *Talk Therapy* - Talk therapy is what many of us think of as "therapy." This is when a trained professional uses verbal sharing, processing, and reflection techniques to help people work through their mental health challenges. Talk therapy can be done individually or in duos and groups. Talk therapy is effective for general mental health challenges and concerns, including depression, family and school challenges, life changes, grief, and emotional regulation. Talk therapy relies heavily on the chemistry and communication between client and therapist or the group, so it is important for kids to find a talk therapist they can trust.

- *Cognitive Behavioral Therapy (CBT)* - CBT blends cognitive therapy with behavioral therapy. This approach focuses on challenging thoughts and beliefs, with the identifying behaviors that perpetuate them. CBT is a direct, specific, and goal-oriented therapy type. CBT can be extremely effective for a range of childhood mental health challenges including depression, eating disorders, and addictions. It is the treatment of choice for anxiety, phobias, and OCD.[12]

  - *Acceptance and Commitment Therapy* (ACT) is a targeted CBT strategy that can be used to help kids accept their thoughts and feelings and commit to making behavioral changes that are good for them, no matter how they feel about those changes at the time.

  - *Exposure and Ritual Prevention* (ERP) is a targeted CBT strategy that can be used to help kids overcome obsessions and compulsions.

  - *Dialectical Behavior Therapy (DBT)* - DBT is a variation of CBT used to manage overwhelming and destructive emotions and behaviors. It can help kids develop distress tolerance, mindfulness practices, emotional regulation skills, and relationship/interpersonal skills.[13] DBT is a great option for kids who haven't been helped by other therapy types.

- *Pharmacotherapy (Psychiatric/Psychotropic Medication)* - Pharmacotherapy is the treatment of mental health conditions with medication. This should only

(Continued)

(Continued)

happen under the direct care and supervision of a trained medical professional. Pharmacotherapy can be an effective treatment option—or part of a multipart treatment plan—for kids with attention and hyperactivity disorders, severe depression, bipolar disorder, and other serious mental illnesses. Medications should be carefully considered, chosen, monitored, and adjusted if needed.

- *Eye Movement Desensitization and Reprocessing (EMDR)* - EMDR is a specific therapy type used to heal from trauma and painful life experiences. During EMDR sessions, a specially trained therapist supports a young person who talks through a painful memory while simultaneously watching a repetitive outside stimuli, like the therapist's fingers going back and forth or tapping.[14] EMDR is a proven therapeutic intervention for children who survived traumatic events.

- *Play Therapy* - Play therapy is an interactive and interpersonal therapeutic technique where a therapist uses play to help children prevent or resolve difficulties and encourage healthy development and life skills. Play therapy is an effective treatment for children experiencing developmental and learning delays, disabilities, and for younger children.[15]

- *Art and Music Therapy* - Art and music therapies are interactive and expressive therapy types that use creating and viewing art and music to tap into and express deep emotions, which can be unspoken and unrealized. Art and music therapists provide young people with materials to create, view art, or listen to music and then use those experiences to help them process feelings and worries. Art and music therapy can be good for kids experiencing situational stressors like illness, divorce, or grief. It can also be helpful for kids who already consider themselves artistic or musical, or for those who don't want to talk about their problems.

- *Dance and Movement Therapy* - Dance/movement therapy focuses on body movement. It is highly individualized and aims to help young people improve self-esteem, body image, and strengthen their coping skills. Dance and movement therapy can be a great option for kids with developmental delays, those who are nonverbal, those who live in hospital or residential settings, and those with chronic or serious health issues.[16]

For more information on specific mental health conditions and recommended treatment options and guidelines, check out the book *Child & Adolescent Mental Health: A Practical, All-In-One Guide* by Dr. Jess P. Shatkin.

 Available for download at **www.wholechildwholelife.com**

Emotional Wound Care

The following strategies are like the emotional equivalent of a bandage and salve to cover and heal a cut. These are specific techniques kids can use when they experience negative emotions or mental health challenges. This is not an exhaustive list, but these strategies are worth trying and putting into a mental health toolkit if they work.

When Feeling Overwhelmed and Overloaded

Think about brains like smartphones. The more apps that are open, the slower they run. If a smartphone is due for an update or upgrade, it gets glitchy. Unfortunately, brains might be at maximum cognitive capacity, but there's no new update to download or better brain to buy. Kids need strategies to manage cognitive bandwidth issues by turning off the "apps" they are not using.

A counterintuitive but effective way to manage cognitive bandwidth is to build in breaks and times without tech or distractions. My friend Maddy Day calls this taking time to "pause and pace." When we shift to rest and get rid of the noise around us (especially digital device dings), we can sort through what really needs and deserves our limited time and attention.[17]

When Feeling Anxious and Worried

Fears and worries are huge distractions. It's hard for a child to focus on an assignment or activity when they are on high alert. There is an effective CBT technique developed by Dr. Aureen Pinto Wagner that teaches kids how to face everyday fears and worries. It's called RIDE—a four-step acronym standing for *Rename, Insist, Defy, Enjoy.*

Let's use RIDE to imagine a child with test anxiety who is afraid of failing a quiz, so they refuse to take it. First, work with that child to rename the thought they are having as a fear or worry, not reality: "It's only a fear. It is not a fact." Next, have the child insist they are in charge: "This fear is not in charge of me. I am in charge of what I do." Then, encourage them to defy the fear by doing the opposite of what the fear wants: have the child take the quiz. After, enjoy the success and celebrate meeting the challenge.

When Overcome With a Sense of Doom or Dread

Sadness and dread can weigh kids down and dim their light. These feelings can be situational, clinical, or both. In pediatric hospitals, guided imagery is a technique used to help kids get a break from their feelings or surroundings and to lighten mental load or pain. Guided imagery works well for kids who feel anxious or sad, or who experience stress and pain.

Here is a simple protocol for guided imagery from Children's Health Orange County (CHOC) that you can practice with children. Read each instruction aloud and take your time with each step:

- Get comfortable and close your eyes.
- Take four to five deep breaths, feeling your belly rise and fall with each.
- Imagine you could go anywhere in the world right now, where you can feel safe and happy. Picture yourself there. Give yourself permission to imagine this is really happening.
- Look around. Where are you? Who is with you? Take in the sights. What can you see? Smell? Taste? Hear? Touch? Feel?
- Now it's time to come back to your body and this present moment. How do you feel?

When Feeling Panicky

I have had panic attacks, and they are terrifying. The first time I thought I was having a heart attack and ended up in the emergency room. Panic is all consuming and symptoms can make it feel like you are going to die. Kids can have panic attacks that last minutes to hours. They can experience a racing heart and shortness of breath, among other symptoms. Panic attacks can create strong avoidance behaviors because young people don't want to go back to the place or situation where they previously had an attack and may have thought they were dying.[18]

If panic is caught early, kids can ward off an attack by practicing the 5-4-3-2-1 grounding method. This refocuses children on their present surroundings instead of panicky feelings. Grounding can regulate breathing and heart rate and soothe the nervous system. With 5-4-3-2-1 kids tap into all 5 senses, starting with sound. With this technique, children pause when they feel panicked, breathe, and find 5 things they can hear, 4 things they can see, 3 things they can touch, 2 things they can smell, and 1 thing they can taste.

When Feeling Overstimulated

Too much noise, movement, and other stimuli can cause some kids to become overstimulated. This is especially true for children with attention sensitivities and those who are neurodivergent. When children feel overstimulated, they can find relief by taking a short break and temporarily leaving the environment. Jennie Ellsworth is a special education teacher in St. Louis whose brother has autism. Knowing the importance of this technique, Jennie has a "calm down corner" in her classroom, which has a large tent with soft pillows, a bean bag, headphones, books, and privacy. You can also let kids walk the halls or take a bathroom break for a set amount of time—anything that immediately reduces noise, light, and stimulation and gives them the privacy, quiet, and autonomy they need to reset and return when ready.

When Feeling Strong Emotions or Exhibiting Self-Destructive Behaviors

Like the RIDE technique for fears and worries, there's an action acronym from the DBT therapeutic approach called REST to help kids disrupt strong and harmful emotions and behaviors. REST stands for *Relax, Evaluate, Set an Intention, Take Action.* When kids are overwhelmed by emotion or the impulse to lash out or self-harm, they need help stopping the action. By teaching and practicing REST in advance—like a fire drill—kids have a strategy to use in scary moments.

Let's use REST to imagine a child experiencing rage and wanting to hurt themself. First step, tell them it's time to relax. This is the signal to freeze, pause, take a breath, step away, and create some space. Next, tell them to evaluate the situation. Ask them what's happening. Don't push them to solve the problem, just try to have them consider what is going on. From there, have them set an intention. This one requires prework, because intentions are coping skills or distractions that can be done instead of the destructive behavior. The final step is taking action where a kid puts that intention into action.

Some examples of coping skills and distractions include holding an ice cube, squeezing a stress ball, exercising, throwing a soft ball against the wall, stretching, playing a card game, watching a short video, praying, singing, writing, drawing, going for a walk, or listening to the radio.

Soul Wounds

Some young people inherit their parents' and grandparents' stress and survival responses brought on by historic harms and trauma—what social worker Resmaa Menakem calls "soul wounds" and scientists refer to as epigenetics (for more, see Chapter 3, "Brain and Body"). This is especially true for young people who are in racial, ethnic, and religious minority groups, because of the historic, multigenerational maltreatment their parents and ancestors endured. A growing body of research shows how inherited trauma changes us at a cellular level and increases the risks that young people will experience mental health challenges.[19] Some children may need emotional wound care for injuries and survival responses passed down from one generation to the next.[20]

Consider Your Own Mental Health

We now have a range of options that help young people tend to their everyday mental health challenges. As with most things, not all will work for every kid, and they are only a starter list. Emotional wound care should be explored and practiced with an understanding that only some will become regular parts of life.

Before moving on to the next section, take time to reflect on your own mental health and emotional wound care strategies and examine what works for you and why. Are there areas you need to address and want to learn more about? If so, take a few minutes to put down this book and do some research for your own self-care.

TRY THIS
- Go through the "wound care" strategies and choose one you want to try with a child and one you want to try yourself. Decide when and how this can happen.

- Identify one "wound care" strategy from the list, or elsewhere, that you want to practice regularly. Share your commitment with someone who can hold you accountable and with whom you can share your experience.

Mental Health Habits and Emotional Hygiene

In 2015, clinical psychologist Dr. Guy Winch gave a witty TED Talk called "How to Practice Emotional First Aid," which has been watched by millions. In his speech, Winch claims children are taught to favor physical health over mental health. He uses the example of a young child who knows to brush teeth twice a day and shower regularly. Winch argues that life would be better if we all practiced preventative mental health care (emotional hygiene) to avoid and attend to daily emotional dirt and damage.

He has a point. Kids experience emotional injury as often as they get physically hurt. In an hour, afternoon, or day, they can feel lonely, get their feelings hurt, feel the sting of rejection, and more. These are expected parts of life and not mental illness. Young people need skills and practices to face whatever emotional "weather conditions" they experience during the day and in their relationships.[21] Emotional hygiene can strengthen their mental and behavioral health and may even prevent or delay the onset or severity of mental illness. This hygiene includes self-care habits and activities that can be used with the *Big 6 "BBB" Essential Health Activities* described in Table 6.

Mind and Soul Care

Think of mental health habits and emotional hygiene as everyday "tips, tricks, and tools"[22] that support cognitive functioning and mental health. They can be done individually, or in a group. Give children plenty of opportunities to try different care strategies and create their own. Kids need a toolbox full of tips, tricks, and tools to fix or prevent a sudden hurt.

Organizational Planners and Journaling

Using a planner is a great way to help children strengthen and develop executive functioning skills like planning and cognitive flexibility. Journaling can help kids process daily events, experiences, and emotions. All of these connect to executive functioning skills, which don't fully develop until our mid-20s, but are in high demand much earlier, especially at school. Planners provide a structured way for kids to manage overwhelming cognitive demands by being able to write down and follow a schedule, establish priorities, organize tasks, and monitor progress. Journaling is a regular ritual that can help kids manage emotions, process thoughts, create time for themselves, and reflect.

I am a huge fan of bullet journaling, which is a hybrid planning/journaling tool. I use it every day and also do it with my kids. It is endlessly modifiable and creative, and it incorporates journaling and trackers, which are great for organization and processing. I start a new bullet journal every year, with monthly overviews and annual goals. Every month I create a month-at-a-glance with important events and deadlines, as well as various trackers for health, work, and writing. At the start of each week, I create a week-at-a-glance and to-do lists for my personal and professional projects.[23]

Language Lessons

One time in elementary school I was sent to the school counselor for something that happened between me and a friend. I remember she didn't let me tell her what happened but pointed to a paper of 1980s-style emojis and asked me to tell her how I was feeling. It was awful; the emoji faces didn't capture what I felt inside, and I didn't have the language or permission to describe it myself. We need to empower children with words that attach to the complex and intense feelings they experience.

I love Brené Brown's book *Atlas of the Heart: Mapping Meaningful Connection and the Language of Human Experience*. It's basically an encyclopedia of human emotions. While it's written for adults, you can translate many—if not all—of the feelings into kid-friendly language. Consider instituting a "word of the day" or "word of the week" that is a complex human emotion and build in time every day to talk about it.

Mindfulness Practices

I was a reluctant mindfulness enthusiast, but now I think it's one of the most important tools we can teach and practice with older kids— especially teens. There is so much research on the benefits of mindfulness for helping young people deal with stress, suffering, attention, pain, illness, trauma, and more.[24] Mindfulness is indispensable, portable, accessible, and inclusive. Long-time mindfulness advocate Professor Mark Greenberg once told me that by teaching teens and young adults mindfulness, we equip them with ways to listen, be present, and be intentional about what they want and who they want to be each day.

One of my favorite mindfulness resources for young people is Uz Afzal's *Mindfulness for Children: Practicing Mindfulness With Your Child Through the Day.* Here's one exercise from her book you can try to help children refocus: Have everyone take out a piece of paper and pen and close their eyes. Then play a song. It can be anything. Everybody keeps their eyes closed and draws what they hear (draw to and with the rhythm). Afterwards share your drawings and talk about the experience.

Body Care

There are other strategies that strengthen the brain and body connection. In addition to these practices, mental health and emotional hygiene requires proper nourishment and hydration.[25] These body care techniques should be done along with meeting the body's physical needs. These practices can be a great way for kids to calm themselves down, stabilize mood, and reduce the stress response in the body.

Body Scan

A body scan is a regular practice kids can do on their own or in a group. While it is initially a guided practice, kids can learn to do it on their own. Body scans teach us to pay attention to what is happening in each part of the body. With regular practice, body scans can stop racing thoughts, sync up the brain and body, and activate positive emotions.[26] Children should only do a body scan in environments where they are safe and comfortable.

Here is a simple protocol for doing a body scan with young people:[27]

- Have kids get comfortable in a seat or lying down.

- Invite them to find something on the ceiling or in front of them to stare at. Tell them it's ok to zone out and relax.

- Invite them to notice the seat they are sitting in or the ground they are lying on. Ask them to notice how it feels.

- Now invite them to place one hand on their hearts and the other on their bellies. Ask them to take two to three full breaths, feeling their belly rise and fall with each.

- Ask them to think of someone or something that makes them feel good and safe. Once they have that person or thing in mind, ask them to capture that feeling of warmth and goodness. Next, tell them to have that feeling start to spread through their body. Start at the top of their head and go down their arms to their fingertips. From their shoulders, down past their heart, and into their bellies. Then down one leg to their foot and toes, and then the other leg, foot, and toes. Once you have gone through the whole body, ask them to imagine the feeling getting warm and bright. Ask them to sense it in their entire body.

- Let kids rest and relax with that feeling for a few minutes, and encourage them to whisper, "I am safe," and "I am calm."

- After a few minutes, invite them to open their eyes and put both hands on their heart. Have them find the spot they stared at in the beginning, and end by having them take a moment to notice how they feel.

After finishing, transition to an activity where kids can stay in a relaxed and restful state.

Calming Breath

Breathing is something we do to survive, and it is easily changed by how we feel; it can also change how we feel. Anxiety can cause us to hold our breath or take shallow breaths. This can trigger hyperventilation and panic. In extreme cases, this change in oxygen sends emergency signals to the nervous system, and we can pass out.[28] By doing regular breathing exercises, kids can support and strengthen their nervous systems, and stabilize their stress and threat response.

Here is a daily practice children can do that takes less than five minutes. Go through steps 1 through 5, reading each step aloud, and then repeat 10 to 15 times.

- Get comfortable in a seat or lying down.

- Relax your shoulders, and put a hand on your belly.

- Breathe in deeply through your nose, filling up the belly with air.

- Now hold your breath while I count to three: 1-2-3.

- Slowly breathe out your mouth.

Beyond this practice, you can have kids do a "breath check" the same way you might give them "brain breaks." During a breath check, kids take a one-minute break to focus on their breathing and check how they feel. At the end, invite kids to take two to three big breaths with one hand on their bellies and another on their hearts. Tell them to try and fill their bellies up with air on the inhale and notice any changes as they breath. This quick exercise gets children in the habit of checking in with their breath and making minor adjustments to take better care of themselves.[29]

Silent Dance Party

Kids are made to move. Sometimes we need extra movement and motion to distract, reenergize, or help kids get their jitters out. Children often sit for too long and their bodies need to shift and stretch. Movement can stimulate and improve mood and attention, while reducing stress and anxiety.[30]

There are lots of ways to integrate movement into your schedule. For example, you can have kids stand up and do jumping jacks, stretch, or hop up and down. One of my favorite examples is the silent dance party. For kids to feel comfortable with the silent dance party, you need to have an established culture of safety, fun, and acceptance. You also need to provide personal headphones and music if kids don't have their own. In a silent dance party, young people connect their headphones to a playlist or song online. They can choose whatever they want to dance to, and because they are using headphones, no one can hear or judge their dancing style. Everyone presses play and the silent dance party starts. Make sure to lead by example.

Prioritize and Practice

To thrive, young people need to feel healthy and whole. Sometimes that takes therapy, treatment, and/or medications. It should always include emotional wound care and hygiene. Mental health challenges are easier to address when children are surrounded by adults who believe them, and who are kind and caring.[31] While this chapter focused inward and on the individual, emotional well-being is deeply impacted by the quality of relationships and having spaces to experience collective care and belonging.[32]

Most young people will go through a season or situation where they need specific and individual support for an active mental health challenge or illness. While this section explored a variety of techniques and exercises, it is not exhaustive or complete. Mental health care also includes exercise, spending time with friends and loved ones, physical affection, reading a good book, doing art, cooking, and more. There's no set number or combination of practices that guarantee mental health or emotional healing. Young people will spend their lives learning what works for them and why. One of the best ways to prioritize mental health and promote emotional wellness is to model it yourself. You can help kids explore what it means and looks like for them while trying out new techniques and practices yourself.

WHOLE LIFE PRACTICE

Prioritize Mental Health

Learn

- Young people's mental health is an area of growing concern. In 2021, America's pediatricians and the U.S. Surgeon General declared youth mental health a "national emergency."

- *Mental health* refers to someone being positively and productively engaged in relationships, responsibilities, and activities, while *mental illness* refers to disturbing thoughts, emotions, and behaviors that interfere with or impede those positive engagements.

- There are many signs and symptoms of a mental health challenge or condition. It is important to learn the red flags and know what to do if you see them.

- Mental health first aid (MHFA) is a free course that helps teens and adults learn how to be mental health first responders. MHFA teaches a five-step action plan, ALGEE, which stands for *Approach and assess risk of suicide and harm, Listen nonjudgmentally, Give reassurance and information,* and *Encourage appropriate professional help.*

Reflect

Mental health is health and it's critical for children to live, learn, and thrive. Your mental health is also important. Using the information and tools from this chapter, take time to reflect on your mental health.

Look through the red flags and see if you have any of them. If you do, is there anything you need and want to do about it? Do you see these in the children you care about? Take note of what comes up for you.

Now look at the section on mental health habits and emotional hygiene. Which mind, body, and soul care practices do you want to try? What are your other self-care strategies? Reflect on what emotional hygiene looks like in your life and how you want to maintain or improve it.

Act

As you absorb what you read and reflected on, consider how you can put insights into action. Take time to set a few commitments and intentions on how to *Prioritize Mental Health*.

- What is one small action you can take *today* to put this practice into action?

- What is one larger action you can take *this month* to put this practice into action?

- What is one big action you can work toward *this year* to put this practice into action?

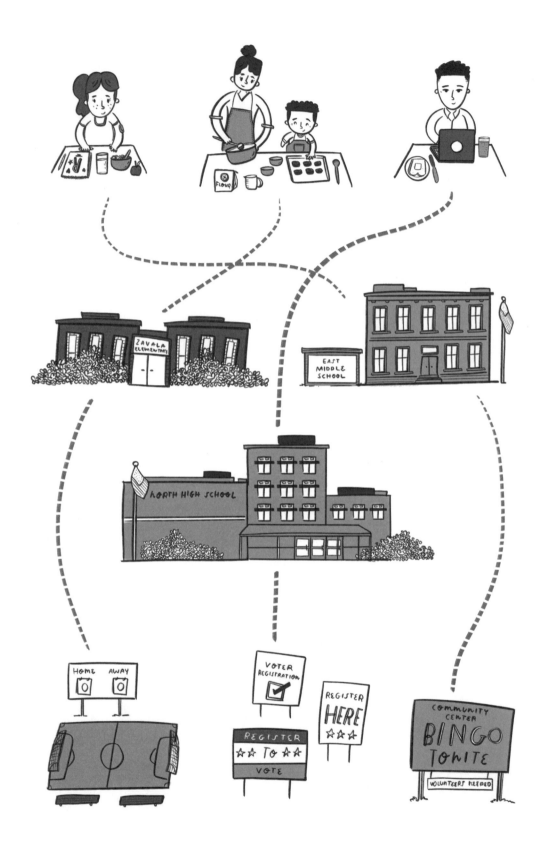

Invest in Personal Interests 8

"When people are in their Element, they connect with something fundamental to their sense of identity, purpose, and well-being."

—Sir Ken Robinson

Sitting on the banks of the Hampton Roads harbor, where the Chesapeake Bay meets the Atlantic Ocean, is the city of Newport News. A coastal community of nearly 200,000 people, Newport News is a racially diverse hub and home to the largest public school district on the Virginia Peninsula.

Bridget Adams is the school district's program administrator for the Office of Youth Development. Originally from Boston, Bridget moved to the area in 2004, leaving a life in corporate management for a career in public education. Before becoming program administrator, Bridget spent a decade as a marketing teacher at a Newport News high school.

As soon as you meet Bridget, you can tell she loves her work. More than that, she exudes care and commitment for the students she serves. Bridget is on a mission to see every student in Newport News active in a sport, club, or activity—and she's doing it. Over the past 6 years, the school district has assigned a youth development lead to every school and hired an activities director for every high school. This youth development team oversees recruitment and sign-ups for clubs and activities and makes sure kids have positive options during and after school. Under Bridget's leadership, the district has reduced activity fees[1] and established after-school busing for anyone who needs it. The district prioritizes youth development and has included it in their strategic plan and school improvement plans.

Listening to Bridget makes me want to move my family to the tidewaters of Virginia. Under her watchful eye, "all students have the opportunity to lead, serve, and be involved in the decision making and planning" of the district's youth development activities. All schools offer sports and national affiliate clubs (e.g., DECA, Girls on the Run) as well as student-led clubs that inspire and equip. Bridget told me about STAND, a district-wide and student-led campaign that discourages bullying and promotes positive school culture; students started it after a classmate who was bullied committed suicide. Then there's The Vibe, a student talk show, and Live Well, a student wellness program. A clear favorite of Bridget's is a girls' empowerment club:[2] Blossom for elementary school students, Bloom for middle schoolers, and Flourish for high schoolers. "Bloom Nation" brings the girls together to support each other, dream big, connect with local women leaders, and take care of their collective and individual well-being.

Bridget and her team honor student perspectives and interests through clubs and activities, knowing it directly impacts their well-being and futures. The sheer volume of opportunities—more than 600—ensure students have opportunities to engage in activities that are fun, build skills, and foster friendships. By removing activity fees, providing free transportation, and offering opportunities during the school day, every kid in the community can participate.

You Can Only Be What You Can See

In 2018, one of my mentors, Greg Darnieder, collaborated with Stanford University professor Milbrey McLaughlin to publish *You Can't Be What You Can't See: The Power of Opportunity to Change Young Lives.* This book tells the story of a successful youth program Greg founded and ran on the Near North Side of Chicago from the late 1970s to the mid-1990s. I met some of the alumni from that program in 2016 at a White House event, and their life stories were stunning. Each pointed to the transformative role the CYCLE program played—ranging from the community and connections to available resources and opportunities to the agency and authority they had as participants and junior staff.

When Greg told me the title of the book, I liked it right away. I used to run a high school for older youth with adult responsibilities who didn't have time or money to do much beyond school and supporting their families. Their future horizons were limited to immediate, eclipsing needs. Their career ambitions went only as far as their employed friends and family and whatever those individuals did for work. Joining sports teams and clubs were a luxury reserved for people with extra time and money.

My students would have loved a program like the one Greg ran in Cabrini Green—it combined school supports (e.g., tutoring) with leadership development and career awareness opportunities (e.g., junior staff program, scholarships, mentorship). Clubs and field trips were available at no cost for kids who could swing it, and the program kept an open-door policy because they understood how crowded kids' lives were and the pressing responsibilities they had at home.[3] CYCLE combined programming and people power. It was as relationship centered as it was youth centered.

Interests-Based and Kid-Centered Programming

Whether it's Bloom in Newport News or CYCLE in Cabrini Green, the best activities for kids combine personalization around who they are and what they care about, with exposure to and exploration of new experiences; these activities also focus on building skills and strengthening healthy relationships.

Investing in kids' interests is about giving them accessible and enjoyable opportunities to explore what is important to them, to introduce them to activities you think they would like, and to show them you care about their interests because you care about them. This is done through programs like CYCLE, clubs like Bloom, sports, after-school clubs, one-time experiences, and everyday interactions. We must expose kids to all kinds of possible interests, make space for them to try them out, and provide time and training for them to become skilled in the ones they enjoy.

Exposure

Greg was right—you can't be what you can't see. For a child to pick up a hobby or pursue a career path, they need to know it exists. It is a gift to introduce and connect a young person to an interest that ends up being a core part of their life journey.

Informally, we expose kids to new interests by listening and making recommendations. When my older son was in first grade, my mom noticed he spent a lot of time creating structures out of any materials he could find. She wondered whether he might like architecture, so one day she showed him a video of a baseball stadium being built. Ever since, Justice has been a baseball stadium history buff. He creates his own stadiums with magnet tiles and LEGO bricks based on his hand-drawn designs. That building interest led him to a deeper one—his love of baseball. He eventually became more interested in the baseball part of baseball stadiums and is now a true fan of the game.

We expose kids to new interests by introducing them to people who do those activities—this can be done in real life, online, or even by watching videos. For older kids, this can happen during a career fair or by inviting a guest speaker to class. For younger kids, this can be at a club fair, where older students pitch various activities and tell younger students why they should sign up. That same baseball-loving son showed no interest in playing an instrument until his band director visited classrooms with instruments and a video of each one being played. Suddenly, he wanted to be a percussionist.

Exposure is also about access and availability. It's easier for young people to try different sports if their family can afford a membership to the YMCA or a local recreation center. It's more likely a student will develop an interest in music or theater if their school has a band, strings program, and annual school theatrical performance. Budget constraints and staffing shortages cause nonprofits and schools to stop offering the "extras," which are essential for kids to discover their interests. Advocate for and inquire into financial assistance and fee waiver programs. If you're able to advocate to a school board or state legislator, push for continued or increased funding for programs like music or art, or afterschool programming for all grade levels. If you are somewhere without these types of activities, look for virtual options. Between YouTube, social media, apps, and websites, there are ways kids can explore various interests and connect with people online and from a distance.[4]

Exploration and Experimentation

After exposure comes exploration and experimentation. This is when kids participate in activities, go to club meetings, try a sport, or learn more about a topic. There are many ways to make this happen in schools, youth programs, and at home. We should all consider this an essential part of our work.

Two hours down the road from Newport News is Cumberland County—a rural community outside of Richmond—where school leaders have spent the past few years tinkering with a class for juniors and seniors: Dukes Discover Passion Projects. This student-driven course is an independent study, with facilitated support from the district curriculum lead, Sheri Almond. Passion projects help older students explore personal and professional interests before deciding what to do after graduation. These projects connect them with local leaders, employers, and organizations and give them space to explore interests in a safe and low-stakes way.

I was fortunate to meet the first Dukes Discover class and hear about their projects. Each student came up with a project that blended leadership with service, personal passion with possible professional pursuits. Take, for example, Chase, who spent the semester teaching basketball to younger students with disabilities; Maleeyah, who started a mentoring program for middle school girls; Nathan, who designed and welded his own BMX bike; and Justin, who organized and sent care packages to soldiers overseas.

Dukes Discover Passion Projects included all the premium ingredients kids need to explore and experiment with their interests. These are the same defining characteristics of student-centered learning. That's because this type of exploration and experimentation is personalized. Student-centered learning can be characterized as follows:

- Young people have *voice and choice* over their projects and are able to *personalize them* to match interests and abilities
- Adults act as *facilitators of learning* rather than direct instructors of content
- Projects are *appropriately challenging* with *real-world relevance and impact* that can be done *anywhere, anytime*
- Experiences support kids' identity development and their social emotional growth
- Engagement fosters lifelong learning and pursuits[5]

Student-centered learning—and its education cousins, experiential and project-based learning, and work-based and service learning—are excellent ways for kids to explore and experiment with personal interests. Across these learning strategies, kids get customized, hands-on learning that is relevant, relationships based, and skill building.

Enjoying the Experience and Building Expertise

Once young people discover their interests, they need opportunities to practice and play. This can happen independently or through organized activities, like class projects and clubs. This phase focuses on skill building. In a group context, it's also a chance to build teamwork, camaraderie, and community around shared interests. With enough practice and experience, kids build mastery—eventually becoming accomplished musicians, athletes, actors, debaters, mathematicians, builders, activists, and more.

Creating ways for young people to enjoy and develop expertise in their interests is a way to support the wide and long of their lives. The *wide* means ways we help them find and explore interests across the places where they spend time. For example, if a child is interested in science, we help them find ways to do it at school, home, and in after-school or summer programs. The *long* of their lives refers to ways we help kids cultivate an interest they can do across a lifetime, like swimming, reading, painting, or chess.

Building expertise means providing kids with opportunities to not only enjoy their interests but also to be appropriately challenged by them. For athletes, this means exercises and coaching that develop more complex skills and higher levels of performance. For musicians, it's practicing and performing more demanding songs and scores. And so on. This works best when kids have a knowledgeable teacher or coach who can evaluate, guide, and support them. That "coach" should be actively engaged and enthusiastic about the activity, imparting their own wisdom and learning and ensuring the child is actively doing the activity, not just absorbing the instruction. As Sam M. Intrator and Don Siegel say in *The Quest for Mastery*, we want kids connected to programs with people who have a "mastery mindset."[6]

TRY THIS

- Write a list or print rosters of the young people in your life. Next to each name, note whatever interests you know they have. If you're not sure, jot down different topics they talk about or activities they like. Once you're done, review the list and ask yourself what you can do to increase their exploration of those interests.

- Consider an activity or interest you want to learn more about or try. This could be a physical pursuit (e.g., rock climbing, hiking, or weightlifting), or a new hobby or experience (e.g., painting, writing, or cooking). Actively work to increase your exposure and then plan to try it out.

Invest in the Individual

Beyond programs, classes, groups, and teams, there are everyday interactions we have with kids and interests they share with us. Consider the child who always talks about the same video game or the content they created on social media; the athlete who wants you to watch the tricks they learned over the weekend; the client who spends each session talking about an invention they came up with; or the budding thespian who believes "all the world's a stage" and never stops singing and dancing.

We hold power that shapes and shifts kids' interests based on our attention and responses. Imagine a child who loves art and wants to pursue it. They pour their heart into their sketchbook and finally get up the courage to ask you to look at their drawings. What happens if you go over each drawing with awe and wonder? What about if you breeze through, busy and distracted? What if you say you don't like their art, or sarcastically suggest they find a new hobby?

Investing in kids' personal interests is an investment into everyday interactions with kids themselves. It's choosing to be present when they share and really listening to what they have to say. Showing interest in what interests them is sometimes easy and other times more difficult. When my younger son explains an online game, my immediate reaction is to shut down the conversation, but I know that shuts him down too.

Investments of time and attention are as important as connecting kids to programs and offering them new opportunities. Many kids pursue and practice interests privately or try new things and look to adults for affirmation. They may share these interests with you at any time, and you need to be ready to listen and respond when it happens.

Pursuits of Passion and Purpose

Another part of investing in kids' personal interests is investing in things they care about—from social causes to family responsibilities. In an interview with Professor Heather Malin, director of research at the Stanford University Center on Adolescence and author of *Teaching for Purpose: Preparing Students for Lives of Meaning*, I learned the distinction between supporting young people in finding their passions and helping them pursue purpose.

Here's how Heather explained it: All kids can benefit from a sense of purpose in their lives[7] and want to feel purposeful in things they do. Some kids might have a specific interest they are passionate about, but passion is not necessary for having purpose. Passion invokes strong emotions and energy that aren't necessary for purpose. When passions are pursued with a singular focus, they can cause kids to miss out on key parts of childhood—like friendships, school, or certain social activities. Passions should only be pursued if it is what kids want and when the passion brings them joy and purpose.

Purpose is an ongoing exploration and process in which kids ask themselves what gives them joy and energy. It's the active exploration of what they are willing to work for, commit time to, and give attention to. Purpose can be passion and it can also be a sense of responsibility—to the world, to a cause, or to family. In her research, Heather found that many young people name family as their top priority and their biggest source of purpose. Family, she says, is not a passion or an interest that can be cultivated in a club or youth development activity. It should not be diminished or minimized in value.

In the schools and programs Heather studied, she found that adults who do the best job helping kids pursue purpose are the same ones pursuing purpose themselves. She recommends we engage in active exploration of the things that bring us joy and meaning, of what we are willing to give our time, talent, and treasure to. Then, we share that enthusiasm with kids. That enthusiasm and energy is contagious.

Lifetime Pursuits

I was a teacher who let kids design class projects around interests to learn content and master academic standards. I was a school leader who had students take interest surveys and do internships to determine college majors and career pathways. I am a parent who has signed my kids up for sports and camps because their friends were doing it, or because—to be honest—I needed childcare.

With what I know today, I wish I could go back and engage my students in interests that brought them joy and purpose, not just ones that improved their class performance or made them more employable. If I had a do-over, I would encourage them to pursue interests that would last a lifetime.

We get to help children find their "Element," as Sir Ken Robinson called it—the space when kids are "doing the thing they love, and in doing it they feel like their most authentic selves. They find that time passes differently and that they are more alive, more centered, and more vibrant than at any other times."[8] The joy of doing those things will inspire novelty and creativity, strengthen identity and purpose, activate accomplishments and pride, and offer ongoing enjoyment and well-being.

WHOLE LIFE PRACTICE

Invest in Personal Interests

Learn

- Youth development opportunities help kids explore and engage in personal interests. These activities combine fun, skill building, and the chance to build and strengthen relationships. These can be sports, clubs, groups, after-school and summer programs, one-time experiences, and one-on-one relationships.

- Exposure to positive youth development opportunities and new interests requires access and availability. Kids can't be what they can't see, and they can only do what they can afford or access. We must create barrier-free opportunities that all kids can enjoy.

- Investing in personal interests includes exposure to what's available, opportunities to explore and experiment, and sufficient space and time for young people to enjoy interests and develop expertise.

- When done well, interests-based programming and practices are also student-centered learning: Kids have voice and choice over what they do; opportunities are personalized; adults are facilitators focused on skill building and relationships; activities are challenging with real-world relevance; and kids engage in lifelong learning that supports identity development and social emotional growth.

Reflect

Heather Malin, author of *Teaching for Purpose*, found that adults who are most effective at helping kids discover personal interests and purpose are those who can model their own purpose. With that in mind, take time to think about your purpose(s).

- What brings you joy and purpose?

- What are you willing to commit your resources, time, and attention to?

- What are the most meaningful parts of your life?

- Do you have specific interests and passions?

After reflecting on your purpose(s), consider how you can help kids cultivate their personal interests, purposes, and passions.

(Continued)

(Continued)

Act

As you absorb what you read and reflected on, consider how you can put insights into action. Take time to set a few commitments and intentions on how to *Invest in Personal Interests*.

- What is one small action you can take *today* to put this practice into action?

- What is one larger action you can take *this month* to put this practice into action?

- What is one big action you can work toward *this year* to put this practice into action?

NOTES

Nurture Healthy Relationships 9

"The good life is built with good relationships."

—Robert Waldinger

David Shapiro and I spoke days before he announced his transition from CEO of MENTOR to the YMCA of Greater Boston. For nearly 2 decades at MENTOR, David was at the helm of the nation's organizational champion for the positive power of healthy adult-child mentoring relationships.[1]

David walks the talk. When we spoke, he told me how—despite a grueling work and travel schedule—he coaches his kids' youth baseball teams and makes sure practices and games are protected on his calendar. He shared how the transition from national to local work enables him to invest more deeply in his community, family, and children. He described one of his best friends to exemplify the qualities of positive relationships, and later shared that this friend started as his mentee.

Although I interviewed David remotely, he actively engaged and remembered what we discussed. I told him my son had baseball tryouts later that day and we commiserated about the pressures of youth sports and David and Justice's shared love of the game. I mentioned Justice would love talking with him about baseball. Later that week, David emailed to check on Justice and tryouts, saying he hoped they could meet. The next time we talked, Justice was there, ready with baseball questions. At one point, the two took over the conversation and I watched a real-time masterclass on how to nurture healthy relationships.

David has spent more time than most thinking about what high-quality adult-kid relationships require. That is after all, the essence of good mentorship. I asked him what he has learned matters most in these relationships.

Here's what he shared:

- **When you are in a relationship with a child who is not your own, you inherit all similar relationships a child had before yours.** For example, if you are a sports coach, you will be compared to every coach a kid had. As kids get older, you will be measured against the greats (e.g., their favorite teacher) and worst (e.g., the teacher who made fourth grade terrible).

- **There is power in showing up in mundane moments.** What might seem boring to you could be life changing for a kid. You might be the only one who has shown up a third or fourth time, the only person to never yell, or the only one to give the child space to be introspective. Allow relationships to form in everyday moments without an agenda. Be willing to engage young people on their level and terms.

- **Connect with kids joyfully and around interests.** Kids want adults to have fun with them. Do things you both like. They might enjoy doing something you loved when you were young. Think about jumping rope or playing four-square together, join a kickball game, or teach them a favorite card game or magic trick. Don't force conversations about hard and heavy stuff every time you connect. Be present, have fun, and find what feels right.

These three lessons are important parts of a child's social architecture because they create lasting memories and a strong bond. My hope is that every child has more than one adult who shows up for them and lives out these truths—adults who demonstrate concern about and awareness of where a child has been, where they are now, and what they want and hope for in the future.[2]

Webs of Social Support

Kids need more than one positive adult relationship. They need networks—webs—of social support. That's been an area of study for

Jonathan Zaff, who directs the CERES Institute for Children & Youth at Boston University's Wheelock College of Education & Human Development, just 15 minutes down the road from the MENTOR headquarters.[3]

In 2017, when Jonathan and his research partner Shannon Varga ran the Center for Promise at America's Promise Alliance, they developed a framework to describe the *web of support* young people need to survive and thrive.

Through their work, Jonathan and Shannon explored the complex range, organization, and content of young people's relationships. They considered buildings and programs where young people spend time, and they studied the quality of social connections and capital.

Jonathan and Shannon's framework showed that the right people and actions can convert a young person's web of relationships into a *web of support*.[4] From their perspectives, this happens when a young person has at least one "anchor"—a strong relationship that provides unconditional support. Here's how developmental psychologist Urie Bronfenbrenner described it in his book *Making Human Beings Humans*: "A child needs the enduring, irrational involvement of one or more adults in care of and in joint activity with that child. In short, *somebody has to be crazy about that kid*." Young people should also be in charge of their learning and development, benefit from a network of people connected to them and each other, and finally, every person in the *web* must be in a position to offer some social support without having to provide everything.[5]

In a *web of support*, people support children from wherever they are and whatever positions they hold. These supports can help a child form **social bonds**—experience close connections and care from those in their network—and **social bridge** opportunities—connecting kids to people and resources outside of their web of support.

This builds on a long-held understanding in education and youth development that young people need at least "one caring adult" to make it in life. While young people do need *at least* one caring adult, Jonathan and Shannon integrated research across disciplines and decades to show how young people benefit from a support network of multiple people providing them social connection, companionship, community, and opportunity.[6]

Figure 4   Webs of Social Support

Built to Last

In 2017, David, Jonathan, and Shannon weren't the only people in Boston talking about the power of relationships. Across the Charles River in Cambridge, a Harvard Medical School team was finishing one of the world's longest-ever studies on life, health, and happiness.

The *Harvard Study of Adult Development,* led by psychiatrist Robert Waldinger, began in 1938 during the Great Depression, in hopes of learning what makes a healthy and happy life. Researchers followed 268 Harvard sophomores over 80 years, collecting data on their health, relationships, and life circumstances. At that time, Harvard students were white men, so over the years the research team diversified the pool by adding the subjects' children and hundreds of other Boston city residents.[7]

When the study ended, the team concluded that positive relationships might be the most powerful predictor of people's lifetime health, happiness, and longevity. In a viral TED Talk about the study, Waldinger said, "It turns out that people who are more socially connected to family, to friends, to community, are happier, they're physically healthier, and they live longer than people who are less well connected."[8]

DANGERS OF LONELINESS

While positive relationships help us to be happy, healthy, and live longer,[9] being lonely has the opposite effect. Loneliness increases chances of getting sick and may lead to premature death.[10] Loneliness begets loneliness, spurring antisocial behaviors and social anxiety that makes it harder to connect with others, resulting in more isolation. Some researchers believe loneliness is a root cause of depression and anxiety.[11]

Physical and psychological responses to loneliness are probably an evolutionary survival strategy, like the *fight or flight* mode we enter when we are stressed or afraid. In hunter-gatherer times, if a person wandered away from the tribe, they were more vulnerable to attack, injury, and death. The body's physical and emotional response to loneliness could be our body's way of telling us to go back to people, because it's safer.[12] Some refer to this as our *tend and befriend* response.

Experiencing loneliness is a normal childhood experience, but chronic loneliness threatens children's quality of life and learning.[13] If young people feel they have no friends, no one to talk to or turn to, they need help.[14] These feelings, in addition to social isolation, require immediate attention and intervention.

How to Nurture Healthy Relationships

The relationship experts in Boston make this clear: Kids need caring adults who provide unconditional love and support along with a network of people who provide resources, connections, and companionship. The quality of relationships and networks have short- and long-term benefits and bolster young people's health and happiness across their lifetimes.

It's hard to narrow down research on relationships because there is a ton, and I have come to believe relationships matter more than anything else. I started this chapter with David because he reminds us how important it is to foster individual relationships with kids. Jon and Shannon show how a young person lives and learns inside an interconnected and intersecting network of people and places that can be a web of support. The Harvard Study reveals that our social health and wealth make a major difference in the quality of our lives across our entire lives.[15]

Relationships profoundly impact how young people live and whether they love their lives. We must approach relationships with curiosity, intention, sensitivity, and respect. For this, I turned to longtime mentors and friends Karen Pittman and Merita Irby, cofounders of the Forum for Youth Investment. Karen and Merita have a gift for taking complex ideas about young people and describing them in ways that are accessible and actionable.

The three of us mulled over everything we know about youth development and the importance of relationships and agreed that "nurturing healthy relationships" must be a practice that is applied across four dimensions (see Figure 5):

- Your direct relationship with a child

- Your relationship with other adults in the child's life

- The child's relationships with other people

- The child's relationship with self

Figure 5   Four Dimensions of Healthy Relationships for Children

RELATIONSHIP TO SELF

RELATIONSHIP TO ADULT

RELATIONSHIPS BETWEEN ADULTS

RELATIONSHIPS WITH PEERS

Your Relationship With a Child

The relationships you have the most responsibility for and control over are the ones you're in. In direct relationships with kids, your interactions land on a spectrum of transactional to transformational—from fulfilling a task to being in a more intensive and intimate role.[16] The type of relationships you have may also change and evolve over time.

- You might be a *steady relationship*: someone who is a constant in life. This can include family, friends, and mentors.

- You might be a *seasonal relationship*: someone kids see during a specific time of year or life. This can include teachers and summer camp counselors.

- You might be a *situational relationship*: someone kids connect with for specific support and services. This can include doctors and therapists.

Whatever kind of relationship you have with a child, strive to make your interactions positive and developmental. We are often more important to a child than we realize, and—as David Shapiro reminded me—we may never know the full impact and influence we have on the children in our lives. His advice is to do what you say you're going to do, no matter the relationship you have. Children's experiences of self-worth, stability, trust, and positivity directly tie to your behavior, interactions, and reliability. Seek to build and nurture relationships that are mutually beneficial, offer authentic connection, empower, and equip.[17]

A year before Jon and Shannon released their framework and Robert Waldinger's team concluded their 80-year study, Karen Pittman, our colleague Caitlin, and I released *Ready by Design: The Science (and Art) of Youth Readiness*. For 2 years prior, we studied what kids need to be ready for a changing world. Positive and healthy relationships emerged in the research more than anything else. We put a chart in the report that described the two core responsibilities adults have in relationships with kids: to build connections and build competence. Table 16 is an adapted version of that chart, which can be used as a self-assessment or guide.

Table 16 Practices to Nurture Healthy Relationships With Kids	
BUILD CONNECTIONS	**BUILD COMPETENCIES**
• Focus on the young person	• Be planful and predictable
• Be a coach and offer encouragement	• Offer opportunities that strengthen abilities
• Be engaging and interesting	• Be strengths based
• Be intentional and present	• Empower and equip
• Be socially and culturally responsive	• Create space and time to practice skills
• Be honest and trustworthy	• Make real-world connections
• Cultivate community and belonging	• Model what you want to see
• Encourage teamwork and collaboration	• Provide healthy challenges and risks
• Assign appropriate roles and responsibilities	• Provide information, resources, and tools
• Respect agency and autonomy	• Offer structure with clear boundaries
• Offer psychological and physical safety	• Nurture a sense of self and independence
• Show care and concern	• Create the chance for young people to shine
• Support personal growth	

online resources
Available for download at **www.wholechildwholelife.com**

As you consider Table 16, think about your relationships with children. Are you in steady, seasonal, or situational relationships (or some combination)? When and where are interactions more transactional or more transformational?

TRY THIS

- Reread David Shapiro's three lessons about relationships from the beginning of the chapter. This week, remind yourself that showing up can be enough. Focus less on getting through an agenda or activity and more on meeting the kids where they are.

- Inventory the relationships you have with young people. How would you describe those relationships? Choose one relationship with an individual child or group and assess it with the characteristics in Table 16. Based on that self-assessment, decide how to increase or improve one characteristic from the list.

Relationships With Other Adults in a Child's Life

Your relationship with a child exists in the context of others. As Jon and Shannon's research showed, you are one point in a constellation of connections that are life-wide, stretching across the places where young people live, learn, and play. That social web is also lifelong, stretching from the past into the future. Young people are influenced in the present by their past relationships and by current ones. As David described it, "You may think you want to be *that person* in a child's life, but you actually want to be a part of a network of people. Strive to be *that person* who unlocks relationships to other adults, or who shows the power of what a healthy relationship to an adult can look and feel like."

An important part of your relationship with kids is your connection to and engagement with other people in their lives. For example, with the exception of young people who are homeschooled, children go to school in environments where adults have assigned expectations, roles, and responsibilities. Kids connect with school staff in the context of being a student, athlete, client, mentee, etc. That defines and drives various aspects of the relationship and sometimes limits the view of the young person. When school staff get to know other adults in a student's life, they strengthen their relationship with the student, which can positively impact the student's learning and behavior.[18]

Connected adults across a child's life help in other ways too. Recently, Karen told me about a transactional interaction that can become transformational. Across the United States, first responders are adopting a program called "Handle with Care" to help young people who have witnessed or experienced something traumatic. In participating communities, first responders send schools a daily list of students who were involved in a traumatic incident. No specific details are shared, just a message to handle that student with care. Think through the implications. If that child acts out or seems withdrawn, staff are better prepared to respond with kindness and compassion, rather than correction and punishment.

In Chapter 4, "People and Places," we explored how to map where kids spend time, and with who. These adult-to-adult relationships make these maps come to life by providing a network of support where information can be shared, responsibility distributed, and concerns uplifted. For teachers and youth workers, these adult-to-adult relationships help you understand how young people behave in other settings, including at home. For parents and caregivers, these relationships make it easier to check in on concerns or share celebrations. Networked relationships happen naturally or by design. They may be easier to foster in small communities where teachers also coach and everyone plays at the same park, belongs to the local recreation center, shops at the same stores, and attends the same faith institutions. This is also present with *team teaching* approaches, where teachers share students and regularly meet to discuss student needs.

The Search Institute—a leader in positive youth development—developed a *Developmental Relationships Framework* with five research-based characteristics for healthy relationships with young people. These characteristics are individually and collectively powerful. As you participate in a child's web of support, try to embody these five characteristics:[19]

- Express care
- Challenge growth
- Provide support
- Share power
- Expand possibilities

To build adult-to-adult relationships that support a specific child, start with the relationships closest to you. If you're a caretaker, that's the other people responsible for your child. If you're a teacher, that's school staff. If you're a youth worker, that's fellow counselors and program leadership. Ask the young person to connect you to the people they care about. You can initiate conversations by sharing information, then move toward regular interactions, building a relationship over time that benefits the child.[20]

Supporting Relationships Children Have With Others

Another part of this practice is creating environments and experiences where kids are free to form relationships and where they can learn and practice skills needed to nurture those relationships.

In *Ready by Design,* we went beyond what adults can do to build connections and competence to ask how they can design spaces and situations that prioritize **social health**—positive relationships and social interactions—and build **social wealth**—new relationships, opportunities, and resources. Table 17 details what we found in the research.

Table 17 Environment and Experiential Conditions That Nurture Healthy Relationships	
PLACES THAT ARE	**PEOPLE WHO ARE**
• Safe and secure	• Empowering and equipping
• Clear on routines, roles, and responsibilities	• Loving and caring
• Welcoming and inclusive	• Coaching and motivating
SPACES WHERE KIDS CAN	
• Connect with each other and explore their shared interests and tasks	
• Be challenged and engaged in social interactions	
• Observe and explore social interactions	
• Practice, fail, and learn from their mistakes	
• Actively use relationship, communication, and emotional management skills	
• Connect with people who are similar and different	
• Reflect and grow	

If you work with groups of children in any capacity, you're in charge of promoting and protecting these conditions, and ensuring they work for every child. This requires knowing who your kids are, how they relate to each other, and what they need. You can gauge that through observations and interactions as well as through individual conversations and surveys. Regularly check in on how kids feel about group dynamics and culture.

Navigating High Conflict

At times, you might need to help young people work through conflict. This could happen in real time—requiring your conflict negotiation and mediation skills—or after something happens. When these situations occur, be an active listener and learner. Consider the facts and take a broad view. A conflict is often an outward symptom of something larger. Look for root causes that may have set off disagreements and seek common ground between the child and the person or people with whom they had a conflict. When the child is in the wrong, seek connection instead of or along with correction.

It's possible that a conflict will arise that looks like what author and journalist Amanda Ripley calls *high conflict*. These are us-versus-them arguments that dehumanize, demoralize, and become all consuming.[21] This happened during the COVID-19 pandemic when people wearing masks believed those who didn't were acting with nefarious intentions, and vice versa. These conflicts can be scary and seem unsolvable, but based on what Ripley described in her book *High Conflict*, teaching kids to name these conflicts and work toward resolution or reconciliation may be one of the most important challenges of their lives.[22] The world seems increasingly polarized, but our biggest problems require working together, seeing each other's humanity, and extending both empathy and care.

In *High Conflict*, Ripley provides a list of traits that associate with high conflict—personal characteristics like certainty, rigidity, righteousness, and zero-sum thinking—as well as those describing good conflict— curiosity, humility, and novelty. If we recognize tendencies of high conflict in kids, we can intervene early and coach them toward the attributes associated with good conflict. We can also help them learn to apologize, accept forgiveness, and pursue reconciliation.

TRY THIS

As we support young people in their relationships with others, we may need to coach them on when and how to apologize. In our house, we have a simple process for seeking forgiveness inspired from the Hawaiian word ho'oponopono, which means to correct and make things right.

This is what I do when I've wronged my children, and it is what we have taught them to do. When they are ready to mend a relationship, I tell them to "go ho'oponopono."

Here is the four-step process inspired by the definition of ho'oponopono:[23]

1. Say "I'm sorry," and describe what you did wrong.

2. Ask the person, "Can you forgive me?"

3. Express love and care.

4. Say "thank you." (In our house, we hug)

In our family, this simple practice is sacred. If both people are wrong, they go back and forth on each step. At first it felt silly, but now we appreciate having a structure and process for apologizing. With this practice, forgiveness is requested and not required. One time, my son told me he would "think about it," and I had to reel in my desire to demand forgiveness. I'm glad I didn't. He found me later that day and told me he accepted my apology. His authenticity made the wait worthwhile.

The next time you owe someone an apology, try to practice this four-step process of seeking forgiveness. Consider how you could use it at home and work.

Teaching Relationship Skills

Relationship skills can be learned, practiced, and strengthened. Young people must be able to use them in person and online. Without specific instruction, kids will relate and respond to people in ways that have been modeled for them, whether those are healthy or not.

Here are important relationship skills for kids to learn and strengthen over time:

- Exhibiting self-control and self-awareness

- Being able to listen and respond

- Practicing diplomacy and conflict management

- Being adaptable

- Staying open-minded and curious, even in arguments

- Demonstrating empathy and compassion

- Being able to pay attention and be present[24]

To teach these skills, model them and provide opportunities for kids to practice. This can happen through coaching or group activities. You can practice it in simulated scenarios, like role playing, improv, and debate. You can always support and strengthen these skills by providing real-time constructive feedback.

Supporting the Relationship Children Have With Themselves

The final dimension is helping kids form and sustain healthy relationships with themselves—who they are now, who they are becoming, where they come from, and what makes them unique. This ties into the other whole life practices, especially *Embrace Identities and Cultures* and *Build Community and Belonging*. That's because a child's sense of self connects to their family, community, cultures, identities, and overall sense of belonging. We nurture a child's relationship with self by encouraging the development of a healthy self-image and ensuring they have positive role models and representation within their web of support.

Nurture and Nudge

Relationships are foundational for children to live, learn, and thrive. They might even matter the most. Our relationships with kids suffer when we are too busy and distracted to slow down, be present, and invest in our interactions. It's easy to walk through the motions and not pause to consider the quality of our time together and relationship overall. It can feel like too much work to prioritize relationship building with kids and the people in their lives. Make time. The research is abundant and clear: positive relationships keep us alive and enable thriving. My dear friend Gena Keller always tells me to "nurture and nudge" my way into things, and that rings true for this: Nudge your time, attention, and effort in the direction of relationship building, and nurture your relationships and those children every chance you get.

WHOLE LIFE PRACTICE

Nurture Healthy Relationships

Learn

- There are more than two people in your direct relationships with kids. Young people bring their past and similar relationships with them. You will be compared to the people like you and with similar roles (e.g., past coaches, teachers, another caregiver). Be sensitive to young people's lived experience and take time to learn about it.

- Young people need caring, consistent adults *and* a web of support to thrive. Webs of support are the full range of relationships kids have, activated to provide ongoing support and opportunity. Some of these relationships are transformational—defined by care, love, and support. Others are more transactional—defined by assigned roles, responsibilities, and tasks. Many relationships will slide back and forth, depending on the situation and season of life.

- Positive relationships might be the most powerful predictor of health, happiness, and longevity. Meanwhile, loneliness can shorten your lifespan, make you vulnerable to illness, and impede your quality of life.

- There are four dimensions of healthy relationships to nurture with kids: (1) your relationship with them, (2) your relationship with the other adults in their lives, (3) their relationships with others, and (4) their relationships with themselves.

Reflect

Reflect on your childhood and think about the web of relationships you had, across all the places where you spent time.

- Which steady, seasonal, and situational relationships were most impactful, and why?

- Who embodied the three lessons David shared with me, and what difference did that make?

- Were there experiences where your web of relationships became a web of support? What happened and how did that feel?

After reflecting on your early relationships, think about what parts of your experience you want children to experience.

(Continued)

(Continued)

Act

As you absorb what you read and reflected on, consider how you can put insights into action. Take time to set a few commitments and intentions on how to *Nurture Healthy Relationships*.

- What is one small action you can take *today* to put this practice into action?

- What is one larger action you can take *this month* to put this practice into action?

- What is one big action you can work toward *this year* to put this practice into action?

NOTES

Build Community and Belonging 10

"Today, we find ourselves at a critical juncture, divided on the fault lines of politics, class, gender, and race. In its silent way, belonging is the central conversation of our times."

—Toko-pa Turner

I live 30 minutes east of St. Louis City, in a mid-sized college town surrounded by farm country. When I started writing this book, I took to social media to crowdsource recommendations for interviews and places to write about. Among local friends, Liberty Middle School was a constant suggestion. Liberty is one of two middle schools in our community, serving about 1,000 students and located next door to the elementary school where my kids went to preschool and catty-corner to our local YMCA.

I was curious about what was happening down the street, so I reached out to the principal, Allen Duncan, to schedule a visit. I was in the building the next day. I was greeted by smiling staff and sidewalks full of encouraging chalk messages from families and students. Upbeat music played in the hallways and the atmosphere was warm and welcoming.

When Principal Duncan took me around the building, I noticed clusters of framed photos of staff and students and ceiling tiles filled with handwritten advice from graduates. There was an outdoor courtyard with a parent-painted mural reminding kids "U Are Loved," like the one in the entryway that said "In this school . . . We belong. We are a family. We are Liberty."

Beyond decor, I was told school staff gets together for regular social outings, something started during the COVID-19 pandemic that has continued ever since. The school community is divided into eight houses, an idea inspired by the Ron Clark Academy and Harry Potter, making it possible to form close communities within an otherwise large student body.

Every year, Liberty organizes around a central theme. When schools shut down in 2020, the theme was "Whatever It Takes," and then during the next year of pandemic schooling, it was "Better Together," and when kids returned to school in 2022, the motto was "Be Legendary." This motto carries across the community and instills noticeable pride in staff, families, and students. Since learning about it, I have seen social media posts that end with #BeLegendary, students seeing each other at community events and using the "L" sign (pointer and middle finger raised to signal "Be Legendary" and oppose the "Loser" sign). School leadership has successfully tapped into the power of positive school climate, rituals, routines, handshakes, and signs.

During my visit, I saw how strong culture creates the conditions communities need to thrive. After interacting with Liberty students—including one who survived brain cancer, a classroom of students with intellectual and developmental disabilities, and one who was new to the school—I was reminded how strong culture builds strong community and how strong community is necessary for building belonging.

Different Kinds of Community

Communities are places and spaces where people gather. Some communities are assigned and others children choose for themselves. While communities should usher in a sense of belonging, it's not guaranteed. Many of us have experienced being in a community but feeling like we didn't belong. Our job is to build and support communities where kids know they are welcome, experience belonging, feel known, and can be themselves.

We are wired for social contact and have a primitive need to form groups. In ancient times, social cohesion kept people from injury, illness, and death. Our instincts favor quality connections over quantity. That's because we are more likely to survive with people who know us, want us to be safe, care about us, and take care of us.[1]

Research and experience point to five kinds of communities kids participate in. Generally, young people will be active in multiple communities, some that intersect and others that stay distinct. These communities are (1) ones of convenience, (2) cohorts and crews, (3) cultural, (4) organized around causes and convictions, and (5) formed in a crisis or around shared struggles. Table 18 provides descriptions of each.

Table 18 Five Kinds of Community	
TYPE	**DESCRIPTION**
Convenience	Communities formed from proximity. Examples include neighbors and family.
Cohorts and Crews	Communities formed from programs and placements. Examples include school, classrooms, youth programs, and sports teams.
Cultural	Communities formed around heritage, race, ethnicity, and other identities. Examples include informal and broad affiliations (e.g., the Black community) and formal and specific affiliations (e.g., the Asian-American Student Association).
Causes and Convictions	Communities formed around social causes and faith. Examples include churches, mosques, temples, community organizing groups, and coalitions.
Crisis	Communities that form around a disaster or shared suffering. Examples include disaster response and support groups.

Within these communities, young people engage in multiple relationships that help them develop their sense of self and place in the world. These relationships intensify as children get older and enter adolescence. In childhood, communities mostly determine where kids spend time, what they do, and with whom. In adolescence, identity formation becomes increasingly important and young people have more choice about which communities they participate in. Community membership is a key part of helping young people figure out who they are, what they believe, where they belong, how to behave, and what they want in life. This whole life practice intersects with two others: *Nurture Healthy Relationships* and *Embrace Identities and Cultures.*

In my experience, young people search for and form communities out of a need to belong and not be alone. When groups at school and youth programs fail to include and embrace kids, they go elsewhere for community. I dropped out of school, in part because I felt I didn't belong at my high school. Out of school, I was in community with a close group of friends who swore to protect and be there for me, no matter what. I was desperate to belong, and I found that with other young people like me. When we see young people connecting to peer groups or people that worry us, we must ask ourselves, "Why?" There are needs for connection, community, and belonging that are probably being met through these relationships that aren't being met in school, at home, or elsewhere.

Sometimes young people experience groups that fit all four community types. For example, the Polynesian Voyaging Society engages young people in Hawai'i and on the island of O'ahu (convenience) around ancient wayfinding traditions, values, beliefs, and practices (cultural). Young people join intergenerational crews who train and paddle together (cohorts and crews). In recent years, the Polynesian Voyaging Society has been raising global awareness about climate change (causes and convictions).

TRY THIS
- Think back to your childhood and the communities you were a part of. When and how did you join those communities? What benefits or challenges came with being associated with each group?

- Over the next few days, pay attention to how, where, and why kids gather and organize. For example, if you work in a school, pay attention to where kids sit in the cafeteria or who they play with at recess. If you run a youth program, pay attention to the different feel and vibe of each group. If you're a caretaker, ask your child about their group or group of friends. What types of communities do you notice? To what degree does it seem like kids belong and can be themselves?

Communities as Currency

While communities are a way for kids to experience care and companionship, they are also a way for them to connect to valuable opportunities and resources. This social capital helps young people move ahead and pursue their interests. We get ahead in life because of who we know and who knows us.[2]

When community connections are limited, so is social capital. For example, when a child lives in a racially segregated community, connections may not carry across racial divides. This can limit resource access and connections to opportunities available to people of other races. Historic and persistent exclusion, racialization, and marginalization can lead to what Beverly Daniel Tatum described as "reduced community helpfulness."[3]

This also happens across economic divides. In his book *Dream Hoarders: How the American Upper Middle Class Is Leaving Everyone Else in the Dust, Why That Is a Problem, and What to Do About It,*

Richard Reeves describes how wealthy families purchase social and economic opportunity enhancers for their kids (e.g., club memberships, private schools, elite sports, fraternal organizations) which leads to lucrative connections, which leads to more lucrative connections. As Richard describes it, Americans loves to tell the story of "rags to riches" and pulling oneself up by their bootstraps, but we operate according to a reliable system of economic and social class reproduction.

We can build young people's social capital through intentionally designed social environments and experiences. An August 2022 study published in *Nature* found that economic connectedness through friendships that cross class lines had a profoundly positive impact on young people's ability to move out of poverty. The study found that future incomes increased up to 20 percent for children who grew up poor but lived in neighborhoods where at least 70 percent of their friends were wealthy. The study analysis showed these friendships were more impactful for economic mobility than school quality and family structure.[4]

One of my favorite examples of this is Live Oak Camp in New Orleans. Live Oak is a beloved summer camp for local New Orleans kids ages 8 to 18. The camp is intentionally designed to bring together young people from all parts of the city who might not meet because of different demographics and determinants. As program director Lucy Scholz told me, campers form lifetime friendships with kids who are different from them and experience collective community as early as 8 or 9 years old. By adulthood, those friendships are fully formed, generating social connections across the city that bridge racial, ethnic, economic, political, and geographic lines. Through camp, young people diversify their social network, expand the reach of their relationships, and bridge divides that lead to othering, oppression, and other forms of harm and hate.

Live Oak prioritizes diverse community building and bridge building. They have created structural and financial ways for any child to attend. By separating campers from the city and digital devices the camp experience becomes an equalizer. It is a closed yet diverse community, with many cohorts and crews. Lucy says this leads to campers feeling responsible for each other and camp, leading to a powerful sense of camaraderie and community that lasts for years. Through regular check-ins and meet-ups during the school year, camp staff see how summer bonds extend and support campers back home, creating more openness and empathy for children who are different from them, but like their Live Oak friends.

TRY THIS   • Plan an "equalizing" experience for kids. While you may not be able to take them camping, create some type of team-building experience where they can work together, strengthen bonds, and depend on one another in new ways. After you're done, process the experience as a group.

Climate, Culture, and Community Building

Whether we are thinking about Liberty Middle School, the Polynesian Voyaging Society, or Live Oak Camp, there are consistent characteristics among vibrant communities that are obvious, even to outsiders. These positive "community builders" move people from congregating to belonging.

- **Sense of pride and collective identity:** Strong communities are easily recognizable and kids have ways of acting, dressing, and behaving to show off membership and see themselves as visible and valued members.

- **Rituals and routines:** Handshakes, chants, dances, songs, and celebration ceremonies are some ways a community can feel sacred. Strong communities have ways of marking special occasions or regular events that are memorable and meaningful.

- **Time-tested traditions:** From shared meals and chores to ways of coming together, strong communities show up for each other, and find ways to spend time together, sharing mundane to momentous experiences.

In his book *Better Together: Restoring the American Community,* scholar Robert Putnam said community building and social capital take time and effort. His research shows that community building works best when it happens through intensive in-person interactions that facilitate trust, build mutual understanding, and create bonds that are reciprocal and mutually beneficial. There is early research on the benefits of technology to enable and encourage community building and build social capital. Research suggests that technology should support community and connections rather than drive them. Virtual platforms like Zoom or Slack enable online meeting spaces where relationships and communities can be in regular contact and meet when in person isn't possible. These online platforms can facilitate connections between young people and prospective mentors and employers, especially those who live far away. Nothing, however, can replace the power and quality of in-person interactions.[5]

In her landmark book on building social capital in schools, *Who You Know: Unlocking Innovations That Expand Students' Networks,* Julia Freeland Fisher notes that schools—and youth programs—deal every day in the power of relationships and importance of social connectedness. She recommends doubling down on relationship- and community-building experiences, integrating and investing in student supports that deepen and expand young people's connections, and carefully using technology when it helps expand a child's communities, especially in instances where divides and disparities create limits that are hard to overcome.

Building Belonging

Brené Brown is my go-to expert on belonging. In 2010, she wrote *The Gifts of Imperfection* and described belonging in this way:

> Belonging is the innate human desire to be part of something larger than ourselves. Because this yearning is so primal, we often try to acquire it by fitting in and by seeking approval, which are not only hollow substitutes for belonging, but often barriers to it. Because our true belonging only happens when we present our authentic, imperfect selves to the world, our sense of belonging cannot be greater than our level of self-acceptance.[6]

In 2017, in *Braving the Wilderness: The Quest for True Belonging and the Courage to Stand Alone,* she went one step further, saying that belonging cannot be achieved or accomplished, rather it is something that is felt and that enables us to endure the brutal conditions of uncertainty, vulnerability, and criticism.[7]

With children, belonging is primal and visceral. We cringe at the absence of belonging when a child is chosen last for a team or rejected by classmates on the playground. We feel the absence when teens confess to not fitting in and hating school or themselves. We see kids seek belonging when they contort and change how they act, dress, speak—sometimes dimming the best parts of themselves—to fit into a friend group or be more socially acceptable. Sometimes young people even lie about who they are, where they're from, and what they like, to try and find belonging and acceptance.

Belonging is warm and powerful. There's a palpable energy in spaces where young people belong, have ownership, and are free to be themselves. These are places and relationships where young people feel known and seen. These are spaces that are welcoming, inclusive, and affirming. They seem less stressful and more intimate. Kids are fortified and nourished by being there. In indigenous cultures, these spaces emphasize belonging to each other *and* place. As Hawaiian cultural leader Noelani Goodyear-Kaopua described it to me, the line between human and not human is more porous than in mainstream culture. Because of this, belonging to place helps young people understand their own story, history, and heritage in connection with ancestors, animals, and nature.

Belonging deeply intersects with identity and culture. According to my friend and youth development expert Dave Martineau, when we invite kids to bring their full selves into a community, they must be able to trust us, and we must trust them back. True belonging requires good listening, acceptance, mutual trust, and unconditional support. Belonging also helps young people endure hardship and conflict and explore how they can be a part of a community even when there are disagreements.

Dave explained that conflict and dissent are an expected part of building and being in community. In these situations, a young person's sense of belonging extends to a sense of responsibility for the community and the care of people within it. Belonging doesn't require sameness of views and opinions, but it does require a standard level of care and safety so everyone can continue to be a part of the community and belong even when situations arise that bring out differences, dissent, and discomfort.[8]

Threats to Belonging

There are personal reasons why a young person might believe they don't fit in. Sometimes it's circumstantial—for example, a child moves to a new community and enrolls in a small school with students who have grown up together and whose families know each other. Sometimes it's contextual or generational. For example, many tweens and teens have a distorted view of community and connectedness because of social media. The distance between what is curated online and what is happening in real life creates a discontent between reality and something filtered. There are also broader, more systemic threats to belonging. Two highly interconnected ones are *othering* and *lack of representation.*

Othering

Othering is a natural occurrence with dangerous consequences. A part of our primitive wiring is to associate positive attributes to groups we belong to, and negative attributes to everyone else. According to Shawn Ginwright—a leading scholar on belonging and healing—this us-versus-them thinking leads to *othering,* which he defines as "the process of labeling groups of people with negative attributes and then identifying with the positive attributes of your own group."[9] When this occurs, it can lead to dehumanization and isolation. This divides across all the fault lines Toko-pa Turner described in her book *Belonging, Remembering Ourselves Home*: politics, class, gender, and race. Othering gives rise to the "isms": racism, sexism, adultism, classism, ableism, along with other forms of exclusion, suppression, and oppression.[10]

Shawn Ginwright's research and writing suggest that this threat can only be extinguished by belonging that goes deeper than the one Brené Brown described. He describes this level of belonging as the "capacity to see the humanity in those who are not like us and to recognize that the same elements that exist within them also exist within us. It means that we must see the humanity in others, even if they refuse to see the same in us." This is a practice, which can and must be taught to our children.

Lack of Representation

Othering dehumanizes, stripping away the opportunity and inclination to experience and express empathy toward people who are different. This worsens with false narratives and lack of representation. If young people only interact with people like them and hear stories like theirs, it is easy to buy into fear and falsehoods about "other" people. Relatedly, if a young person is a part of an underrepresented community and can't see themselves in curriculum, books, media, classroom activities, or school celebrations, then it's easy to believe they don't belong and that their differences set them too far apart to ever fit in.

One of the more promising ways to increase representation is through reading and honest conversations. In St. Louis, a group called We Stories formed to equip families with the tools and support to start and strengthen conversations about race and racism. We Stories used an intergenerational approach to help parents and children bolster their skills, comfort, and confidence in learning history, analyzing multiple perspectives, discussing difficult topics, and advocating for equity in their communities. Caretakers learned how to use the power of diverse children's literature to lay a foundation for learning about people with different lived experiences in ways that neutralize or celebrate differences, which humanizes others and builds empathy.

We Stories began in a heavily segregated community that consistently ranks as one of the most racist cities in the United States.[11] By using children's books, a parent training program, and curriculum, We Stories introduced families to a variety of different characters and authentic voices, exposing young people to children who looked different and lived differently from them. This cultivated empathy and initiated conversations around diversity and inclusion. Meanwhile, We Stories provided parents with the space to process and the practices to build their understanding of race, racism, and other experiences of prejudice and oppression. As a community and with guidance from We Stories staff, these families engaged in collective learning and supported one another as they put their practices into action.

Belonging Across the Long and Wide of Life

Communities can create conditions for belonging, but young people also attend schools and youth programs or live in places where they feel they might not belong, and where messages—ranging from people's attitudes and behaviors, visible images, and policies—reinforce that reality.

To confront this, and cultivate belonging with kids we care about, we must double down on teaching and encouraging empathy, compassion, courage, and conflict resolution. We must prioritize and make time for relationship building and team building, nurturing meaningful connections, and helping young people form a sense of shared identity and purpose.[12]

This is especially important and difficult in areas that are homogenous or segregated by beliefs, race, and/or ethnicity. If you are in a place like this, think about how to bring together different groups around common experiences. In the past, I've seen this work with buddy programs between mostly white and mostly Black schools, or interfaith coalitions coming together for a day of service.

In *Belonging: Remembering Ourselves Home,* Toko-pa Turner explores longing to belong in this way:

> There are many different kinds of belonging. The first kind that comes to mind is the feeling of belonging in a community, or to a geography. But for many of us, longing to belong begins in our own families. Then there is the longing we feel to belong with an intimate other in the sanctuary of relationship, and the belonging we yearn to feel in a purpose or location. There is also spiritual longing to belong to a set of ways or traditions, the longing to know and participate in ancestral knowledge . . . and if we take a broader view, there is a belonging with the earth itself, which is felt (or not felt) at the heart of us all. Finally, there is the great belonging, which may be the most nebulous and persistent of all, the longing to belong to that "something greater" which gives our lives meaning. [13]

Belonging is more than a human need. It is the substance that connects children to each other, to the people around them, to the places where they live and come from, and to something greater than themselves. Belonging extends to beliefs and aspirations. Like loneliness, the loss of belonging makes it hard to live, and when it is accompanied by othering and a lack of representation, it becomes life threatening.

We must build and nurture communities that care for one another and show common concern, respect children's humanity, and facilitate close connections without perpetuating an us-versus-them mentality. This whole life practice is crucial across every sphere of a young person's life for health, wholeness, and well-being.

WHOLE LIFE PRACTICE

Build Community and Belonging

Learn

- Communities are the places and spaces where people gather. Some are assigned and others are chosen. We form and join communities because we are biologically wired for social contact and social cohesion. Communities reveal a lot about who young people are, what makes them safe, where they or others think they belong, what they believe, and how they identify.

- There are five kinds of communities that young people join. Many intersect and overlap, although some are distinct. They are communities of (1) convenience, (2) cohorts and crews, (3) culture, (4) causes and convictions, and (5) crisis.

- Communities offer more than care and companionship; they also bring status and wealth. Social capital is when social connections and relationships generate advantageous opportunity, access, and resources.

- Belonging is our innate human desire to be a part of something. It is about fitting in, self-acceptance, and being able to bring our authentic selves into the world. For children, belonging is a primal and visceral need. It can be threatened by othering and lack of representation, and it can be nurtured by empathy, compassion, courage, and conflict resolution.

Reflect

Reflect across your life. Think about the communities you were a part of as a child, tween, teen, and young adult. Consider the communities you feel most connected to today.

- Where and with whom have you experienced true belonging?

- In what instances have you felt othered or unrepresented, and what impact did that have on your self-worth and self-acceptance?

- To what extent do you prioritize community building and belonging with kids?

After reflecting, find someone to process with. If what emerged feels private, write about what you are thinking and feeling.

Act

As you absorb what you read and reflected on, consider how you can put insights into action. Take time to set a few commitments and intentions on how to *Build Community and Belonging*.

- What is one small action you can take *today* to put this practice into action?

- What is one larger action you can take *this month* to put this practice into action?

- What is one big action you can work toward *this year* to put this practice into action?

Embrace Identities and Cultures 11

"Knowing that we can be loved exactly as we are gives us all the best opportunity for growing into the healthiest of people."

—Fred Rogers

In West Kauaʻi, there is a small nonprofit with big vision and impact. Kūmano I Ke Ala is a community organization that is a teaching and training facility, farm, business, paddling club, summer camp, afterschool program, cultural hub, and more. On a recent trip to Hawaiʻi, I met the team at their offices in the town of Waimea to learn about their youth programs and cultural restoration projects. During our time together, we sat under a traditional hale (Hawaiian house) built by local kids, eating bananas, and learning—for the first time in my own life—about the farming and food practices my ancestors used, and that Kūmano I Ke Ala staff continue to teach today.

Later, in the pouring rain, I watched more than 30 middle and high schoolers divide into crews and carry canoes into the river. As I watched them, the organization's founder, Kaina Makua, told me these were the same kids who work the farm, built the hale, and grew the bananas. To them, I was Auntie Malia, a welcome elder, in spite of not feeling old enough to be one. They greeted me with respect and hugs, putting their foreheads to mine to share hā—breath—creating a sacred space where we could connect to each other and the land we share, Hawaiʻi.

A few days later, I went back to see Kaina on his loʻi (taro farm) farther up-country. To get there, I drove to a bridge and waited for a truck to pick me up. We drove through the gulch, up a hill, and through the woods until we reached an area surrounded by cliffs, with restored lo'i, other native crops, and more youth-built hale. For hours, Kaina talked with me about the Hawaiian values they teach kids through farming, food production, traditional construction, language lessons, and paddling.

In Hawai'i, this cultural and experiential learning is known as 'āina (land)-based education. For Kaina and his team at Kūmano I Ke Ala, this includes daily language lessons that kids practice as they work together. It is teaching Hawaiian values through experience. For example, young children work with older youth to harvest taro and make poi (a Hawaiian staple food), and then give it away; the lesson they learn is to give to others the first of your harvest. Another example happens in the canoe: there are six seats, and everyone—no matter their positions—has a kuleana (responsibility) to fulfill. The lesson is about everyone needing each other and doing their part to finish the race.

Learning steeped in culture is rich, vibrant, empowering, and equipping. It can also heal. On O'ahu—a neighboring island to Kaua'i, and home to Honolulu—there is another lo'i, this one on the Kawailoa Youth and Family Wellness Campus, where Hawai'i's last juvenile detention facility is located along with safe housing for youth experiencing homelessness or human trafficking. Kupa 'Āina is a farm run by Partners in Development Foundation, which uses 'āina-based practices as a restorative and trauma-informed approach to healing. It is a powerful model to see in action, one which I hope many will use.

The farm uses indigenous and regenerative agricultural practices, combining ancestral knowledge systems with the modern science of circular ecologies. Through farming, young people get to aloha 'āina (love and steward the land) and mālama honua (care for the earth). Farm manager Zachary Huang told me one of the most powerful parts of the work is watching young people grow and support thriving crops, and through the process begin to thrive themselves. Through participation, young people have space to learn, heal, and develop knowledge and skills they can use to build a strong and food-secure future for themselves, their families, and Hawai'i.[1]

'Āina-based education has been on the rise since the 1970s when Native Hawaiian-led social movements sparked a wave of policy change, including provisions for Hawaiian language, culture, and history to finally be taught in public schools. Before then, children could not speak their language at school and they received little to no formal instruction on Hawaiian history, geography, agricultural and aquaponics science, navigational arts and maritime practices, or cultural traditions and stories.[2]

Today, more of Hawai'i's children experience their culture and history in schools and youth programs, which is accelerating and deepening their own identity development. Although there is still work to be done, educators and youth workers are finding ways for native kids to see themselves and their language in education and extracurricular activities, building a sense of self and purpose through place, people, and ancestral values.

Embracing Community and Culture

Around 2011, Cheryl Ka'uhane Lupenui was appointed as the only Native Hawaiian to the Hawai'i State Board of Education. The board tasked her with overseeing the few policies that had to do with Hawaiian language, history, and culture. Through her work chairing the state Student Achievement committee, which was in the process of revisiting learning outcomes, Cheryl started thinking about what it would take to have Hawaiian culture integrated and infused into both curriculum and context across the K–12 experience.

This led to a small group of Hawaiian cultural and education leaders coming together to design a framework to reflect and represent Hawai'i and offer a holistic approach to teaching Hawaiian cultural values and history to students in elementary, middle, and high schools. The group looked to other native communities across the globe, asking what cultural and 'āina-based education should look like on the islands.[3]

In the end, the group developed Nā Hopena A'o—HĀ, for short. This outcomes framework, with guiding statements originally written in Hawaiian, masterfully reflects the unique values and traditions of native culture while supporting the cultural and identity exploration and expression of all students, regardless of background. Hawai'i is, after all, one of the most racially and ethnically diverse places in the United States.[4] The result was a guiding structure for learning that helps students strengthen their sense of Belonging, Responsibility,

Excellence, Aloha, Total Well-Being, and Hawaiʻi (BREATH). It reflects Hawaiʻi's roots and branches of cultures, customs, and communities.

Kaʻanohiokalā Kalama-Macomber—who oversees HĀ for the Hawaiʻi Department of Education—told me this framework brings together being and belonging. Through cultural experiences and community connections, young people develop a sense of self and place, understanding who they are, who they are in relationship to where they are from, their gifts, and how they can use those gifts for individual and collective well-being.[5] These experiences connect schools and community partners like Kūmano I Ke Ala—bringing students and educators into the community and bringing the community into schools.

Kaʻanohiokalā described the power of seeing children from different walks of life come together around the thing they have in common, living and growing up in Hawaiʻi—sharing an island and its finite resources. As she described it, it's teaching young people to answer the question, "How can I be the best me, for the collective we?" With intentional design, Hawaiʻi educators use HĀ to nurture students' relationships to one another, the land, and the broader community. When it works, young people find purpose and belonging through a connection to place and story.[6] This type of power and community-building happens across the United States, in many community centers and congregational spaces that run after-school and summer programs.

Celebrating Community and Teaching Culture in Freedom Schools

Across the continental United States, children spend afternoons and summers learning about and celebrating their cultures in similar ways to Hawaiʻi. CDF Freedom Schools®, a longstanding program of Children's Defense Fund, was born out of the civil rights movement in Mississippi during the "freedom summer" of 1964. Back then, Freedom Schools were a place where Black children could learn about their culture from young adults who looked like them, cared about them, and wanted to see them do well. Today's CDF Freedom Schools® are true to the same spirit but open to children of all backgrounds, providing them with transformational literacy and cultural enrichment.

CDF Freedom Schools® use intergenerational leadership, positive energy, and joy to cultivate children's love of learning, reading, and culture. Young people teach and counsel younger children, with the expressed purpose of teaching them culture and history they may not get in school.

For Freedom Schools, this starts with reading. This has been described to me as "windows and mirrors." Through books, children in CDF Freedom Schools® meet characters who look like them and their families and who reflect their cultures and identities. This doesn't happen enough in U.S. public schools, and when it does, it can be about traumatizing events (e.g., slavery, the Holocaust), inaccurate (e.g., Thanksgiving), or incomplete (e.g., only studying Martin Luther King Jr. during a unit on civil rights). CDF Freedom Schools® also read books about children and cultures from around the world. These books become "windows" into cultures kids may be unaware of. Program staff help children explore these cultures and find common ground with the characters.

In addition to windows and mirrors, CDF Freedom Schools® provide children with joy in gathering with cheers, chants, and recognition. Harambee, a Swahili term meaning "let's come together," is the start of every Freedom School day. Kids and staff come together to sing, dance, cheer, chant, and hear a community leader read aloud to them. This is a time for recognitions, giving children the chance to encourage and celebrate one another. At CDF Freedom Schools® children get to see and be themselves, and they learn from people who look like them, live in their communities, and who they want to be like.[7]

Five Stages of Cultural Connections

HĀ and CDF Freedom Schools® are inspirational models of cultural appreciation and representation, which benefit kids from every background, especially those who don't see themselves well represented in schools, teachers, books, and curriculum. Together, they illuminate five stages for embracing children's cultures and helping them create cultural connections (see Figure 6). The first, Harambee, comes from Freedom Schools. The remaining four come from Nā Hopena A'o (HĀ).[8]

Figure 6   Five Stages of Cultural Connection

Harambee

"Let's come together" calls for cultural connections by creating sacred and set-aside spaces to gather, recognize, and celebrate who we are individually and collectively. For CDF Freedom Schools®, it's a chance to let go of the negativity of the outside world and embrace the positivity of the program and its people. Harambee is when kids recognize and name each other's gifts. It is full of ritual and routine, which makes it a memorable and meaningful experience. Harambee is a big reason why kids keep coming back to Freedom Schools®.

We can all create Harambee experiences. In schools and programs, this can happen through morning meetings, advisories, cohort experiences, "houses" within a school or camp, assemblies, rallies, and affinity groups. At home, this can happen during mealtime, to start a weekend, to begin a break, to celebrate a holiday, and in gatherings with family and friends. These are times when we come together as a welcome, inclusive, and affirming community to celebrate the collective and individual well-being of every person.

Connection to Self

Ka Hanu means breathing, and it is the first stage of the HĀ cycle. Ka Hanu is about a personal connection to culture and history. It is helping ourselves and children reflect on our own stories and experiences, exploring how they impact who we are and how we see the world.

This stage begins with us. We must learn our own stories, cultures, and identities, reflecting on how they form and shape us, and exploring how they color how we see ourselves and the world. This extends to children, helping them learn about themselves, their gifts, and their own stories. This can be done through reading, writing, movies, media, or through facilitated and guided reflection.

Connection to Each Other

Ke Ahe means deeper breath, and it's about relationships. This second stage of the HĀ cycle is about our exchanges with one another. Ke Ahe is learning each other's stories and being mindful of how others' experiences shape who they are and how they experience the world.

This stage reminds me of how Brené Brown describes *empathy* in her book *Atlas of the Heart:* "We need to dispel the myth that empathy is 'walking in someone else's shoes.' Rather than walking in your shoes, I need to learn how to listen to the story you tell about what it's like in your shoes *and* believe you even when it doesn't match my experiences."[9] This is done through relationship and honest sharing. This can happen organically, or by designing spaces where young people and adults come together to have facilitated cultural connections, experiences, and conversations.

Connection to Community

Ke Aho means a deep breath you hold and that sustains you. This third stage of HĀ is like the South African concept *ubuntu*, which means *I am who I am, because of who you are.* This is about interdependence, when we move from learning each other's stories to seeing how we are a part of each other's stories. As Kaʻanohiokalā described it, this is realizing that we inhale and exhale together—that HĀ (breath) is shared.

Ke Aho is about collective well-being and reciprocity. It is fostering community conditions where children feel safe and welcome to explore their cultural questions and identities. This stage moves from intermittent interactions about culture to integrated experiences where culture is woven into everything. This is done by shifting from cultural responsiveness to cultural experiences and immersion.

Connection to the World

Ua Hāloa means a far-reaching breath, where HĀ is sustained. This final stage is developing a deeper understanding of HĀ. It is having a larger worldview and seeing the connection between us and the world. We begin to understand the impact of our actions, together and apart, on all communities, past, present, and future. This is what happens when kids in a CDF Freedom School® in St. Louis, Missouri, learn about a freedom fighter named Malala in Pakistan, and what happens when kids in Pakistan learn about freedom fighters in St. Louis, Missouri.

We all live on the same island in the universe, and we must work together to take care of it. Just like children in Hawaiʻi have their small Pacific islands in common, children everywhere share planet Earth. Together, they will face and fight existential threats and steward a global home that houses all our cultures and communities.

TRY THIS

- A respected Hawaiian elder, Puanani Burgess, tells a story about the power of our names and what they reveal about cultural roots and connections. This week, consider the story of your name. What does it tell you about who you are and where you are from? If you don't know, take time to investigate. If you work with older youth, consider offering this as an independent project.

- Choose one of the five stages of cultural connection you want to focus on. Take time to evaluate how you're already putting this into practice and what new strategies you would like to try. As you plan, consider what this stage looked like for you growing up, and now as an adult.

Identity Development

Through culture, kids explore who they are in the context of where they come from. Culture is only one part of identity development. Through childhood and especially in adolescence, young people discover who they are and what that means demographically and preferentially. Identity formation is a primary task of adolescence and young people spend their tween and teen years exploring and experimenting with their sense of self.

There are different signs young people are exploring their identity. Symbolic changes include new ways of expressing themselves through dress, hair, and speech. Relational changes include spending time with different peer groups, based on who they feel they fit in with. Sometimes young people become more or less engaged in school and extracurricular activities because they associate aspects of their identity as being more or less studious, smart, or involved.[10]

As identity development happens, young people need adults who extend unconditional love and support. This is true regardless of whether you agree with or understand the identity. As young people discover and own who they are, they look for trustworthy adults to provide guidance, affirmation, resources, and connection. They need adults who can protect and advocate for them, fighting against unfair treatment, discrimination, and bullying. Our actions and attitudes with young people should always lead with love and never leave kids afraid of or disgusted by who they are or think they might be.

Identity development is a process, and young people deserve our care, belief, and empathy as they go through it. In adult-child relationships, adults hold incredible power and sway. Our misuse of that power can lead young people to suppress, reject, or deny pieces of themselves because they feel they are in danger, unsupported, and afraid. This suppression or rejection of who they are is traumatizing and makes it hard for young people to learn[11] and thrive.

Group and Personal Identity

Throughout childhood and adolescence, young people develop group and personal identities. **Group identity** is a young person's understanding of who they are in the context of groups and communities they are assigned to, choose, and are perceived to be a part of. **Personal identity** is a young person's understanding of who they are individually, including how others perceive them.[12] **Intersectionality** is how group and personal identities come together and result in unique experiences of prejudice and privilege, based on a history of advantaging some groups and people above others.[13] Young people deserve to be seen, supported, and understood for their holistic identity. When we break young people's identity into separate categories and see them as only part of themselves, we risk missing the complexities and challenges as well as the community and belonging they may experience at the nexus points.[14]

Young people's group and individual identities—and the ways in which they are intersectional—orient young people to who they are, where they belong, and how they fit into the world. Young people's developing identities are real-time reflections of what they care about, believe in, and aspire to become. These identities are influenced by family, friends, media, culture, and society. As young people move from childhood to adulthood, we see their identities shaped and reshaped by time, experience, and experimentation.[15]

Racial and Ethnic Identity

A young person's racial and ethnic identity is complex and takes time to develop. For young people who belong to historically marginalized racial or ethnic groups, it's a necessary part of early and ongoing identity exploration because race and ethnicity are often the first thing other people notice and acknowledge, and that brings bias and assumptions. Professor Joanna Williams at Rutgers University—a scholar of racial and ethnic identity development for adolescents—told me this is especially true for Black youth, who cannot escape from the everyday impacts of racism and the risks of anti-Black violence.[16]

Joanna shared that people often assume race is the most important part of a young person of color's identity. This assumption can diminish the fact that kids are trying to figure out the rest of their identities too (e.g., who they're attracted to, what they believe in). Racial and ethnic identity become salient for children at different times and for different reasons. Young people must be allowed to assert and define whatever parts of their identities are most important to them at a given time.

Researchers like Joanna have found that racial and ethnic identity development is linked to positive self-esteem, engagement in learning, and fewer depressive symptoms. When kids feel connected to and good about their racial or ethnic group membership, it improves their mood, self-concept, pride, behavior, and school connectedness.[17] Schools and other youth settings can nourish or diminish racial and ethnic identity exploration and strengthen feelings of pride and connectedness.

A few years ago, Joanna interviewed middle schoolers to better understand how their racial and ethnic identities were shaped by being in racially diverse or homogeneous schools. One of her survey questions asked middle schoolers what they learned about their race and how they learned it. As she went through the results, Joanna saw that Black youth often mentioned slavery as the only topic connected to their history and culture taught in school. Many other students, especially immigrants and refugees, didn't see themselves represented in what they learned at school at all.

School environments and academic curriculums can leave kids of certain racial and ethnic groups feeling boxed in, misunderstood, underrepresented, and judged. Schools can be places where young people experience racism and ethnocentrism as well as racial bullying or violence. It can help to bring students of the same race or ethnic background together to talk about their experiences and encounters in a safe way with those who may be going through the same thing.[18] This validates and honors the unique challenges these young people face and fulfills their needs to be authentically supported and understood.

We must do our part in offering or asking for a full and fair representation of young people's race, culture, and backgrounds in the books and media they have access to, assignments we give them, and examples we use. For example, if a place or program bans a book that represents a young person's individual or group identity, it sends a clear message that the young person is not welcome and does not belong. Research shows that young people who are a part of marginalized and stereotyped groups will end up experiencing personal marginalization and stereotyping. Help young people find and see themselves in what they are learning, reading, watching, and doing, so they can explore those parts of their identity, and enjoy the gifts that can come from them.[19]

TRY THIS

- Consider your own story of racial and ethnic identity development. Reflect on when you first realized there were different racial and ethnic groups. Discuss or write about how that impacted you.

- Consider your educational experience. Reflect on what you learned about different racial and ethnic groups, especially your own. Discuss or write about how that shaped your attitudes, perceptions, and biases.

Gender and Sexual Identity

Every person has a sexual orientation and gender identity. For young people, affirmation and support around gender and sexuality is as important as every other part of identity and personhood. It can also be uncomfortable to talk about. I am super uncomfortable talking about sexuality with kids, especially my own. I'm working on it, but like many adults, I didn't grow up talking about it, especially with people who were older than me. It felt secret and shameful. Professor Stephen Russell, who studies LGBTQ+ youth health and well-being at the University of Texas at Austin, told me young people are embracing this conversation more openly and these aspects of their identity more flexibly and fluidly than most adults.

Here's a parallel example Stephen used to help me understand this growing openness: years ago, there was incredible rigidity within the Christian faith about which denomination you belonged to. If someone left one denomination for another—let's say Methodist for Lutheran—it was a big deal. Changing denominations could result in discrimination and negative treatment or rejection from friends and family. Over time that changed. Today, there is more openness about which church people go to and which denomination it's a part of—many people choose a church based on individual fit, regardless of denomination.

Stephen shared that a similar thing is happening among young people with gender and sexual identity. There is more openness to explore, change, and try various identities for fit. When young people have space to explore and experiment, they more fully form those aspects of their identity, just like they would with faith and community. This requires us to accept the in-between and hold back from jumping to conclusions—young people might show an attraction to one gender or change their pronouns, and then change their minds, maybe more than once.

A young person who identifies as sexually and gender diverse is the same young person they were before, but now with the risks of homophobia, transphobia, stigma, and prejudice. This increases their need for safe and supportive adults who recognize and accept them for who they are. If they experience rejection or feel the need to suppress or hide these parts of their identity, it changes their physiology. According to Stephen, this rejection can heighten their stress response, change cognitive processing, and damage their sense of self-worth and self-esteem.[20] This is bad for their health, learning, and life outcomes. Young people who are transgender and gender nonconforming face heightened risks during middle and high school when puberty leads to the fear or development of physical characteristics that may not match their gender identity.[21]

Like racial and ethnic identity, young people who are marginalized because of gender and/or sexuality can benefit from coming together with others like them and those who support them. Young people deserve to be with people who listen, believe them, and treat them with respect. LGBTQ+ youth are at higher risk of suicide and poor mental health than their peers. They need adults and peers who strengthen their health and well-being.[22] For example, a Genders and Sexualities Alliance (GSA) group is beneficial for those who are involved in the group—LGBTQ+ students and students who are straight and cisgender[23]—and those who are not in the group. Research shows there's a spillover effect with improvements in how young people feel and are treated even outside of the group experience.

Striving to Be an Identity-Safe Person

As young people explore and experiment with their independent and intersectional identities, they need adults to provide and promote environments that are safe, inclusive, and affirming. It's ideal if those environments are responsive to and representative of the identities young people have and are developing.

I spoke about this with Laura E. Hernández, a senior researcher at Learning Policy Institute and the coauthor of the report, "Creating Identity-Safe Schools and Classrooms." We discussed how identity safety in schools extends beyond integrating diverse materials and resources into instruction in meaningful and authentic ways. Research shows that being an identity-safe person and offering an identity-safe environment also means being relationship centered and empathetic, trusting that young people are who they tell you they are, and giving them agency and voice.

Laura and I discussed the evidence around the competencies adults can embody to cultivate identify safety and support identity development as a normal and healthy part of learning and life. I shared our list with Professor Katie Johnston-Goodstar, a scholar of indigenous youth work at the University of Minnesota, who added to it. The result is a set of characteristics all adults should aspire to. When we demonstrate the attributes described in Table 19, we protect and respect young people's cultures and identities, which means we protect and respect young people themselves.

Table 19   Characteristics of Identity-Safe Adults
Deep listener
Empathetic
Self-aware and self-appraising
Socially and contextually aware
Accepts identity development as a process
Looks to children and community for answers
Authentic
Open-minded
Willing to learn and change
Humble
Trustworthy
Honest
Considerate
Curious

In recent years, identity politics and policies have had a chilling effect on adults who work in schools and other youth-serving systems and settings. This has kept them from being able to freely and fully support, advocate for, and protect all young people they serve.[24] These politics and policies jeopardize young people's well-being and threaten their lives. Identity development and exploration is a big part of growing up. It happens at home, in school, in community, and wherever else young people spend time—it can't be stopped or slowed down. We must support young people while they experience it—even when we don't totally agree or understand. We do this because it supports kids' healthy growth and development. If we cannot or will not, then we should not work with kids.

TRY THIS
- How identity safe are you? Go online and read the Learning Policy Institute's report, *Creating Identity-Safe Schools and Classrooms.* Assess yourself and the environments where you spend time with children. Talk about your reflections with someone you trust or explore your reflections privately through writing.

WHOLE LIFE PRACTICE

Embrace Cultures and Identities

Learn

- Cultural connections combine being with belonging and bring young people together around the people, places, and values they share.

- Reading can offer young people "windows and mirrors" into cultures. Windows introduce children to characters from different places and cultures, while mirrors introduce children to characters like them.

- Five stages of cultural connection are (1) coming together, (2) connection to self, (3) connection to each other, (4) connection to community, and (5) connection to the world.

- Identity development is a core task of adolescence and a vital part of youth development. Young people form group and individual identities, some of which are intersectional. Identity development includes but is not limited to culture, race, ethnicity, gender, sexuality, faith, and community.

Reflect

Think about your own culture and identity development.

- What are your cultural connections, group identities, and individual identities and how and when did they form?

- How have your individual and group identities impacted how you are treated and accepted by others? In what ways were they represented and reflected in school and other programs you participated in?

- To what extent do you prioritize culture and identity development with kids? Are there opportunities to elevate and honor young people's heritage and native languages through your work?

After reflecting, find someone to process this chapter with. If what emerged feels private, write about what you are thinking and feeling.

(Continued)

(Continued)

Act

As you absorb what you read and reflected on, consider how you can put insights into action. Take time to set a few commitments and intentions on how to *Embrace Identities and Cultures.*

- What is one small action you can take *today* to put this practice into action?

- What is one larger action you can take *this month* to put this practice into action?

- What is one big action you can work toward *this year* to put this practice into action?

NOTES

MY FAMiLY 2022

Me at church 2017

baby Marcos 2014

Momma 1998

Abuelo + Abuela Mexico

Attend to the Past and Present 12

"The great teachers understand that where we come from affects where we go, and that what sits unresolved in our past influences our present."

—Mark Wolynn

Jessica Pittman is a respected pediatric pulmonologist at St. Louis Children's Hospital and an associate professor of pediatrics at Washington University School of Medicine in St. Louis. She is also my son's doctor. The first time we took him to see "Dr. Jess," as we affectionately call her, we spent nearly an hour together.

During that initial visit, Jessica asked questions, listened intently, and typed notes while we talked about my son's years-long struggle with asthma. Whenever I mentioned a medical event, she pulled it up in his chart to review the details. She went beyond his experience with asthma to ask how he was doing in school, sports, at home, and with friends. After we talked, she examined him, and asked additional questions before making recommendations for asthma management and medications.

In less than an hour, Jessica weaved together my child's life story with his health history and determined which environmental, social, and family factors might contribute to his respiratory and overall health. She knew how he was doing in real time and what had happened since his last exam—she had reviewed his major medical moments starting with the time he got respiratory syncytial virus (RSV) and was hospitalized as a baby.

Today, Jessica knows my son's history and personality well enough to make visits a positive experience. She goes above and beyond, like the time she visited him in the hospital after he got his tonsils out or called me in the spring of 2020 when we didn't know how COVID-19 would impact children, especially those with asthma.

Jessica has mastered the art of addressing whatever is happening now and considering the role the past might have on the present. This is something medical and mental health professionals are trained in and expected to do, but surprisingly it's less commonly taught to education and youth development professionals, and not taught to parents or volunteers.

This training gap means many of us are more prone to reacting to what we see a child do without asking why they are doing it. Knowing the "why" can explain so much. An exploration of root causes and context activates empathy and points us toward effective solutions and supports. For example, imagine a child who can't focus at school and struggles to finish assignments. She is easily distracted, constantly fidgeting, and quick to anger. Her teacher has been conditioned to treat these behaviors as problematic, even disrespectful. When the student misbehaves, she is redirected, and eventually receives correction and consequences. Without investigating the root causes of the behavior, the child might continue to be disciplined for something out of her control. This combination of behaviors might be the result of trauma,[1] untreated attention deficit disorder, a learning disability, vitamin deficiencies, or problems sleeping—none of which are deliberate disobedience.[2]

Kid Specialists

I reached out to Jessica to better understand her process for getting to know patients, identifying root causes of health problems, and providing ongoing care. I suspected that some of it was her signature approach, but I hoped plenty was what she learned in school and on the job.

Besides being a respected pediatric pulmonologist and professor, Jessica is a mom to two school-aged children. That made our conversation personal. Like me, she wants her boys to be surrounded by adults who get to know them by considering their lived experience, family history, and other factors that could impact learning and development.

Jessica walked me through her approach to initial intake, making rounds at the hospital, and how she partners with children and families in ongoing care and treatment decisions. As we talked, we were both struck by the powerful lessons this pediatric approach has for anyone who works with kids.

All of us can seek information and insights to better understand what is helping or hurting a child's ability to thrive. We are kid specialists and, as much as possible, our prevention and intervention strategies should remedy or respond to the root causes of whatever challenges kids face.

Intake

When Jessica first gets to know a child, she plans for a detailed encounter with lots of questions and listening. This establishes her relationship with the child and family and informs her initial diagnoses and treatment recommendations. As she shared, she brings some expertise in medicine but no expertise in that child. Her highest priority is learning from the child and their family and matching that with what she knows from medicine and experience. From there, she builds a plan and offers possible solutions.

This intake process should take place in all youth settings. When we take time to get to know kids, including who and what they care about, we are in a stronger position to contextualize and customize environments and experiences to meet needs and address concerns. Early conversations and interactions are a chance to build trust and talk about problems that might require specialized care, like special education or therapeutic interventions.

Intake can occur naturally or be deliberately designed. In the Maplewood Richmond Heights School District (MRH), a suburban district in St. Louis, educators are trained and paid to meet with students during the summer at their homes or in a preferred community setting (e.g., playground, park). This is a way to establish relationships, to meet students and families where they are, and for school staff to see where and how students live.

In a 2019 program evaluation of the MRH home visit program, almost every educator reported being comfortable or very comfortable conducting visits.[3] Visits were viewed as an opportunity to learn about students' interests and hobbies, discuss strengths and struggles, and get background information that might help make the student's school experience a success. Educators reported leaving visits with a better understanding of students and their families. Families valued home visits, and since the program started, the district has seen increased family engagement and decreased discipline issues and dropout rates.[4]

Meeting in a student's living room or favorite park is an intimate experience that lends itself to deeper conversations, active participation, and building relationships on equal footing. It shifts power, with families and kids as experts and teachers as learners. This is healing for caregivers who have bad memories of and experiences with school. For them, going to school for student conferences can be triggering or retraumatizing. By having intake conversations at home and in the community, students and families can engage with school staff safely and comfortably.[5]

If you work with children and home visits are not an option, create intake opportunities through family questionnaires, phone calls, or conferences. Meet one-on-one with kids and attend community events where they'll be (e.g., soccer games, neighborhood celebrations). With my children, we have had summer camp counselors meet with us before camp started, sports coaches chat on the sidelines, and teachers hold conferences with in-person and virtual options. If you are a caregiver and think this would be beneficial for your child, extend the invitation yourself.

Funneling Questions

For Jessica, intake conversations are youth- and family-centered and organized around questions that start big and get increasingly narrow and specific. She usually begins with something like "What brings you in today?" followed by a request for more details: "When did this problem start?" or "Tell me more about the cough."

For those of us who aren't doctors, parallel questions might be "How are you feeling about this upcoming school year/summer camp/sports season?" This can be followed by requesting more details: "Why do you think you're anxious about sixth grade?" or "How long have you been thinking about quitting soccer?"

Jessica lets kids and families decide where to start and how much to share. She prompts them for more details while giving them space to tell their own stories. Jessica's job is to listen for important details and concerns. For example, does the cough keep the child from playing a sport they love? Are they missing too much school? Is a parent missing too much work? Context clues fill in the bigger picture and help Jessica make informed recommendations and decisions.

Intake is how we start building the whole child portrait explored in Part 1. We ask questions and learn about what's going on in every area of a child's life, including their hopes and fears. As Jessica shared, the impact of certain behaviors can be more serious or as important as the behaviors themselves. Think back to the fidgety child who can't focus at school. Those behaviors might make it hard for the child to form friendships or see school as a place where they belong.

- The next time you have a serious relationship with a child, start with intake. Plan it out: Where will you do it? When? How will you create a level playing field? What types of questions will you ask?

- Consider a child who is presenting a concerning behavior. Identify strategies from this section that can help you move from reacting to the behavior to responding to the root cause.

TRY NOW

Making Rounds

In addition to seeing kids in her clinic, Jessica spends time making rounds—what hospital staff call "rounding"—at the hospital. In this setting, she may take care of an existing patient or work with someone she has never met before. Rounding is a way teams of professionals (e.g., nurses, physicians, social workers) connect with the patient and family and work together to address a pressing problem or concern.

In the hospital, Jessica relies on the rhythm and routine of rounds to get to know patients and their families. She is working against the clock to address urgent issues while trying to rapidly develop an understanding of history and context. To be safe and successful, Jessica needs reliable information from the child, family, and other adults responsible for the child's care.

To do this, she and the medical team follow the same steps of rounding each time:

- Meet with the child and family to talk about the primary concern (e.g., asthma attack)
- Review the history of the presenting problem (e.g., symptoms of the asthma attack)
  - When did it start?
  - How frequent/severe is it?
  - Description of situation/symptoms
- Consider context: Anything else that might be contributing to or causing the problem (e.g., allergies, recent construction, smoke, virus)

- Review of other systems (e.g., cardiovascular, nervous)
    - High-level screenings to see if it's more than the presenting problem and chief complaint (e.g., could this look and sound like asthma but be something else?)
- Learn the broader history
    - Personal history
    - Family history
    - Environmental history
    - Social history
- Physical examination (e.g., check vitals, evaluate present situation)
- Make an initial assessment and plan
- Chart everything (often digitally or through dictation), including thoughts, reasoning, and a possible plan of action
- Be ready to review and revise as more is learned or changes

Rounding is a practice any "kid specialist" can use when a child is struggling. Some aspects of rounds that are particularly useful include (1) starting with and centering the young person and their family, (2) coordinating and sharing care with other people, (3) considering history and context, and (4) creating a plan that can be reviewed and revised.

Start With and Center the Young Person and Their Family

Science backs up what Jessica learned in her clinic and on the hospital floor: you cannot be an expert on every child you meet, because no two are the same. Developmental scientists and professors Richard M. and Jacqueline V. Lerner demonstrated those differences when they studied more than 7,000 young people who participated in the 4-H Study of Positive Youth Development (PYD). This project followed youth (about 2,500 of whom participated in 4-H programs) across eight waves of testing, from fifth grade to senior year of high school. The average scores for the group as a whole (all 7,000 young people) did not vary much across grades. However, when they looked at the specific pathways of development followed by these youth, as well as subsamples, they were able to see impressive variations in each child's specific developmental journey.

As Richard told me, "Development and human life fluctuate every day for everything. Young people live according to the daily rhythms of their life circumstances, health, development, learning, and well-being. Change can happen at any point and for many reasons. By starting with and centering a young person and their family as individuals, you open the possibility of being able to meet and support the whole child."[6]

Coordinate and Share Care With Other People

Too often, adults are put in charge of children without sufficient background information on who they are, what they need, or what they're going through. Past and current teachers or counselors don't have an opportunity to meet and compare notes. Caregivers don't talk to a new coach. Coaches meet families briefly, but conversations are limited to pleasantries.

During rounds, Jessica knows that the survival and health of her patients depend on strong communication and working with her colleagues. During shift changes, there are lots of sign-offs and hand-offs, where the medical team connects to update each other on patients' progress and status. This is an opportunity to check in on immediate concerns and important context. Unfortunately, these conversations can be breeding grounds for bias, so the medical team must hold each other accountable, being alert to any judgments, prejudices, or false assumptions made about children, their families, or their care.

Every day, sign-offs and hand-offs are facilitated by parents and caregivers. A child wakes up feeling sick and Mom emails the teacher to give them a heads-up. A teen had a rough day at school and Dad tells the coach before practice starts. Equally important but less frequent is when professionals connect with each other about a child and situation. For example, this could be fourth grade teachers meeting with fifth grade teachers to talk about a group of students, or a pediatrician meeting with a teacher and therapist to talk about a patient.

For Jessica, sign-offs and hand-offs always include the child and family because information can get lost or misconstrued in translation and transition. She has made it a practice to go over what she learned about a child with the child and family and ask them three questions: Does this sound right? Did I miss anything? Is there anything else I need to know?

Consider Broader History and Context

The past lives on in the present. It shows up in our reactions, behaviors, and even our cells.[7] Just as we should map the "people and places" in children's lives, we should plot their timelines with historical events and contextual details.

Lived Experience

When I discussed the 4-H study with Professor Richard Lerner, I asked him what role the past has on young people's present developmental state. He told me that no kid is ahistorical. From his perspective, you can't know a child without understanding them in the wholeness of their individuality. Richard suggests getting to know young people by seeking out the answers to these questions: "Where are you now? Where have you been? Where do you want to go?" This helps to understand what's happening for kids *right now*, in *recent history*, and in their *life experience*.[8]

Richard Lerner's colleague Dr. Pamela Cantor put it this way: "We are our histories. Every cell in the body carries the history of what it has experienced in its lifetime and the history of what has happened to us."[9] Young people's lived histories manifest in their bodies and behaviors. When challenging life events and stress build up and exceed a young person's ability to cope, they experience **allostatic load**. However, adversity is not destiny, as Dr. Cantor emphasizes. Positive relationships, experiences, and opportunities also become embodied; they nourish and can even heal young people from the impacts of trauma.

By taking trauma-informed and healing-centered approaches to our work with children, we can repair or reverse the negative impacts of adversity and reduce allostatic load. Young people's embodied selves will carry the cumulative benefits of nourishing and healthful relationships, experiences, and opportunities.[10] The more healing is centered and children are nurtured, the better off they'll be.

TRAUMA-INFORMED CARE

Trauma-informed care is a way of engaging children that recognizes the pervasiveness and presence of trauma and promotes interactions, experiences, and environments that are healthy, healing, and safe.

According to the National Child Traumatic Stress Network (NCTSN), trauma negatively impacts school performance, learning, development, and physical and emotional health.[11] Young people often respond to trauma behaviorally. Here are some signs children may have experienced or may be experiencing trauma:

- **Preschool:** separation anxiety, regression, slow or stalled development, difficulty sleeping, unexplained outbursts, signs or complaints of illness or injury, over- or underreacting to touch, whiny, irritable, worried, fearful, frequent talk of death and dying.

- **Elementary School:** preoccupation with safety, worries about violence, irritable, moody, major behavioral changes, distrust, difficulties responding appropriately to social cues, signs or complaints of illness or injury, changes in school performance, hyperarousal, avoidance, difficulties with authority.

- **Middle and High School:** preoccupation with safety, anxiety, worries about violence, major behavioral changes, discomfort with feelings, increased risk of substance abuse, difficulty trusting others, over- or underreacting to loud noises and lights, thoughts and comments about death and dying, hyperarousal, avoidance, emotional numbness.

As with warning signs of mental illness, these behaviors are not always related to trauma, and some kids experience trauma with no external signs of distress. Even so, these are behaviors that interfere with kids' abilities to live, learn, and thrive, and they can be helped by trauma-informed practices. In NCTSN's Child Trauma Toolkit for Educators, the following strategies are recommended to support children who have experienced trauma:

- Maintain routines and consistency. These communicate safety and normalcy.

- Give choices. Trauma often robs children of choice and control. Try to restore both.

- Increase verbal support and encouragement.

- Before reacting to problematic behaviors, consider whether they could be a trauma response.

- Set and communicate clear limits for inappropriate behavior with logical and related consequences.

- Be sensitive to possible trauma triggers like loud noises, bright lights, or stormy weather.

- Understand that children may cope by reenacting trauma (e.g., hitting someone if they were hit).

- Anticipate difficult times and bring in additional resources and supports.

- Warn children before doing something unusual, like turning off the lights or making a loud noise.

This information is adapted from the National Child Traumatic Stress Network Schools Committee. (October 2008). Child trauma toolkit for educators. Los Angeles, CA & Durham, NC: National Center for Child Traumatic Stress.

online resources Available for download at **www.wholechildwholelife.com**

Family History

Before our appointment with Jessica, we got a lengthy questionnaire in the mail about family health history. There were questions about various disorders and diagnoses throughout our family tree, with a specific focus on respiratory ailments, like asthma and pneumonia. According to Jessica, this family history is one part of a multidimensional look at a child. With asthma, this is helpful because children whose parents have asthma are more likely to develop it themselves.

Children inherit more than predispositions to physical illness from parents and previous generations. Studies show that children of trauma survivors carry the physical and emotional symptoms of survival even though they did not experience trauma themselves.[12] In the book *It Didn't Start With You: How Inherited Trauma Shapes Who We Are and How to End the Cycle*, Mark Wolynn writes that we share the same biological environment as our parents and grandparents, meaning we inherit genetic rules and directions about how to act and respond to life. Intense and repeated emotions that parents and grandparents experience imprint on their cells and get passed down to their children, leading to a preprogramming in subsequent generations for how to cope and respond to stress.[13] We can be reprogrammed, but it takes strong prevention and intervention strategies. In his book, Mark gives an example of a child born to a parent who survived a violent war; the child was born preprogrammed with a heightened sensitivity to loud noises. Stressful and traumatizing life events before and during pregnancy and through infancy can also alter a child's stress response.

Family history also includes past experiences with systems and settings. For example, a child's parents may have negative associations with schools or hospitals because of historic and persistent racism, prejudice, or some other traumatizing event. This can lead to avoidance of or anxious behavior in that system or setting.

Unless we are genealogists or geneticists, we don't have training on how to document the complete family histories of every child. It's also not always appropriate, and some families don't want to talk about it. Even so, we can approach a child's problem or predicament by understanding that family history might be at play. As you learn more about what children are going through, ask these questions: Do I know what the family's experience is with this situation or setting? Is it possible this has been passed down from parents or grandparents? Is there anything

I need to know about the child's family to support this child and solve this problem?

Social and Environment History and Context

Young people grow up in place and time. The environments they live in and events they live through impact everything about them. When Jessica got to know my son, it mattered that he lived in St. Louis, a city which—according to the Missouri Department of Health and Senior Services—has disproportionately high rates of childhood asthma. It mattered that his asthma was virally induced, and he attended school, which increased his exposure to colds and viruses. It mattered that we were managing his asthma at home. Later, it mattered that COVID-19 was spreading as a deadly respiratory virus.

The conglomeration of past and present social and environmental factors influences how Jessica treats my child and every other patient. Similarly, our knowledge of young people's demographics and determinants and their current circumstances should influence and adjust the supports we put in place, the services we seek, and the personalized plans of action we come up with.

Create a Plan That Can Be Reviewed and Revised

The information gathered from rounding helps us develop a plan for prevention and intervention. Personal information plus context and history should illuminate root causes that may be responsible for seemingly disconnected behaviors and difficulties. The plans we create should name root causes and current circumstances and include the input, involvement, and buy-in from the child and other important people in their life.

Jessica's plans include the diagnosis of the problem, a rationale, an assessment of what has been learned, and next steps. Our plans can follow a similar breakdown: problem, rationale, assessment, strategies, and solutions. Strategies and solutions should address what needs to happen right away, and recommendations and options should address what to pursue down the road.

As the Lerners discovered in their 4-H study, plans become outdated in an instant because development can be diverted by anything new to a child's lifescape. We must view plans as evolving, always up for reevaluation, adjustments, and additions. If something happens to a child and a plan no longer works, we shouldn't wait to meet and talk about it.

Young People Should Hold
Their Own Histories

Something I admire about pediatricians is their thoughtful planning for a young person's transition from pediatric to adult care. Starting around middle school, doctors start to incrementally give young patients more privacy and autonomy in their medical care and treatment decisions. They might ask family members to step outside during a visit so patients can talk about issues they're uncomfortable discussing with family members present. Young people might be encouraged to take on more responsibility for medications and overall management. This helps them get ready for a time when their families aren't there to monitor, advocate, and manage.

Something similar happens in well-run personalized and competency-based learning environments. For example, in the Kettle Moraine School District in Wisconsin, students are the primary communicators to parents about what they are learning and where they are struggling academically. Younger children send daily or weekly update videos and photos on digital platforms like Seesaw and Classroom Dojo. Older children send emails. By graduation, Kettle Moraine students know how to talk about their learning and show what they know and can do.

Over time, young people must learn and own their histories and be able to talk about them when it's important. As a mom, I want my kids to own their past experiences and understand our family history and the gifts and risks those histories bring. Personal histories are the foundational architecture of life stories and bright futures.

WHOLE LIFE PRACTICE

Attend to the Past and Present

Learn

- Intake should be a priority practice in any youth setting. When we take time to get to know kids and their families, we are better able to contextualize and customize environments and experiences to meet needs and address concerns.

- When talking to children about an issue they are having, funnel your questions: Start with questions that are big and broad and move to ones that are narrow and specific.

- "Rounding" is a practice done by medical teams in hospital settings that can be adapted and used with children in any setting. To do this you (1) start with and center the child and their family, (2) coordinate and share care with others, (3) consider history and context, and (4) create a plan that can be regularly reviewed and revised.

- Trauma-informed care is a way of engaging with kids that recognizes the pervasiveness and presence of trauma and promotes interactions, experiences, and environments that are healthy, healing, and safe.

Reflect

Reflect on how you react when children misbehave.

- What personal scripts do you have about what it means when a child misbehaves?

- What is the model behavior associated with being "good" in your setting(s)?

- What biases and false assumptions have you made about children who misbehave?

After reflecting, find someone to process this chapter with. If what emerged feels private, take time to write about what you are thinking and feeling.

Act

As you absorb what you read and reflected on, consider how you can put insights into action. Take time to set a few commitments and intentions on how to *Attend to the Past and Present*.

- What is one small action you can take *today* to put this practice into action?

- What is one larger action you can take *this month* to put this practice into action?

- What is one big action you can work toward *this year* to put this practice into action?

Act With a 100-Year Mindset 13

Shortly after I started writing this book, our family celebrated the life of Mary Bruemmer, one of my husband's mentors, who lived to be 101 years old. At her funeral, the priest described the major milestones of Mary's life. I held my boys tight and reflected on how much can happen in the span of 100 years.

Mary was born in 1920, when few women were able to pursue higher education. In 1938, she graduated high school and enrolled at Saint Louis University (SLU), where the student body was 100 percent white and more than 95 percent male. Mary dedicated most of her working life to SLU, returning to the university in 1956 to direct the first residence hall for women, then serving as the first-ever dean of women, and taking on various leadership roles before retiring in 1990 to become a full-time volunteer. During our visits with Mary, she would share stories that showed how much society, St. Louis, and SLU had changed throughout her decades on campus.

Mary arrived at SLU at the start of World War II. She was in leadership during the civil rights movement in the center of a severely segregated city. Her student affairs career began long before the internet and smart technologies and ended with students who got in touch with her by email and Zoom.

The SLU that Mary retired from was much different from the one she started at years ago. My husband met her in the early 2000s when he was the undergraduate president of the student government. By then the university had multiple residence halls for women and increasing racial diversity. In student government, there was the Black Student Alliance, International Student Federation, Hispanic American Leadership Organization, Filipino Student Association, and more. During my husband's time as SGA president, students were fundraising for recovery efforts after Hurricane Katrina and saying goodbye to loved ones in the military who were deploying to Afghanistan and Iraq. Today, SLU continues to diversify its staff and student body, and students are focused on recovering from and responding to a global pandemic and high-profile acts of racial and political violence.

Living Longer Than Ever

Mary is the only centenarian I've known. Until now, living a 100-year life was considered the exception, but many scientists believe that living to 100 will become the expectation. It's possible there are millions of Marys among today's children, and many will live to be older than she did.

In May 2021, Emily Willingham published an article in *Scientific American* called "Humans Could Live up to 150 Years, New Research Suggests." In the piece, Emily describes a group of "longevity" scientists who research how long humans can live—absent accidents, hazards, chronic illnesses, or the end of the world. According to Emily, these researchers agree that humans have the potential to live between 120 and 150 years.[1]

With constant medical and technological advances, people are living longer than ever mostly because childhood mortality rates are down, and more illnesses can be treated and cured. While we have tools and tech to extend life, those same advances don't always improve the quality of life. There are crushing disparities in life expectancy and who is most likely to live to old age. For kids who grow up in poverty and are exposed to violence, a 100-year life may seem impossible; many have seen loved ones killed or pass away before making it past the first quarter. For those who make it to old age and remain poor, they predictably die 10 to 15 years earlier than someone the same age who is wealthy.[2] Inequality, demographics, determinants, relationships, and genetics determine a lot about whether someone will have a long life, and if that long life will be a good one.[3]

Since learning that science may give our kids longer lives but not better ones, I have been looking for what will. This has taken me into research on aging and longevity, as well as the work of future forecasters. It has caused me to confront my own fears about the future and learn about the forces shaping it, including climate change and technology. Over time, I have reoriented and started acting with a 100-year mindset, always asking what (my) children need now and might need throughout their prospectively very long lives.

I think of Mary, living from 1920 to 2021. I imagine my boys, born in 2010 and 2013, and the possibility of them living to see 2110, even 2150. I remember when my boys were born—during the Great Recession and the emergence of smart technologies—and what has defined their childhoods so far—a love of baseball, LEGO, the COVID-19 pandemic, the Marvel universe, mass shootings, family and friends, economic crises, racial reckonings, technology advances, and "tech time." I worry about what it means for them to inherit a world with a changing climate, radicalized politics, scarcity, shortages, and divided communities. I wonder what life will be like in a hundred years and how we can prepare them for the possibilities of it. We may discuss "21st-century skills" like they are still new and debatable, but by this calculation it's time to decide on 21st-century skills and start determining 22nd-century ones.

Raising Future Centenarians

It's daunting to think about preparing kids for a 100-year life because it's hard enough to meet their needs now, let alone for a future so far away. Many of us are focused on getting young people through the program they're in, into the next grade, or—if we're especially ambitious— successfully launched into adulthood. Setting a time horizon and success metrics for 100 years may seem like too much, and yet we are the ones who can help kids acquire skills and supports in childhood that will last them a long lifetime.

As I learned about aging and longevity, I was struck by how many successful aging skills and supports emerge in the early years. For young people to be ready and well across their whole lives, we must attend to their future selves. The same *whole life practices* that enable young people to thrive in childhood will enable them to thrive in adulthood and elderhood. In Marta Zaraska's book *Growing Young: How Friendship, Optimism, and Kindness Can Help You Live to 100*, she says it this way: "[T]he very same efforts that rejuvenate our bodies and help us live long also help us grow as people."

Longevity Skills and Supports

The prospect of a 100-year life means young people will not only live longer but work longer. Today's kids could have a 60- to 70-year career—a seeming lifetime of work. Across those years they will experience multiple jobs and job changes. Many will be parents and grandparents—even great-grandparents—while working. They will work while sick or taking care of someone who is. They will work while in relationships and enduring loss. They will work through disasters and disruptions, and work with ever-changing technologies. Almost all will have times where they don't work, work too much, or work multiple jobs at once. Many will go back to school, perhaps multiple times, to update and upgrade their knowledge, skills, and credentials.[5]

Knowing this, let's not pressure kids when they're young to choose a single career path or passion to pursue. Instead, let them discover the causes, questions, and careers they want to explore. In a long life, the first credential will probably not be the last, and we should adjust our expectations accordingly. With time the technical skills kids learn in school and on the job will become outdated, making it important for them to be able and open to learning skills that endure with time and transitions.[6] Kids also need to learn how to pause and pace themselves because their journeys will take time. They will need skills to navigate transition and pursue personal transformation because longer lives means more life stages and changes.[7]

Among those who have lived a long life, there are commonalities to consider. These individuals tend to be physically active and healthy eaters. They engage in activities they find meaningful and have purpose in their lives. These are people with lower levels of stress and strong support among friends, family, and community.[8] Research shows they have longer telomeres than others—the caps on DNA that help determine how fast cells age and die. Telomeres can be shortened and lengthened according to lifestyle, making longevity and livability dynamic, and something young people (and adults) can change if they know how.[9] The long-lived also tend to be kinder and more empathetic, valuing and prioritizing relationships and the people around them. Longevity is strengthened even more when social connections have been present across a lifetime.[10]

Aging well also means staying cognitively fit and mentally sharp, attributes increasingly important for young people in a world constantly demanding their attention and full of distractions.[11] The novelty, creativity, and curiosity we want kids to have remains important into their later years.[12]

I spoke with Warren Wong, a geriatric doctor in Hawai'i, about the stages of early and later life and how similar the skill and support needs are. Here are strategies from the research and that conversation that can help us act with a 100-year mindset with young people and ourselves:

- Practice pausing and pacing

- Learn to weather transition and change

- Stay cognitively fit and focused

- Always learn something new

- Extend empathy and kindness

- Keep moving and eat healthy

- Prioritize relationships and social connectedness

- Reduce and manage stress

To set young people on a path for long and lovable lives we must prioritize their social, emotional, and cognitive health. We must encourage and equip them to imagine many possible futures, helping them acquire the skills and supports to succeed in each one.

- Think about what it would mean if the children you care about grow up to be centenarians. What could you do today to support their longevity? Read back through this section and think about skills and supports you want to prioritize.

- Choose one longevity skill or support to focus on this month. Take a few minutes to jot down strategies and activities you can implement to engage that longevity builder for kids and yourself.

TRY NOW

Forecasting Possible Futures

In addition to helping young people build skills and supports that will last a lifetime, we can aid them to envision and embrace their possible futures. This is especially important given the amount of change and challenge with which they are growing up. It's easy for kids to get overwhelmed by it all and, as one young person told me, "How do you expect young people to look into a future they can't see and that adults have no answer for?"[13]

That's a question I asked Katherine Prince and Peter Bishop, two professional future forecasters. I wanted to understand whether **forecasting**—the practice of identifying multiple possible futures—could help young people cope with their fears of the future and face whatever is to come. Specifically, could forecasting build the resiliency and adaptability young people need to navigate the challenges they know (e.g., changing weather) and the ones that are harder to anticipate (e.g., impacts from extreme weather)?

Peter described this as teaching kids to be "future historians." It's the opportunity for young people to imagine a range of possible futures and decide why they care and what they can do to make the world better today and tomorrow. It also provides young people with a way to examine looming threats and break them into smaller parts where they have more control and ability to act. Future forecasting is a form of organizing and healing: young people envision their ideal future, engage with related problems, and take actions that move toward a better world than the one we're in.

For Peter, this is storytelling work. Young people are living in a story with three chapters: past, present, and future. They are the main characters, and to do well, they have to study for their role. Like a play, the story changes depending on their performance. In Peter's experience, this mindset shift offers young people agency over their lives and leads to a belief they can influence the world rather than becoming victims of their circumstances. With time, young people learn that the world changes them, and they change the world— an interactive relationship that comes with lessons and requires sensemaking and imagination.

Future Forces and Forecasting

When my kids were very young, we experienced a tornado at a T-ball game. The weather changed quickly, and even though we were ok, it left them with a fear of storms. Afterwards, my older son wanted to spend every storm in the basement. We would hunker down and wait for the thunder and wind to stop while he would come up with different doomsday scenarios. One day, I showed him how to read the radar and encouraged him to use it plus whatever he saw outside to make his own weather predictions.

Teaching my son to read a radar didn't remove his fear, but it helped him rightsize it and respond in ways that were healthier and more helpful. Future forecasting can do the same thing. When I talked to Katherine, she walked me through six practices she uses to develop a professional future forecast. These are practices we can teach and encourage kids to try themselves:

SIX STAGES OF FUTURE FORECASTING

1. **Expect change:** This is about situating ourselves in change. While it's easy to think things will stay as they are today, they won't. The present, however you define it, is always a temporary condition.[14] This practice asks us to think about inbound changes—what's happening to us—and outbound changes—what we are doing to change things. We can teach kids to *signal scan*, which is the practice of looking around for signals of change—early indicators that things are shifting, including new patterns and trends. Over time, this practice helps kids embrace uncertainty and become more aware and open-minded.

2. **Question assumptions:** This is thinking through changes that are happening and which ones might persist and increase. It's shifting language from "this can't happen" to "what if this were possible?" or "What if there could be a different way?" We can work with kids on their "what if" thinking based on the signals of change they uncovered in the first stage. Questioning assumptions builds an imaginative space where young people can safely explore and consider how to shape the future, building their self-efficacy and sense of power over it. During this stage, young people explore the space between now and the future, which helps them discover ways to act and respond.

3. **Play with alternative futures:** This is examining what the future might look like, by studying and contemplating the impacts of different assumptions. It's understanding our baseline assumptions and working through possible alternatives if things change. With children, we can think through scenarios about one aspect of the future (e.g., education, environment, health) if the current state continues or if one or more things change. They can act out these scenarios creatively, through a play, song, in writing, or art.

4. **Create multiple scenarios:** In this stage, we step back and wonder what all the possible futures could be, because it is unlikely the future we imagine will be the one we get. The purpose of this stage is to explore and examine a range of possibilities. Ask kids to answer these questions for each possible future: How would I succeed in this one? What skills and supports would I need? This stage builds young people's belief that they can live in uncertainty and that there are strengths and strategies they have that will work across them all.

(Continued)

(Continued)

5. **Envision how to endure and thrive:** This is naming personal strengths and strategies that will last. This helps kids understand and give language to their timeless needs and the things about their lives that will be true no matter what happens, and it provides an emotional anchor for them to tap into when they feel frightened by a change or challenge. Once those timeless values and needs are identified, you can help young people work to strengthen them and know how to access them when they're needed.

6. **Make sense of what these futures mean for today:** This final stage is about empowering young people as storytellers and creators. This is where we make sense of the world and find ways to monitor, manage, and act in the present. You can have kids try the "three horizons method," which is when a forecaster answers these three questions: What are we doing now (near-term future)? What is our ideal future (long-term future)? How do we get there (mid-term future)? This is an exploration of the similarities and differences between the present and future, and what transitionary steps are needed to get from the near term to long term. Think of this as a forecasting GPS, showing various routes you can take and how much time you might spend on various parts of the journey.

 This list is available for download at **www.wholechildwholelife.com**

As Katherine walked me through these six practices, I kept thinking about the game Disruptus, one of our family favorites. In this game, players learn to use **disruptive thinking**—ways of thinking differently to challenge the status quo and come up with novel ideas and inventions. A player might pull a card with a picture of a refrigerator. Depending on the roll of the dice, players must *add on* to the refrigerator, *combine it* with some other appliance, *improve it*, or *disrupt* the way we keep food cold and fresh. At first, our family struggled with the *disrupt* rounds. It was hard to imagine something other than a fridge keeping food cold and fresh. The game got easier with time and practice.

Where disruptive thinking has been an important 21st-century skill, I believe forecasting will be an imperative 22nd-century one. The future is barreling down on us, and young people feel the pressure and unpredictability of it. By giving them forecasting tools, we can equip them with a lifelong strategy of operating in and making sense of an uncertain future so they can be the authors and actors of their own stories.

In the next few weeks, try future forecasting with kids.

TRY NOW

- Choose a domain (e.g., education, pop culture, technology, healthcare)

- Decide on a forecasting question (e.g., what might school be like in the year 2050?)

- Have kids use the six stages of forecasting as guidelines for coming up with a range of possible futures

- At the end, have kids present their ideal futures and what they might do to get there

WHOLE LIFE PRACTICE

Act With a 100-Year Mindset

Learn

- Medical and technological advances mean that people are living longer than ever. Many of today's kids may live to be 100 or older.

- Living a 100-year life means the possibility of a 60- or 70-year career. In this "lifetime" of work, young people will likely experience multiple careers, as well as experience working through a range of life stages and events. We must prepare young people for their working journeys, not just specific jobs.

- Future forecasting can be a way to help young people deal with their uncertainty and fears of the future, in addition to identifying ways they can act and contribute positively to the world around them.

Reflect

Reflect on your own life and feelings about the future:

- How and where did you see yourself in this chapter? Are there longevity skills and supports you want to build into your personal or professional life?

- How do you hear young people talk about the future? How do they feel about it? Do they express a sense of being able to change what will happen?

(Continued)

(Continued)

- Consider the six stages of forecasting. How might these help you and the children in your life deal with the present and prepare for the future?

After reflecting, find someone to process this chapter with. If what emerged feels private, take time to journal or record what you are thinking and feeling.

Act

As you absorb what you read and reflected on, consider how you can put insights into action. Take time to set a few commitments and intentions on how to *Act With a 100-Year Mindset*.

- What is one small action you can take *today* to put this practice into action?

- What is one larger action you can take *this month* to put this practice into action?

- What is one big action you can work toward *this year* to put this practice into action?

NOTES

Be a Force for Good 14

"Change in ourselves and in the world in which we live may not take place in a hurry; it will take time. . . . [P]lease keep in mind that as human beings, equipped with marvelous intelligence and the potential for developing a warm heart, each and every one of us can become a force for good."

—Dalai Lama

On Valentine's Day in 2018, a 19-year-old boy entered Marjorie Stoneman Douglas High School in Parkland, Florida, with an automatic weapon and brutally killed 17 students and staff. A group of students who survived the shooting directed their terror and trauma toward action in the aftermath. Within a month, these young people had organized March For Our Lives, a global movement of demonstrations calling for an end to school shootings and laws to protect against gun violence. Our family, incensed by recurrent school shootings in the United States, donated, marched, and talked about this student-led movement. My dad sent the kids a blue March For Our Lives T-shirt, which became a favorite of my godson's.

Nearly 4 years later, a different 19-year-old boy entered Central Visual and Performing Arts High School in St. Louis. He also had an automatic weapon, and he used it to brutally kill a student and teacher while seriously wounding others. Among the victims was my godson— the same boy who wore his March For Our Lives T-shirt until it was soft and faded. The shooting happened hours after I emailed David Hogg, a survivor of the Parkland shooting and gun control activist, asking to interview him for this chapter.

I did speak to David the week I reached out, but instead of talking about this book, I was seeking advice on how to respond to the horror of a school shooting and the global attention on my injured godson. I met with his team at March For Our Lives and asked them how to handle media and begin dealing with and healing from what happened.

Less than 4 years after David was hiding from a mass shooter in his high school, he has become an internationally known spokesperson and advocate for a generation growing up with so much trauma and tragedy. In his foreword to the book *Fight,* by John Della Volpe, David describes today's young people this way:

> We are a generation forced to grow up in fear of becoming victims of gun violence in our neighborhoods and schools. Heavily in debt, we enter an economy that reduces young people to commodities and squeezes us for profit. We inherit a natural world that may have already reached its tipping point. At every turn, our institutions are failing us, and we are paying the price. Half of our generation reports feelings of depression and/or anxiety. The government reports our stress levels are twice those of adults over thirty.[1]

Powerlessness in the face of these risks and realities will lead to suffering. We must find ways for young people to feel and be powerful. They should not live in fear for their lives, and they should have control over their lives.

At 11 and 9, my children know the causes they care about. They want school shootings to stop, racism to end, our planet to heal, and mental health for all. After their godbrother got home from the hospital, I asked my older son what message he would write on a protest sign. His response was immediate: "Let us live and have a future."

Civic Engagement and Sociopolitical Youth Development

If we consider kids in context—the whole picture of who and how they are and the ways their environments and experiences shape them—we can see how toxic conditions like school shootings and live shooter drills impact them. Experiences with violence, oppression, suppression, trauma, tragedy, and disaster poison children's well-being and jeopardize their development.[2]

Young people deserve supports and skills to solve the problems that hurt them. We can help them learn to use their gifts, stories, and experiences for good. Becoming a force for good is profoundly powerful. It moves young people from being passive and feeling helpless to becoming active agents in their own healing and transformation. This can strengthen their identity, confidence, and willingness to take risks—all essential for healthy development.[3] It can also alleviate some of their angst and anxiety. Young people tell me they are frustrated with their circumstances and afraid for their lives and futures. They want ways to make things better.

We can teach kids strategies for identifying, interrogating, and fighting the conditions and challenges that cause harm. Young people will come up with different solutions from adults because their perspectives are fueled by experiences that are uniquely their own. Their childhoods have been defined by global problems that are personal and proximate. This positions them to be what Zoe Weil calls **solutionaries**—young people who bring their knowledge and skills to solve pressing problems and create positive change. This "solutionary thinking" requires us to help children learn to

- Focus on problems that can be solved
- Make choices based on what does the most good and least harm
- Invite and listen to others' perspectives with a focus on strengths and solutions
- Recognize the interconnections and intersections of problems, systems, and situations
- Seek and engage in collaboration and collective action[4]

Solutionary thinking is more than what young people need; it is what they want. Amanda Shabowich is a leading voice on youth and inter-generational engagement. She has been directly involved in numerous youth leadership experiences, including as a young fellow for the Youth Transition Funders Group, a network I help staff. Through her personal experiences and professional work, Amanda has spoken to hundreds of young people involved in social change. She has never met a young person who isn't interested in making the world a better place—for themselves, their loved ones, their community, and future genera-tions. Amanda told me young people often feel in the dark about why problems persist and what they can do to help.

The October 28, 2022, edition of my children's favorite magazine, *The Week Junior,* backs this up. Every year, the magazine puts out a "Junior Voices" survey, asking young readers what they care about and what's on their minds. Of those who responded to the survey, nearly 9 in 10 said it was important to learn about what's happening around the world. The same number believed they should have a say on issues that affect them and that they wished more adults would listen to them. These young readers overwhelmingly wanted to inspire other children to make positive changes (82 percent) and believed their actions can make a difference (72 percent).[5]

It is not enough to expect children to be resilient or resistant to the circumstances that threaten their lives. We must give them ways to exercise power and participate in rectifying problems and generating solutions. This type of youth engagement will nurture their well-being and set them on a path for lifetime civic and social engagement.[6]

Causes and Civics With Younger Children

The types of activities that support sociopolitical development and civic engagement look different depending on a child's age and developmental stage.

Younger children are less likely to understand or be passionate about complex challenges like inequality or poverty. They can, however, become passionate about helping friends and family in need. Beginning in the early years, we can nurture and encourage the vital connection between compassion and action. For example, when our younger son was in first grade, his best friend was undergoing chemotherapy for leukemia. Their teacher decided to create care bags of toys for each chemo treatment. Harrison was happy to have something he could do to help his friend. We spent hours assembling care bags, and he delivered each one with pride. Thankfully, his friend is in remission, but Harrison still cares about the cause. Each year, he donates to the Leukemia & Lymphoma Society and our local children's hospital "for Steven." Since first grade, Harrison has wanted to help children with cancer and chronic illnesses.

In addition to nurturing connections between kids and causes, we can teach them civics. **Civic engagement** is something people do to increase their interest in, support of, and work to solve a shared, public problem. Civic engagement is more than an act of kindness or goodwill; it requires working across diverse perspectives to come up with the best solution for the context and community. Oftentimes, it is work to change or transform an institution, organization, or policy.[7] By learning civics, children get a head start in understanding how decisions and laws are made, and what they can do to create change themselves.

With younger children, you can simulate a community or neighborhood. Maybe this is an extension of what you already do, like classroom jobs, chores, or team responsibilities. Besides teaching kids how communities work, these simulations are spaces where you can introduce real world problems. For example, you can introduce an issue with littering, or people's pets getting loose and lost. Kids can work together to generate different ideas, listen to each other's opinions and perspectives, and reach consensus on solutions. You can have kids create community rules and contracts, even letting them vote on certain things. This is an entry point into everyday civic life. In a time of increased polarization, it's an opportunity to help children learn to work and live together.[8]

Causes and Civics With Youth and Young Adults

Toward the end of elementary school and through middle and high school, young people increasingly identify and engage in causes that matter to them. Often, these relate to personal experiences and interests. Sometimes, older children become involved in causes their families care about.

Kei Kawashima-Ginsberg runs CIRCLE at Tufts University and is a leading scholar on youth civic engagement. Lucky for me, she is also a friend. As I was researching this chapter, I asked Kei why civic engagement is important for our kids' development and how we can support it.

According to Kei, civic engagement holds intrapersonal and inter-personal benefits for young people. Intrapersonally, civic engagement is a form of self-care. It helps people cope with uncertainty, difficulties, and disagreements. Young people develop emotional tolerance and different ways of expressing themselves and their ideas. Interpersonally, civic engagement invites young people to work with others and participate in collective and creative problem solving.

Kei has found that young people can engage in causes and civics independently, but it is more supportive when it happens within an institution or group. This creates sustained intergenerational opportunities, where young people and adults work together, and adults can offer guidance, facilitation, and support. Through their differences, both young people and adults learn to see things differently and can adapt over time.

Individual or institutional support can be done through a class assignment, group project, guest speaker, field trip, and more. It is anything that feeds a young person's fire and gives them opportunities to do something about it. When young people's interests go beyond what we can support, we can direct them to other people and places that can help. For example, you might notice a young person is passionate about the environment, which you know very little about. You can talk to them about their interest and offer to connect them to a local group or organization that does conservation work.[9]

Student Groups, Clubs, and Chapters

Youth-led clubs, chapters, and groups are another way for young people to be forces for good.

From a young age, Mia Stavarski knew she wanted to be a therapist. She was the kid on the playground who listened to classmates' problems and offered support. Senior year of high school, Mia took an art class, loved it, and learned she could go to college for art therapy. She applied to Temple University for their art therapy and counseling program, which is where she found the student-led group Active Minds.

Active Minds is the leading nonprofit in the United States promoting mental health awareness and education for young people. It was started by Alison Malmon, whose brother lost his life to suicide when she was in college. Bereft, Alison gathered a group of fellow students to raise awareness about depression and change the conversation about mental health. Nearly 2 decades later, Active Minds is at more than 1,000 schools, campuses, communities, and workplaces.[10]

When a classmate invited Mia to attend an Active Minds meeting her sophomore year, she knew it was the club and cause for her. Before long, she took a leadership position, and by junior year, Mia was president of the Temple University chapter amid the COVID-19 pandemic and a growing youth mental health crisis.[11]

At the same time in Kentucky, more than 100 middle and high school students were working with each other and adults to reach fellow students, policymakers, educators, and families to fight for the changes they wanted to see in schools and the public education system. With support of an institutional home—the nonprofit Kentucky Student Voice Team—and adult partners, young people like Solyana Mesfin were able to engage in education advocacy, including Solyana's appointment as the first student to the Kentucky State Board of Education. Solyana used the power of her position, the platform and support of the Kentucky Student Voice Team, and her learned skills in advocacy and communications to push for education issues and raise awareness—through sharing her own story and conducting research—on the mental health needs of Kentucky teens.[12]

Both Mia and Solyana developed personally and professionally through their involvement in these student-led efforts. Each had ongoing support from adults who offered guidance, resources, and information. For Mia, this was her club adviser, Janie. Janie was available and supportive, able to provide historical and contextual information. She gave advice without imposing her own views, and from Mia's perspective, she always treated Mia like an equal.[13] Solyana had the support of the Kentucky Student Voice Team's peer network and staff, including managing partner, Rachel Belin.

Rachel's job is to examine, evolve, and codesign the organization with young people, to reflect and respond to the needs of whoever is engaged. This means her work looks different depending on who is involved, how they envision actualizing their mission to promote more just and democratic schools, and what they need. For Rachel, this is about building and circulating power and enacting organizational norms where young people are centered as collaborative leaders and adults work as partners with complementary capacities to support them.[14]

Youth-led clubs, chapters, and groups enable young people to be socially and civically active with varying levels of commitment. Some kids sign up for clubs because their friends are in them, or their parents need after-school childcare. Others are deeply committed to the issue or interest area. Like the simulated community you might facilitate with younger children, these youth-led groups are fertile spaces for young people to practice collective problem solving, teamwork, decision making, empathy, and more.

- This week, consider interests and issues you know the children in your life have, and research local groups and organizations they can connect to. Introduce a child to an organization, or help a child create a plan to explore an issue of interest independently.

- Let kids take over an activity you normally run. For example, have them design and facilitate a lesson, meeting agenda, daily schedule, sports practice, or weekend outing. Afterwards, debrief and reflect. Ask each other how it felt and what you learned.

TRY NOW

Healing Through Social Action

Through his research and writing, Professor Shawn Ginwright speaks to the ways young people can experience joy, healing, and power over their own lives when they work together to change a system or structure.[15] In many cases, the action itself is a healing intervention. By working with others who have similar experiences and a desire to make things better, young people increase their hope and confidence, develop a more positive view of themselves, form new friendships, and find healthy outlets for expressing and managing emotions.[16]

Healing-centered social action transforms young people's worries into words they can speak and work they can undertake. This is most important for young people who feel powerless over their own lives— those who are marginalized and vulnerable. By working with others to address traumatizing situations (e.g., school shootings) and oppressive laws and systems (e.g., "school-to-prison" pipeline), young people can exercise control over their lives and activate the other whole life practices, especially community and belonging, the embracing of identities and cultures, and nurturing healthy relationships.

This practice might feel beyond your personal and professional purview. Yet our care for kids should extend to the causes that impact them and the actions needed to make their lives better. Knowing that civic and social action can help them heal should inspire us to try and support it whenever and wherever we can.

This is what I talked about with Albert Maldonado, a health funder and former organizer who works for the California Endowment. Albert has funded and been on the frontlines of many youth leadership initiatives and power-building movements. In Albert's experience, he has learned that social action can heal so long as there is hope, joy, and justice:[17]

- **Hope** - Social action can inspire children to imagine what's possible in their lives and the world. They can dream big and know they are not alone while they live in the world as it is.

- **Joy** - It is easy for young people to drown in the barriers they face and the issues that divide us. Life is hard and so is social action. By doing the work with a "crew," it can be fun and celebratory.

- **Justice** - Social action is ultimately about engaging young people as changemakers and bridge builders, getting to the root causes of big problems, and working to make things better and more just. This work builds young people's sense of identity and purpose, helping them to make meaning of their situations and stories.

Rachel Belin from Kentucky Student Voice Team believes the most daunting challenge kids face is not giving in to cynicism. Their childhoods have been hard and the world can seem bleak. Working with others toward the common good can be a "balm for despair." In her experience, service and collective action inoculate young people against giving up.

As adults, we experience our own healing when we support and engage with young people in social action. This happens when we reflect on our past and ask ourselves: "What did I not get when I was in their shoes?" And "What did I desperately need?" This is an opportunity to use our role and authority to champion young people, take them seriously, and offer them the scaffolded supports and opportunities they need to succeed in what they're seeking.[18]

TRY NOW

- Find moments to spontaneously cultivate presence and joy. When Albert worked with young organizers, he always looked for moments to have fun through games, songs, and outings. This week, look for ways to play and promote joy.

- Reflect on what it means that children need a "balm" for their despair. What would it be like to be a child in today's world? What causes would you feel most drawn to and what laws or systems would you want to change?

Caution Before Proceeding

When this practice is done without the other whole life practices, it can have adverse effects and diminish rather than promote thriving. Civic and social engagement can take a toll on young people's health and well-being. The work exposes them to ugliness and evil that can be hard to handle and easy to internalize. Without sufficient support, young people may end up worn out, burnt out, or even more unsafe. We should never ask children to act alone, to stand up for what they believe in without people beside them, or to advocate when they feel mentally or physically unwell.

As adults, we must help kids do this work with health and wellness guardrails in place. Encourage young people to make promises to themselves and each other before taking action. Self-care is also a form of healing and being a force for good.

WHOLE LIFE PRACTICE

Be a Force for Good

Learn

- Young people deserve supports and skills they can use to identify, interrogate, and solve problems that hurt them. By engaging in social action, young people strengthen their identities, confidence, and willingness to take risks.

- Civic engagement and sociopolitical development are healthy parts of growing up—just like emotional and cognitive development. For younger kids, this includes connecting compassion and action. For older kids, this includes teaching them to find root causes to the problems they face and ways to solve them.

- Civic and social engagement are forms of self-care and proven healing interventions. They can help young people improve their hope and confidence, develop a more positive view of themselves, form new relationships, and find healthy outlets for expressing emotions.

Reflect

On your own or in a group, reflect on these questions:

- Who championed you when you were growing up and what impact did that have on your life?

- Who did not take you and your ideas seriously and what impact did that have on your life?

- How can you champion children and the issues they care about? Do you take them and their ideas seriously?

Act

As you absorb what you read and reflected on, consider how you can put insights into action. Take time to set a few commitments and intentions on how to *Be a Force for Good.*

- What is one small action you can take *today* to put this practice into action?

- What is one larger action you can take *this month* to put this practice into action?

- What is one big action you can work toward *this year* to put this practice into action?

Seek Awe and Wonder 15

"Gratitude bestows reverence, allowing us to encounter everyday epiphanies, those transcendent moments of awe that change forever how we experience life and the world."

—John Milton

To get to Idaho Basecamp, you drive 30 miles out of Ketchum down a two-lane road that takes you up a high mountain pass with sheer drops and waterfalls running down rock. After passing the summit, you've made it to camp. Basecamp is 7,000 feet high, smells of wild sage, and has panoramic views of the Big Lost mountains. On the "upper" property there are two yurts, a couple of cottages, and canvas tents where campers sleep. The "lower" part is river and greenery. To reach it, kids cross a bridge with a sign that says, "from here to there" and enter a part of the property that program director Whitney McNees Gershater tells me is called Graceland. Here there are kid-created trails and camping zones. Over time, campers have given these places names like Central Park, the Grove, and Area 52.

Each year, hundreds of fifth graders travel to Idaho Basecamp to spend 3 days with their classmates and teachers. Before entering the property, students line up under an archway, surrender their digital devices, and share one thing they are grateful for.

Over the next few days, students do team building, learn how to make a fire and basic shelter, walk along the river, sing songs, and play games. According to Whitney, this gives Idaho kids an opportunity to immerse themselves in the beauty of the place they call home, an experience they might not have otherwise.

Each fifth-grade camp includes a "solo," which is a half hour where kids sit by themselves on the property. Students often say this was their favorite part of the entire experience. For many it's one of the only times they have been alone in nature for that long and felt the ground beneath them. It is a moving experience that inspires awe and gratitude. Kids connect to the land they live on, gaze at the mountains that surround them, and take comfort in the bigness of the blue skies and snow-covered peaks.[1]

Nine hundred miles south of Basecamp is Neighborhood Ministries, a 40-year-old faith-based organization in a part of the urban core of Phoenix notorious for gang activity and violence. Neighborhood also runs camps and youth programs, but theirs are in the middle of the barrio in industrial buildings on concrete.

Every summer, hundreds of students from South Phoenix flood Neighborhood's eight-acre campus, picked up by counselors in buses and vans. They sing, dance, pray, and play together. It's a space where kids know they are safe at the level of body and soul. It is a different kind of beauty from gathering on a mountain summit, but similarly transformative and transcendent.

At Neighborhood, kids are everywhere. There are games, activities, and many expressions of love and tenderness toward one another. Everyone goes to chapel to be in community together. During these times, campers and counselors share miracles they witnessed, spiritual experiences they had, and gratitude they felt. Neighborhood's founder, Kit Danley, told me this is a resiliency practice for young people, especially for those facing significant challenges. Kids experience being part of a "beloved community" where they are seen, known, and loved. Beauty in this barrio is more crowded than the mountains, but the effect is still the same.[2]

Spiritual Development

We are spiritual beings, hardwired for connection to something greater. Research indicates that spirituality is something we are born with, as natural as eating and breathing.[3] Looking back, I see how this was true in my own life. I was not raised in a religious household but always felt a connection to a higher power. My childhood journals were letters to God. I stole a Bible from my small-town bookstore and carried it everywhere, never reading it, but believing it would keep me safe. I prayed without knowing who I was praying to. I had moments in nature that felt mystical, and interactions with people that felt otherworldly.

Spirituality doesn't have to be religious, although religious traditions and practices can provide language, identity, and community. Spirituality is biological and developmental, like our emotions and cognition. It begins at birth, grows through childhood, and takes off in adolescence when existential questions and curiosity take center stage. Spirituality is the sense of connection fifth graders feel on their solo at Idaho Basecamp and the feeling of awe that comes from hearing a friend describe a miracle at Neighborhood in Phoenix.

Spirituality in Childhood

Younger children express and explore their natural spirituality through awe, wonder, wisdom, and love. It's the look on their faces when they are amazed because something occurred that changed what they believed was possible. We see this when children watch fireworks or react to a thunderstorm. They are big eyed, open-mouthed, and full of curiosity. We also see this when children express unconditional love, like tight hugs for a family member, gentleness with a baby, and affection toward their pets. Children can also show wisdom beyond their age. They might be the first to extend radical acceptance or be moved by compassion to help someone in need.

In the book *The Spiritual Child,* psychology professor Lisa Miller describes five spiritual strengths children share across contexts:

- A love of ritual and prayer
- An intuitive sense of "heart knowing," feeling love and unity with others
- The desire to be helpful, share, and contribute
- Seeing family as sacred and special
- A connection to nature and fascination with the life cycle[4]

It's said that Albert Einstein retained the awe of a child his entire life. In his biography, author Walter Isaacson described it as "standing like curious children, before the great mystery into which we were born."[5] Children instinctively see the world as wondrous. Without effort, this feeling diminishes as we age. Scholars think that if we teach and encourage kids to continuously seek awe and wonder, they will experience lifetime benefits. Awe leaves adults with stronger spiritual connectedness and humility, less stress and sickness, and concern toward people and the planet.[6] Presumably—although not empirically proven—this is true for children too.[7]

Many of us unintentionally squash children's spiritual experiences, not stopping long enough to let them study and soak in something they find wonderful. Financial worries lead us to cancel or skip programs and classes that foster awe and wonder like art, music, and trips. When pressed for time, we pass lookout points, skip visits to see babies or older relatives, or leave sporting events without meeting revered players. This can feel reasonable, even necessary. For kids, though, it may send a message that these moments are not worthwhile.

To support spirituality in childhood, we must embrace moments and opportunities that nourish children's five spiritual strengths. This means slowing down so children can engage in imaginative play, immerse in nature, enjoy solitude, and interact with people and animals. If a child tells you about a spiritual event, something they found miraculous or magical, respond in ways that protect their connection with the transcendent. Even if you don't believe it, respect it.

Spirituality in Adolescence

In the tween and teen years, spirituality surges. Adolescence is a period of intense developmental growth when young people grapple with who they are, why they are here, and what they believe. This is a time when self-awareness and social awareness heighten, and a core sense of self begins to emerge. This is also a time of spiritual individuation and moral development.[8] Young people question what it means to be a good person and wonder if they are good enough. They wrestle with their real and ideal selves and what makes something right or just. Their cares and concerns become more textured and individualized.[9]

For older kids, spirituality is intertwined with relationships and a quest for meaning.[10] Developmentally, young people are hypersocial and emotional, with rapidly developing metacognitive abilities. This makes their interactions and introspection especially important.

To support spiritual development, we must hold space for young people to ask hard questions, wrestle with moral choices, and construct their own beliefs—without imposing our own views. We can encourage their exploration by letting them know it is normal and healthy to be curious or doubtful. We can use books and writing as places for personal reflection, or science to spark awe and wonder. We can promote mindfulness and minimize distractions, so young people have time by themselves and benefit from solitude and contemplation.

A strong spiritual base can prevent and protect kids from suffering. When they bring their worries to a higher power or faith community, express their feelings through creativity, center themselves in nature or sports, feel the guidance of their ancestors, or take comfort in a sense of unconditional love, they are less likely to experience the symptoms of depression, anxiety, or turn to substances and other forms of self-harm.[11] This may be because spirituality activates all the whole life practices. Meaning and purpose are basic needs, soul care is mental health, faith is found in relationships and community, a personal relationship to a higher power invokes belonging and identity, connecting with our ancestors and nature are the ultimate connectors to time (past, present, future), and spirituality overflows externally as compassion and service.

Spirituality as Soul Safety

When a young person sees everyday life as sacred—what Lisa Miller calls the "transcendent experience of nourishing connection"—they tap into a potent form of resiliency and healing.[12]

I get this. When I am terrified or traumatized, I pray. When I feel lost, I seek spiritual connection and guidance. When I go through hardship but believe there's a reason, it's easier to cope and keep going. I see this with my own children, especially as they get older.

I talked to Kit Danley from Neighborhood about this sense of spirituality, and she agreed. She told me how Neighborhood has a program where they help and house children under 12 who have migrated to America on their own. Many have witnessed and survived unspeakable human suffering. Kit told me these kids walk hundreds of miles through desert and dangerous conditions, often going days without food or a safe place to sleep. When she asks them about it, they tell her about the miraculous encounters they had and how they sensed the presence of something ineffable protecting and directing them. These children tell her they're alive because of their prayers and belief in a God who loves them.

Rather than dismiss it, Kit and her team encourage this spiritual connection, hoping it grows stronger. Here's why Kit says that's important:

> Unfortunately, when people say "there is no God. There is no afterlife," children hear "there is no help for you." This leaves kids in the inky, black darkness which they are already in if they live in a tragic and hard environment.

Spirituality and a belief in a higher power can help children feel less alone and afraid. Spirituality provides courage and conviction to keep going when times are tough. A belief in a higher power offers kids a private outlet to unburden themselves, and for those who believe they are praying to a spirit or spirits that are powerful, a place from which to draw strength and stamina.

The ABCs of Spiritual Development

It can be difficult to think of ways to support a child's spiritual development, especially in places like public schools that are expressly nonreligious. However, it is important to make it a priority, because when we dismiss or denigrate this part of a child, we make their lives harder. By generating or sharing experiences that spark awe, strengthen spirituality, and encourage the development of a moral compass, we invest in core assets that will support young people's well-being and wholeness for the rest of their lives. Honor this developmental part of childhood. If you are serving children in a faith-based setting, make sure your dogma and doctrine help it flourish.

When I was a teacher, I always looked for easy ways to remember complex concepts. With the help of my close friend Katie Gholson, I've tried to do the same for spiritual development. Katie is a social worker, chaplain, and former youth pastor. She's the person I interviewed on grief in Chapter 7, "Prioritize Mental Health." Together, we pulled out and prioritized the big pieces of spiritual development, focusing on aspects that can be cultivated anywhere and with anyone.

Here are the "ABCs" of spiritual development:

- **A is for "awe and awareness"** - When children feel a sense of the sacred and spiritual in everyday life, it stretches their understanding of the world, inviting joy, peace, and transcendence.

- **B is for "belief and belonging"** - When children are spiritually grounded, they have meaning, purpose, and a belief in something bigger. Through faith community and a personal relationship with a higher power—whatever it's called and however it's expressed— kids find connection to a community of other believers and an ineffable, everlasting source of love and belonging.

- **C is for "conviction and compassion"** - Children's natural spirituality includes a desire to do and be good. Giving back is purposeful. Spirituality inspires service, advocacy, and social action.

Our behaviors toward children shape their sense of spirituality and the attributes they assign to a higher power. Because of this, we must cultivate and model these ABCs in our own lives and relationships. This means paying attention to young people and expressing awe when they do something amazing. It's believing in them and creating spaces where they know they are welcome and belong. It's also living a life of conviction and compassion, showing young people what it looks like to be of service to others.

- Identify two to three ways you can practice the ABCs with kids this week. This might be for an individual child or a group. What can you model and make happen?

- Reflect on your own sense of spirituality and what you consider to be a higher power. How would you characterize it?

TRY NOW

Nurturing Kids' Spirit and Spark

Whether you engage with kids in a faith-based setting or not, there are many ways to nurture their spirituality. Importantly, children connect to the sacred in their own ways. I feel most connected in conversations, solitude, and nature. For my husband, it's service work. Our kids consider a packed St. Louis Cardinals game with cheering fans to be a spiritual experience. As you read through the strategies in Table 20, consider what you already do and anything else you want to try.

Table 20	Ways to Nurture Young People's Spiritual Development
STRATEGY	**EXAMPLES**
Contribution and Service	Helping others, volunteering, giving back
Art and Music	Creating and composing; attending a concert, the symphony, or art event; visiting a museum; curating art; listening to music
Novelty and Nature	Hiking and being on the water, gardening, sightseeing, stargazing, having immersion experiences, experiencing "solos" in nature, conducting experiments, and engaging in experiential learning

(Continued)

(Continued)

STRATEGY	EXAMPLES
People and Animals	Quality time with loved ones, playing with animals, intergenerational interactions (e.g., conversations with elderly relatives)
Rituals and Traditions	Singing, chanting, dancing, following traditions or routines, celebrating milestones, praying
Fandom and Fun	Meeting someone famous, being surrounded by people who have a shared interest, attending a special event (e.g., sporting event, concert, wedding)
Gratitude and Solitude	Writing a gratitude list, sharing miracles, sending a thank you note, having a device-free day, going for a walk, practicing mindfulness and meditation, journaling
Faith and Cultural Community	Attending faith services, reading religious and cultural materials, engaging in religious and traditional practices

Wholeness Comes From an Integrated Core

The 10 whole life practices cover what young people need internally, socially, temporally, and transcendentally. When I interviewed Kaʻanohiokalā Kalama-Macomber for Chapter 11, "Embrace Identities and Cultures," she recognized these 10 practices not only support a child's whole life but breathe life into the child. Inhale is internal, exhale is social, inhale is temporal, exhale is transcendental. This breath work is our child care work. It sustains the children we care for and about, connecting them to themselves, each other, their pasts, futures, and something greater. As a result, this final whole life practice brings together all the others. It is the integrated and innermost core that weaves a young person's stories into something whole.

WHOLE LIFE PRACTICE

Seek Awe and Wonder

Learn

- Spirituality is biological and developmental. It is different from religion, although religious practices can help nurture (or hurt) it. Spiritual development begins at birth and surges in adolescence when young people are more introspective and interested in existential questions.

- Awe and wonder are natural and common states for children. They happen when children's worldview expands through an event or experience. Awe and wonder diminish as we age, in part because they are not prioritized.

- All young people have five core spiritual strengths: a love of ritual and prayer, an intuitive sense, the desire to be helpful, seeing family as sacred, and a connection to nature and the life cycle.

Reflect

Consider your own connection to this whole life practice.

- What did you feel and think about as you read this chapter?

- What is your story of spirituality, and how did your childhood experiences contribute to it?

- What do you think about us being biologically wired for spirituality and that it should be supported anywhere kids spend time?

Act

As you absorb what you read and reflected on, consider how you can put insights into action. Take time to set a few commitments and intentions on how to help young people *Seek Awe and Wonder*.

- What is one small action you can take *today* to put this practice into action?

- What is one larger action you can take *this month* to put this practice into action?

- What is one big action you can work toward *this year* to put this practice into action?

PART III

Aim for Wholeness

LIVING WITH
JOY AND PURPOSE

SAFE
AND
SUPPORTED

ROOTED
AND
CONNECTED

LEARNING
AND
GROWING

HEALTHY
AND
HEALING

Wholeness 16

"The gardener does not make a plant grow. The job of a gardener is to create optimal conditions."

—Sir Ken Robinson

In 1955, a team of psychologists, pediatricians, and public health workers led by developmental psychologist Emmy Werner began the longest study on record to understand human development. They followed more than 600 babies born on Kauaʻi in Hawaiʻi into midlife. Island life was as close to a control study as the team could find, and for 32 years the researchers watched how participants handled life, including hardship and setbacks. What started as a study on human development became a revelatory exploration of the power of resiliency.[1]

Participants were from different racial and ethnic backgrounds reflecting Hawaiʻi's overall diversity. Roughly half were born to parents with little education who worked as unskilled laborers. Throughout the study, researchers conducted pediatric screenings and psychological evaluations and collected information from medical and school records. They used home visits and interviews to assess emotional support, stress, educational stimulation, and behavioral or learning difficulties.[2] There were extensive follow-ups at ages 2, 10, 18, and 32.[3]

The results revealed three types of potent protective factors among participants who managed to cope with adversity, thrive in childhood, and become competent and caring adults. In her reflections on the study, Emmy Werner said this about those children:

> Their very existence challenges the myth that a child who is a member of a so-called "high-risk" group is fated to become one of life's losers."[4]

Individually, these young people were active, affectionate, agreeable, and sociable. As they got older, they became good problem solvers and enjoyed personal interests. They were helpful to others and believed they could overcome their difficulties.

These children had caring and supportive adults in their lives, proving that nourishing connections and nurturing relationships counteract and counterbalance harmful effects of instability, stress, and trauma.[5] They benefited from close bonds with emotionally stable and strong adults who were sensitive to their needs. These were young people who relied on elders and others in the community for counsel, support, and care in crisis. They had positive role models who were relatives, mentors, teachers, faith leaders, and youth workers.

The Kaua'i study found that even if participants grew up in economically harsh and otherwise vulnerable conditions, they could experience well-being across their lives, as long as these protective factors were in place.[6] Researchers remarked how they were "deeply impressed by the resiliency of the overwhelming majority of children and their potential for positive change and personal growth."[7]

This study gives me hope for our kids. Children growing up on this "island" in the universe are facing unprecedented volatility and vulnerability. These new stressors often worsen persistent ones like inequality, abuse, and neglect. We must remember children's inborn resiliency and act on our ability to strengthen young people's protective factors and provide them with unwavering support.

A Fern That Grows in Lava Fields

This study reminds me of a story told by a Kahu (a Hawaiian minister) as he blessed a summer institute I co-led for teachers on O'ahu. He told us about the kupu plant, which is a fern that is among the first foliage to grow in a lava field. The image is striking. Imagine hardened black lava, which was once hot lava burning and destroying anything in its path, stretching on for miles. For a long time, the lava looked like an impossible place for life to thrive. Then the kupu emerges, standing green, vibrant, healthy, and strong. The kupu, like our children, can thrive in extremely harsh elements if it has the right nourishment.

The story of the kupu took me down a rabbit hole of research on ferns. It turns out ferns are one of the most ancient plants and they grow anywhere except places the sun can't reach. Whether a fern is growing in a lava field, a dense woodland, or a backyard garden, it still needs water and sunlight to survive, and the right amounts of each to thrive.[8]

The survivability of ferns has to do with their adaptability, which has allowed them to endure extremes from global warming to an ice age. Ferns survive and grow with or without us, but they live stronger and longer with the assistance gardeners provide.

As someone who has failed to keep plants alive, I speak from experience that too little *or* too much support (e.g., fertilizer, water, sunlight) can cause "plant stress," or in my case, distress. What plants need—like children—depends on their unique needs, the season, and the condition they're in. I've lost plants by caring for them all the same way, and by not adjusting my care when circumstances change. Several times, a plant has failed to thrive not because it was planted in the wrong place, but because I didn't know what it was or the kind of care it needed.

Optimal Conditions for Thriving

As adults caring for children, we are gardeners of human thriving. These incredibly resourceful and resilient young people will harness ancient instincts to survive in as many different environments as the fern. They will adapt and soak up whatever sunshine and sustenance they can find. Like plants, they will live a longer and more vibrant life with a "gardener's" attention, care, and skill.

To support young people's thriving, we start by learning who they are and where they're planted. By understanding where young people come from (demographics and determinants), their development (age and stage), health (brain and body), environmental ecosystem (people and places), and signature style (strengths and struggles), we develop a whole child portrait. This picture evolves over time, so we must routinely assess and address whatever is new and different.

Once we know about kids and their context, we assess how they are doing. Across the research and literature, there are five dimensions of thriving we can assess and aim for. These are defined and described in Table 21.

Table 21 Five Dimensions of Thriving	
DIMENSION	**DESCRIPTION**
Safe and Supported	Kids are confident and comfortable where they are and who they are with. They know their hearts, bodies, and souls are protected and they can be themselves without punishment or penalty.
Healthy and Healing	Kids are physically, socially, and emotionally nourished—they have what they need for their stage and situation. If there is illness or injury, they are moving toward a healthy recovery.
Rooted and Connected	Kids are connected to family, friends, community, and culture(s) and can abide in a sense of belonging and being welcome and wanted.
Learning and Growing	Kids are acquiring new knowledge and skills. They are encouraged to be creative, imaginative, and curious. They are growing intellectually and developmentally.
Living With Joy and Purpose	Kids feel purpose and meaning in their lives and have regular opportunities to play and enjoy their childhoods. They experience awe, wonder, and the freedom to be a child.

This is not an empirical evaluation of thriving; these five dimensions work as a self-assessment to shine a light on how young people are doing in different systems, settings, and situations. This assessment requires honesty, belief, care, and human judgment. You might find young people feel too safe or so rooted they can't launch. Maybe they aren't safe enough and it's making them anxious and afraid. Maybe the five dimensions are present in ways that make sense for the child, but not us.[9] Frequently these five dimensions are only present with certain people or places.

There's a rhythm and routine to our gardening practice: Who are you? How are you? What do you need? Who are you *today, since that event happened, this school year*? How are you *right now, recently*? What do you need *now, soon, in the future*?

Based on what you know and learn about a child, you can chart how they are and explore what their thriving zone looks like. Thriving is not something to be achieved or accomplished, it is a state of being that young people move in and out of. Events, experiences, and having too much or too little of certain resources will bring young people in and out of their thriving zone. For example, in the same way overwatering can hurt a plant, being overprotective can diminish a child's ability to live with joy and purpose; or, if basic needs can't be met, a child will begin to wither. Consider how you might create and use something like the *thriving tracker* in Figure 7.

Figure 7 Thriving Zones

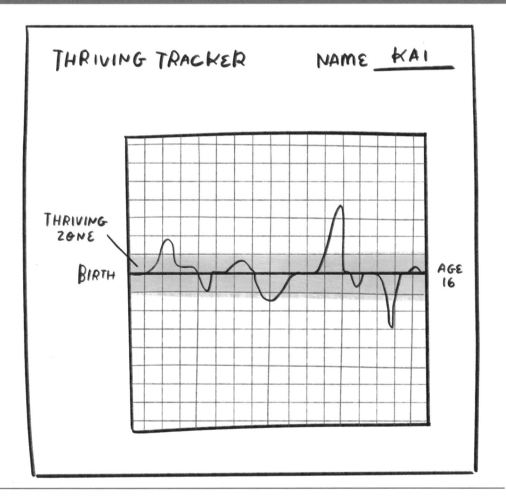

I used to think young people started in a survival state and moved toward thriving. Real life made me realize young people can survive and thrive at once. They may be in the "lava fields" and still have moments of basking in radiant sunshine. They might be in the most fertile environment and an awful storm suddenly makes it hard to stay alive. No matter where kids are planted, the right conditions allow them to experience moments and seasons of feeling whole and being well.

Aiming for Wholeness

Once we know who kids are and how they are doing, we determine what they need. Like sunshine and water, all children need the 10 whole life practices to live, learn, and thrive. These practices are dynamic and personal, changing depending on context and circumstances. For example, if a young person does not feel safe or supported, we might focus on meeting basic needs and prioritizing mental health. If a young person is struggling to find joy and purpose, we may spend time investing in personal interests, building community and belonging, and seeking awe and wonder.

As you interact with kids, ask yourself whether the 10 whole life practices are in place in such a way that children are

- Safe and supported
- Healthy and healing
- Rooted and connected
- Learning and growing
- Living with joy and purpose

When we find ourselves in new situations, we adjust and adapt. When a young child becomes a teen, we modify how we support their evolving identities. If a teenager struggles with mental illness, we double down on prioritizing mental health.

It can be hard to prioritize these whole life practices when there is little time and competing demands. Stay motivated! These are what matter most for kids, and when they're not present, young people struggle and suffer unnecessarily. When they are in place, young people experience health and happiness, and they are better able to learn and develop.[10] The 10 whole life practices are sources of strength, support, and stamina enabling young people to be and become the best versions of themselves.

Cultivating the Garden

Our actions—and inactions—have an outsized impact on a child's ability to thrive. Our behaviors have the power to shape or change the trajectory of their lives.[11] We must cultivate environments and experiences that honor and center the whole of who they are, and that make the 10 whole life practices a core part of their everyday experiences.

There are different levels of *Whole Child, Whole Life* (WCWL) work, and depending on who you are and what you do, you might work on more than one:

- **WCWL People:** These are people who take a whole child approach and prioritize the 10 whole life practices with the young people in their lives. WCWL people are committed to well-being and will do what they can to help young people thrive now and in the future.

- **WCWL Programs:** WCWL program leaders can design or decide on curriculums, program models, and lessons that have a whole child orientation and activate the 10 whole life practices. These programs will lead to positive relationships, safe environments, belonging, rich learning, skill building, and integrated supports.[12] Some programs are natural incubators of thriving. For example, social circus schools and many summer camps are examples of programs that already do this well.[13]

- **WCWL Partnerships and Places:** We can collaborate with others to create a connected and cohesive ecosystem where kids are supported across all spaces where they spend time. Community schools and family engagement are two examples of how this can be done. Individually, this can include child-centered partnerships between teachers and caregivers, special education meetings, and hospital rounds. At the community level, this can happen in neighborhood zones and through collective impact efforts. At the state level, a WCWL orientation can guide the discussions and decision making of children's cabinets, coordinating councils, and lawmakers.

The possibility of classrooms, schools, youth programs, and youth-serving systems adopting a *Whole Child, Whole Life* approach is that young people experience the cumulative benefits of thriving across place and time. Instead of occasional thriving, young people can experience optimal and ongoing thriving.

At the beginning of this book, my son shared a prayer I say to him and his brother each night. I pray for their physical, spiritual, emotional, and cognitive development. I petition for their health, happiness, and joy in the morning. As I pray, I promise to do whatever I can to make that prayer possible.

My hope for all children feels similarly reverent. It is a hope for their well-being and well-becoming, even in challenging times. It is a hope that we, the adults, can be cultivators of thriving, providing the nourishment they need, and celebrating who they are today, tomorrow, and always.

> May our children be safe and supported;
>
> May they experience health and healing;
>
> May they feel rooted and connected;
>
> May they continuously learn and grow;
>
> May their lives be full of joy and purpose.
>
> May our children feel whole and be well
>
> So they can build lives and futures they love.

Whole Child,
Whole Life
Sketchnote

WHOLE CHILD, WHOLE LIFE

10 WAYS TO HELP KIDS LIVE, LEARN, & THRIVE

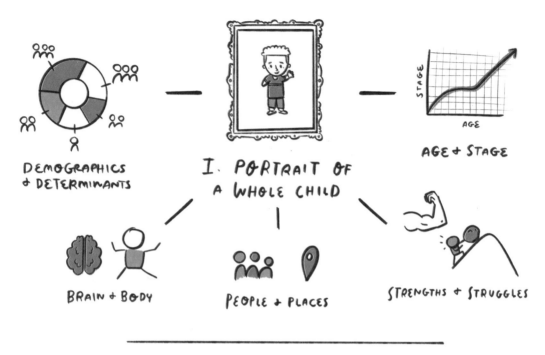

DEMOGRAPHICS & DETERMINANTS

I. PORTRAIT OF A WHOLE CHILD

AGE & STAGE

BRAIN & BODY

PEOPLE & PLACES

STRENGTHS & STRUGGLES

SAFE & SUPPORTED

LEARNING & GROWING

HEALTHY & HEALING

II. AIM FOR WHOLENESS

LIVING WITH JOY & PURPOSE

ROOTED & CONNECTED

II. 10 WHOLE LIFE PRACTICES

MEET
BASIC
NEEDS

PRIORITIZE
MENTAL
HEALTH

INVEST IN
PERSONAL
INTERESTS

NURTURE
HEALTHY
RELATIONSHIPS

BUILD COMMUNITY
& BELONGING

EMBRACE
IDENTITIES
& CULTURES

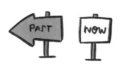

ATTEND TO THE
PAST & PRESENT

ACT WITH A
100-YEAR
MINDSET

BE A FORCE
FOR GOOD

SEEK AWE
& WONDER

Acknowledgments

This is a book that came together through conversations with some of the best and brightest people I know. It was developed during walks with friends, brainstorming with field leaders on Zoom, and reading parts aloud to my family at night.

The result is a collection of stories and advice from people I adore who also happen to be respected changemakers and thought leaders in education and human development. I hope that makes this a personal and powerful reading experience.

Early on, I took my blueprint of ideas to a group of field luminaries. These individuals made sure the "bones" of the book were solid and written in the right order. Special thanks to Karen J. Pittman, Merita Irby, Marvin Berkowitz, Pamela Cantor, Richard Lerner, Elliot Washor, Mark Greenberg, Thomas Hoerr, and Robert Sherman for your willingness to do this and your generosity of time and sharing. Thanks to Roger Weissberg, who passed away before this book began, but whose words and wisdom were with me along the way.

Thank you to my friends and colleagues who served as beta-readers and contributors on key questions and crowdsourcing requests. I'm especially thankful to Meghan Raftery, Corey Green Cliffe, Tara Kierstead, and Alicia Frank for their thoughtful and sensitive early reviews. Immense gratitude to my kitchen cabinet of counselors who read and edited the chapter on mental health; and policy wonks who helped me with the chapter on basic needs and the table on federal benefits programs. Thanks to Katherine Plog Martinez, who listened to me read the entire introduction aloud on a work trip and offered sound advice for how to make it better, and Maddy Day, who was always ready to process what I was learning.

Mahalo to the Kupu Hou Academy cohort from the summer of 2022. You were the first to play with the portrait of a whole child and the 10 whole life practices. I'll always remember our time together, the story of the kupu plant, and our shared commitment to be ready and well so we and our keiki can thrive. Whenever I wonder whether this will work in schools, I remember our discussions.

To my neighbor and dear friend, Katie Gholson. Your thinking and encouragement are tucked into corners of every chapter. I'm so glad your wisdom shines brightly in my sections on grief and spirituality. Thank you for not only believing in the importance of this book but agreeing to take the whole life practices on as a Lenten practice with me.

Thank you to my many other friends, who always asked how writing was going, and who never stopped believing it was worth the work.

Thanks to my husband and kids who embraced the concept of Sunday "Son" Days so I could write in the basement. Evan, thank you for your unwavering belief in me, your consistent encouragement, and the sacrifices you've made to make this book possible. Justice and Koa, thank you for making signs to remind everyone to give me privacy and for feeding me peanut butter honey banana sandwiches when I needed the energy to keep going.

To the people, programs, and places who let me visit and tell your stories—I am grateful for your trust, patience, and permission. This book travels from the islands of Hawai'i to the mountains in Idaho, the barrio in Phoenix to the city center of Norfolk, and in and around St. Louis. Because of you, I get to introduce readers to adults who help kids live, learn, and thrive in classrooms and on canoes, in camps and clubs, hospitals and therapists' offices, during the school year and throughout the summer. I'm deeply grateful to each person I interviewed, who also took time to review chapters, offer feedback, and make each piece stronger.

Manuel Herrera, I knew I needed you to illustrate this book since I fell in love with your Taco Bear. Thanks for being my creative partner in this and for bringing Kai, Riley, and Marcos to life and loving them as much as I do. It was a joy and privilege to work with you on this book and I hope the final product fills you with pride.

To Jessica Allan and the publishing team at Corwin, what a gift you are. Jess, thanks for replying to that first email. I feel like the universe brought us together, and I am overwhelmed by your commitment to me and enthusiasm for what we've produced. I hope you see yourself reflected on these pages and feel like this is your book too.

At one point in this process, I felt overwhelmed with how much there was left to do. Then I remembered that the process is the reward. I have wanted to write books for as long as I can remember. I am so lucky to have the opportunity to talk to passionate people, tell their stories, and help those on the frontlines do the most important work there is—caring for our kids.

About the Author

STEPHANIE MALIA

Stephanie Malia Krauss is a leading voice on what young people need to be ready and well in a rapidly changing world. Her clients include U.S.-based networks, coalitions, philanthropies, nonprofits, government organizations, schools, and community groups. An educator, social worker, and mom, Stephanie regularly contributes to education and parenting outlets, including EdSurge and Scary Mommy. She is the author of *Making It: What Today's Kids Need for Tomorrow's World* and has been featured on PBS NewsHour, StoryCorps, and more. To learn more about Stephanie and sign up for her newsletter, visit www.stephaniemaliakrauss.com.

About the Illustrator

MANUEL S. HERRERA

Manuel S. Herrera is an international speaker, an accomplished illustrator, and a veteran educator. He has illustrated books, publications, and graphics for a variety of organizations, publishers, and schools. Manuel's workshops and speaking engagements focus on sketchnoting, visual thinking, and design thinking. Over the past 19 years, Manuel has keynoted and led workshops across the globe at conferences such as SXSWEdu, ISTE, TCEA, MassCUE, FETC, and the International Sketchnote Camp. In 2018, Manuel became a Google Innovator at LAX18, and in 2016, he was named the Midwest Education Technology Conference Spotlight Educator. You can follow Manuel on Twitter and Instagram at @manuelherrera33.

Glossary

Adverse Childhood Experiences ("ACEs") - a common reference used to describe traumatic experiences that happen in childhood.

Allostatic load - the cumulative burden of chronic stress and life events on a child. When environmental and life challenges exceed a young person's ability to cope, they experience allostatic overload.

Civic engagement - something people do to increase their interest in, support of, and work to solve a shared, public problem. Civic engagement is more than an act of kindness or goodwill; it requires working across diverse perspectives to come up with the best solution for the context and/or community.

Cumulative disadvantage and **marginalization** - when children are born and live with characteristics and conditions that elevate risks of hardship, harm, and adversity.

Demographics - personal characterizations and population-level categories, such as race and gender. Demographics tell us how much advantage a young person experiences in systems and society.

Determinants - the social, political, and historical conditions kids grow up in, including whether they have access to good healthcare and schools, and how safe it is where they live. Determinants give us a sense of the protections and vulnerabilities young people experience.

Development - a highly dynamic, fluid process that is influenced, shaped, sped up, or slowed down by what's happening—from everyday situations and interactions to relationships and broader changes in the world at large.

Disruptive thinking - ways of thinking differently to challenge the status quo and come up with novel ideas and inventions.

Epigenome - a set of chemical markers that decide which parts of our genes (DNA) get activated, and to what degree. The epigenome is responsible for epigenetics, which is when parents and grandparents pass down genetic markers that have been changed because of their adverse environments and experiences.

Forecasting - the practice of identifying multiple possible futures.

Group identity is a young person's understanding of who they are in the context of the groups they are automatically in, choose to belong to, and that people perceive they are a part of.

Intersectionality is how group and personal identities come together and result in different experiences of prejudice and privilege, based on the systematic and historic advantaging of some groups and people over others.

Mental health - being positively and productively engaged in relationships, responsibilities, and activities.

Mental illness - when disturbing thoughts, emotions, and behaviors interfere or stop the engagement in and enjoyment of relationships, responsibilities, and activities.

Mesosystems - the connective space between settings, where two or more of a child's settings overlap and interact.

Personal identity is a young person's understanding of who they are individually, including how others perceive them.

Profiles - the basic picture of a kid, based on whatever available, observable, and reportable data we have. They are constructed from different combinations of demographics and determinants, unique to every child.

Protective factors are characteristics. that minimize or even prevent the damaging effects adversity has on development, allowing kids to do well even when times are tough.

Social bonds - close connections and care from people within a person's social network.

Social bridges - social connections to people and resources outside of a person's social network.

Social health - positive relationships and social interactions that benefit life, learning, and development.

Social wealth - relationships and social connections that provide advantage, access, and other beneficial resources and opportunities.

Solutionaries - people who bring their knowledge and skills to solve pressing problems and create positive change. A term coined by Zoe Weil.

Trauma-informed care - a way of working that recognizes the pervasiveness and presence of trauma, and that promotes interactions, experiences, and environments that are healthy, healing, and safe.

Endnotes

Introduction

1. Office of the Surgeon General (OSG). (2021). *Protecting youth mental health: The U.S. Surgeon General's advisory*. U.S. Department of Health and Human Services. http://www.ncbi.nlm.nih.gov/books/NBK575984/; American Academy of Pediatrics. (2021). *AAP-AACAP-CHA declaration of a national emergency in child and adolescent mental health*. Retrieved December 10, 2021, from http://www.aap.org/en/advocacy/child-and-adolescent-healthy-mental-development/aap-aacap-cha-declaration-of-a-national-emergency-in-child-and-adolescent-mental-health/

Chapter 1

1. Payne, K. (2017). *The broken ladder: How inequality affects the way we think, live, and die*. Penguin Random House.

2. Jennifer, L. E. (2019). *Biased: Uncovering the hidden prejudice that shapes what we see, think, and do*. Viking.

3. Rank, M. (Ed.). (2020). *Toward a livable life: A 21st century agenda for social work* (1st ed.). Oxford University Press.

4. Southern Education Foundation. (2022). *Economic vitality and education in the South: Part I the South's pre-pandemic position*. Southern Education Foundation.

5. Kozol, J. (1992). *Savage inequalities*. HarperPerennial.

6. Marya, R., & Patel, R. (2021). *Inflamed: Deep medicine and the anatomy of injustice*. Farrar, Straus and Giroux.

7. Center on the Developing Child. (n.d.). *How racism can affect child development*. Harvard University.

8. McDermott, C. L., Seidlitz, J., Nadig, A., Liu, S., Clasen, L. S., Blumenthal, J. D., . . . Raznahan, A. (2019). Longitudinally mapping childhood socioeconomic status associations with cortical and subcortical morphology. *The Journal of Neuroscience*, *39*(8), 1365–1373. https://doi.org/10.1523/JNEUROSCI.1808-18.2018; Rank, M. (Ed.). (2020). *Toward a livable life: A 21st century agenda for social work* (1st ed.). Oxford University Press.

9. PolicyLink & PERE. (2018). *100 million and counting: A portrait of economic insecurity in the United States*. https://www.policylink.org/resources-tools/100-million

10. Marya, R., & Patel, R. (2021). *Inflamed: Deep medicine and the anatomy of injustice*. Farrar, Straus and Giroux.

11. Washington University in St. Louis. (2015). *For the sake of all: A report on the health and well-being of African Americans in St. Louis and why it matters for everyone*. Washington University in St. Louis.

12. Araújo, L. A., Veloso, C. F., Souza, M. C., Azevedo, J. M. C., & Tarro, G. (2021). The potential impact of the COVID-19 pandemic on child growth and development: A systematic

review. *Jornal de Pediatria*, *97*(4), 369–377. https://doi.org/10.1016/j.jped.2020.08.008

13. Houtrow, A., Harris, D., Molinero, A., Levin-Decanini, T., & Robichaud, C. (2020). Children with disabilities in the United States and the COVID-19 pandemic. *Journal of Pediatric Rehabilitation Medicine*, *13*(3), 415–424.

Chapter 2

1. Munoz-Rivera, A., Jabbari, J., Roll, S., Kristensen, K., & Grinstein-Weiss, M. (2021). *Impact of Covid-19 on households with children: Family hardships and policy insights.* Washington University in St. Louis.

2. Many schools and educators went above and beyond to get food, digital devices, and the internet to their students. I know of educators who held food drives, fundraisers for digital devices, and who parked buses where there was a strong Wi-Fi signal, inviting students and their families to work from there. Even with those herculean efforts, students living in poverty still experienced incredible uncertainty, resource scarcity, and more barriers to learning than well-resourced peers.

3. Ibid.

4. Houtrow, A., Harris, D., Molinero, A., Levin-Decanini, T., & Robichaud, C. (2020). Children with disabilities in the United States and the COVID-19 pandemic. *Journal of Pediatric Rehabilitation Medicine*, *13*(3), 415–424.

5. Rapp, A., Fall, G., Radomsky, A. C., & Santarossa, S. (2021). Child maltreatment during the COVID-19 pandemic. *Pediatric Clinics of North America*, *68*(5), 991–1009. https://doi.org/10.1016/j.pcl.2021.05.006

6. There were young people whose learning and development accelerated during the pandemic. For some, an at-home and/or virtual learning environment was conducive to their needs and learning styles. For others who were homeschooled or enrolled in virtual schools before the pandemic, with the exception of losing out on some social and extracurricular activities, their learning and development continued without interruption.

7. National Institute on Drug Abuse. (2021, October 7). *More than 140,000 U.S. children lost a primary or secondary caregiver due to the COVID-19 pandemic.* National Institutes of Health (NIH). https://www.nih.gov/news-events/news-releases/more-140000-us-children-lost-primary-or-secondary-caregiver-due-covid-19-pandemic

8. Krauss, S. M. (2021). *Making it: What today's kids need in tomorrow's world.* Jossey-Bass/Wiley.

9. Hendry, L. B., & Kloep, M. (2012). *Adolescence and adulthood: Transitions and transformations.* Palgrave Macmillan.

10. Ibid.

11. Romero, V. E., Robertson, R., & Warner, A. (2018). *Building resilience in students impacted by adverse childhood experiences: A whole-staff approach* (1st ed.). Corwin.

12. Araújo, L. A., Veloso, C. F., Souza, M. C., Azevedo, J. M. C., & Tarro, G. (2021). The potential impact of the COVID-19 pandemic on child growth and development: A systematic review. *Jornal de Pediatria*, *97*(4), 369–377. https://doi.org/10.1016/j.jped.2020.08.008

13. Morris, M. W. (2016). *Pushout: The criminalization of Black girls in school.* The New Press.

14. Epstein, R., Blake, J. J., & Gonzalez, T. (2020). *Girlhood interrupted: The erasure of Black girls' childhood.* Georgetown Law.

15. Fang, J. (2021). *The deadly consequences of hypersexualizing Asian women.* Scientific American. Retrieved March 6, 2022, from https://www.scientificamerican.com/article/the-deadly-consequences-of-hypersexualizing-asian-women/

16. Hendry, L. B., & Kloep, M. (2012). *Adolescence and adulthood: Transitions and transformations.* Palgrave Macmillan.

17. Committee on the Neurobiological and Socio-Behavioral Science of Adolescent Development and Its Applications, Board on Children, Youth, and Families, Division of Behavioral and Social Sciences and Education, Health and Medicine Division, & National Academies of Sciences, Engineering, and Medicine, Bonnie, R. J., &

Backes, E. P. (Eds.). (2019). *The promise of adolescence: Realizing opportunity for all youth*. National Academies Press.

18. This table is adapted from the *Risk and Protective Factors for Youth* table found on youth.gov, a government website designed to create, maintain, and strengthen high-quality youth programs. The original table can be accessed at https://youth.gov/youth-topics/youth-mental-health/risk-and-protective-factors-youth

Chapter 3

1. For more information on the link between common childhood infections, like strep, and neuropsychological disorders, I recommend reading *Brain Inflamed: Uncovering the Hidden Causes of Anxiety, Depression, and Other Mood Disorders in Adolescents and Teens*, by Kenneth Bock, M.D.

2. Barrett, L. F. (2017). *How emotions are made: The secret life of the brain*. Mariner.

3. Sears, W., & Fortanasce, V. M. (2020). *The healthy brain brook: An all-ages guide to a calmer, happier, sharper you*. BenBella Books, Inc.

4. Vaziri Flais, S. (Ed.). (2018). *Caring for your school age child: The complete and authoritative guide* (3rd ed.). Bantam Books Trade Paperback.

5. While researching this chapter, I learned about telomeres, which are the caps on our DNA (like the plastic cap of a shoelace). These microcosmic parts of our body have a deciding role in how long we live and how susceptible we are to disease. To better understand their relationship to children, I used Twitter to connect with Dr. Elissa Epel, coauthor of *The Telomere Effect*. She said, "Health resides in community not just individual bodies." She recommended we focus on creating positive social environments for kids that foster collaboration and safe spaces where they can share and be in relationship, belong, and not feel alone. She ended by saying "Telomeres need social support and love."

6. Breit, S., Kupferberg, A., Rogler, G., & Hasler, G. (2018). Vagus nerve as modulator of the brain–gut axis in psychiatric and inflammatory disorders. *Frontiers in Psychiatry*, 9, 44. https://doi.org/10.3389/fpsyt.2018.00044

7. Levine, H. (2021, January). A user's guide to the gut-brain connection. *Health*, Special Edition, 11–15.

8. These activities are adapted and modified from Big Picture Living and the American College of Lifestyle Medicine. More on this groundbreaking partnership and the "big six" is available here: https://www.bpliving.org

9. For more on child hunger in the United States and globally, see Save the Children's website and resources, available here: https://www.savethechildren.org/us/what-we-do/emergency-response/hunger-and-famine-crisis

10. Dutko, P., Ploeg, M. V., & Farrigan, T. (2012). *Characteristics and influential factors of food deserts* (ERR-140) (p. 36). U.S. Department of Agriculture, Economic Research Service.

11. Sears, W., & Fortanasce, V. M. (2020). *The healthy brain book: An all-ages guide to a calmer, happier, sharper you*. BenBella Books, Inc.

12. Willett, W. C., & Stampfer, M. J. (2006). Rebuilding the food pyramid. *Scientific American*, 288(1), 64–71. https://doi.org/10.1038/scientificamerican1206-12sp

13. Sears, W., & Fortanasce, V. M. (2020). *The healthy brain book: An all-ages guide to a calmer, happier, sharper you*. BenBella Books, Inc.

14. Johns Hopkins Medicine. (2021, August 8). *The science of sleep: Understanding what happens when you sleep*. https://www.hopkinsmedicine.org/health/wellness-and-prevention/the-science-of-sleep-understanding-what-happens-when-you-sleep

15. Gruber, R., Michaelsen, S., Bergmame, L., Frenette, S., Bruni, O., Fontil, L., & Carrier, J. (2012). Short sleep duration is associated with teacher-reported inattention and cognitive problems in healthy school-aged children. *Nature and Science of Sleep*, 4, 33–40. https://doi.org/10.2147/NSS.S24607

16.   Lewis, L. L. (2022). *The sleep-deprived teen: Why our teenagers are so tired, and how parents and schools can help them thrive.* Mango Publishing Group.

17.   Pang, A. S.-K. (2016). *Rest.* Basic Books.

18.   Kohl, H. W., III., Cook, H. D., Committee on Physical Activity and Physical Education in the School Environment, Food and Nutrition Board, & Institute of Medicine. (2013). Physical activity and physical education: Relationship to growth, development, and health. In H. W. Kohl, III, H. D. Cook, Committee on Physical Activity and Physical Education in the School Environment, Food and Nutrition Board, & Institute of Medicine (Eds.), *Educating the student body: Taking physical activity and physical education to school* (pp. 97–160). National Academies Press. https://www.ncbi.nlm.nih.gov/books/NBK201497/; Blackburn, E., & Epel, E. (2017). *The telomere effect: A revolutionary approach to living younger, healthier, longer.* Grand Central Publishing, Hachette Book Group.

19.   Kohl, H. W., III., Cook, H. D., Committee on Physical Activity and Physical Education in the School Environment, Food and Nutrition Board, & Institute of Medicine. (2013). Physical activity and physical education: Relationship to growth, development, and health. In H. W. Kohl, III, H. D. Cook, Committee on Physical Activity and Physical Education in the School Environment, Food and Nutrition Board, & Institute of Medicine (Eds.), *Educating the student body: Taking physical activity and physical education to school* (pp. 97–160). National Academies Press.

20.   Blackburn, E., & Epel, E. (2017). *The telomere effect: A revolutionary approach to living younger, healthier, longer.* Grand Central Publishing, Hachette Book Group.

21.   Krauss, S. M. (2021). *Making it: What today's kids need for tomorrow's world.* Jossey-Bass/Wiley.

22.   For more on this, I recommend *The Art of Screen Time* by Anya Kamenetz, and *Screenwise: Helping Kids Thrive (and Survive) in Their Digital World,* by Devorah Heitner.

23.   Levitin, D. J. (2020). *Successful aging: A neuroscientist explores the power and potential of our lives.* Penguin Random House; Blackburn, E., & Epel, E. (2017).

The telomere effect: A revolutionary approach to living younger, healthier, longer. Grand Central Publishing, Hachette Book Group; Zaraska, M. (2020). *Growing young: How friendship, optimism, and kindness can help you live to 100.* Appetite by Random House.

24.   Harris, N. B. (2018). *The deepest well: Healing the long-term effects of childhood adversity.* Mariner.

25.   Adverse Childhood Experiences ("ACEs") is a common term used to describe traumatic experiences that happen in childhood and adolescence. ACEs can slow or speed up kids' development. For more information, see Chapter 1.

26.   Marya, R., & Patel, R. (2021). *Inflamed: Deep medicine and the anatomy of injustice.* Farrar, Straus and Giroux.

27.   Sapolsky, R. M. (2004). *Why zebras don't get ulcers: The acclaimed guide to stress, stress-related diseases and coping* (3rd ed.). St. Martin's Griffin.

28.   Harris, N. B. (2018). *The deepest well: Healing the long-term effects of childhood adversity.* Mariner.

29.   Blackburn, E., & Epel, E. (2017). *The telomere effect: A revolutionary approach to living younger, healthier, longer.* Grand Central Publishing, Hachette Book Group; Wolynn, M. (2017). *It didn't start with you: How inherited family trauma shapes who we are and how to end the cycle.* Penguin Random House.

30.   Menakem, R. (2017). *My grandmother's hands: Racialized trauma and the pathway to mending our hearts and bodies.* Central Recovery Press.

31.   Lahey, J. (2021). *The addiction innoculation: Raising healthy kids in a culture of dependence.* Harper.

32.   Jessica Lahey's book *The Addiction Inoculation: Raising Healthy Kids in a Culture of Dependence* is a helpful resource. This is an accessible, deeply researched book that provides a hopeful and optimistic view on kids' substance use, abuse, addictions, and sobriety.

33.   Bock, K. (2021). *Brain inflamed: Uncovering the hidden causes of anxiety, depression, and other mood disorders in adolescents and teens.* Harper Wave.

34.   Marya, R., & Patel, R. (2021). *Inflamed: Deep medicine and the anatomy of injustice.* Farrar, Straus and Giroux.

35. Ibid.

36. Ratnapalan, S., Rayar, M. S., & Crawley, M. (2009). Educational services for hospitalized children. *Paediatrics & Child Health, 14*(7), 433–436.

37. Shatkin, J. P. (2015). *Child & adolescent mental health: A practical, all-in-one guide* (2nd ed.). W. W. Norton & Company.

38. American Academy of Pediatrics. (2021). *AAP-AACAP-CHA declaration of a national emergency in child and adolescent mental health.* Retrieved December 10, 2021, from http://www.aap.org/en/advocacy/child-and-adolescent-healthy-mental-development/aap-aacap-cha-declaration-of-a-national-emergency-in-child-and-adolescent-mental-health/; Richtel, M. (2021, December 7). Surgeon general warns of youth mental health crisis. *The New York Times.* https://www.nytimes.com/2021/12/07/science/pandemic-adolescents-depression-anxiety.html

39. Linden, M. A., Braiden, H.-J., & Miller, S. (2013). Educational professionals' understanding of childhood traumatic brain injury. *Brain Injury, 27*(1), 92–102. https://doi.org/10.3109/02699052.2012.722262

40. Prasad, M. R., Swank, P. R., & Ewing-Cobbs, L. (2017). Long-term school outcomes of children and adolescents with traumatic brain injury. *The Journal of Head Trauma Rehabilitation, 32*(1), E24–E32. https://doi.org/10.1097/HTR.0000000000000218

41. Venkatramanan, S., Armata, I. E., Strupp, B. J., & Finkelstein, J. L. (2016). Vitamin B-12 and cognition in children. *Advances in Nutrition, 7*(5), 879–888. https://doi.org/10.3945/an.115.012021; Saloojee, H., & Pettifor, J. M. (2001). Iron deficiency and impaired child development. *BMJ: British Medical Journal, 323*(7326), 1377–1378.

Chapter 4

1. Lerner, R. M. (2005). Foreword: Urie Bronfenbrenner: Career contributions of the consummate developmental scientist. In U. Bronfenbrenner (Ed.), *Making human beings human: Bioecological perspectives on human development* (pp. ix–xxvi). SAGE.

2. Bronfenbrenner, U. (1979). *The ecology of human development: Experiments by nature and design.* Harvard University Press.

3. Ibid.

4. Herz, D. C., Eastman, A. L., Putnam-Hornstein, E., & McCroskey, J. (2021). Dual system youth and their pathways in Los Angeles county: A replication of the OJJDP dual system youth study. *Child Abuse & Neglect, 118*, 105160. https://doi.org/10.1016/j.chiabu.2021.105160

5. Krauss, S. M. (2021). *Making it: What today's kids need for tomorrow's world.* Jossey-Bass/Wiley.

6. Pinker, S. (2015). *The village effect: Why face-to-face contact matters* (2nd ed.). Atlantic Books; Blackburn, E., & Epel, E. (2017). *The telomere effect: A revolutionary approach to living younger, healthier, longer.* Grand Central Publishing, Hachette Book Group; Levitin, D. J. (2020). *Successful aging: A Neuroscientist explores the power and potential of our lives.* Dutton.

Chapter 5

1. Marvin cowrote the chapter on "Fairness." Marvin is also the author of *PRIMED for Character Education: Six Design Principles for School Improvement*, which is a useful guide for schools implementing character education.

2. Peterson, C., & Seligman, M. E. P. (2004). *Character strengths and virtues: A handbook and classification.* Oxford University Press.

3. Krauss, S. M., Pittman, K. J., & Johnson, C. (2016). *Ready by design: The science (and art) of youth readiness.* The Forum for Youth Investment.

4. Rath, T.; Gallup, Inc. (2007). *StrengthsFinder 2.0.* Gallup Press.

5. Reckmeyer, M., & Robison, J.; Gallup, Inc. (2016). *Strengths-based parenting: Developing your children's innate talents.* Gallup Press.

6. Krauss, S. M. (2021). *Making it: What today's kids need for tomorrow's world.* Jossey-Bass/Wiley.

Chapter 6

1. Maslow, A. H. (1943). A theory of human motivation. *Psychological Review, 50*(4), 370–396. https://doi.org/10.1037/h0054346

2. Wahba, M. A., & Bridwell, L. G. (1976). Maslow reconsidered: A review of research on the need hierarchy theory. *Organizational Behavior and Human Performance, 15*(2), 212–240. https://doi .org/10.1016/0030-5073(76)90038-6

3. Benefits programs are determined and funded by public policy. Because policies and available funding change, these provisions change too. Check out Benefits.gov, a U.S. Government resource where you can search for information on specific benefits. This resource even includes a benefit matching questionnaire.

4. Personal interview with Alex Briscoe on May 6, 2022.

5. Krauss, S. M. (2021). *Making it: What today's kids need for tomorrow's world.* Jossey-Bass/Wiley.

6. Ibid.

7. Volpe, J. D. (2021). *Fight: How Gen Z is channeling their fear and passion to save America.* St. Martin's Press.

8. Harris, N. B. (2019). *The deepest well: Healing the long-term effects of childhood adversity.* Mariner.

9. Wanless, S. (2016). The role of psychological safety in human development. *Research in Human Development, 13*, 6–14. https://doi.org/10.1080/ 15427609.2016.1141283

10. These warning signs come from the U.S. Department of Health & Human Services SAMHSA webpage, "Warning Signs and Risk Factors for Emotional Distress."

11. Mori, Y., Tiiri, E., Khanal, P., Khakurel, J., Mishina, K., & Sourander, A. (2021). Feeling unsafe at school and associated mental health difficulties among children and adolescents: A systematic review. *Children (Basel), 8*(3): 232. Retrieved July 31, 2022, from https://www.ncbi .nlm.nih.gov/pmc/articles/PMC8002666/

12. Enskär, K., Isma, G. E., & Rämgård, M. (2021). Safe environments—Through the eyes of 9-year-old schoolchildren from a socially vulnerable area in Sweden. *Child, 47*(1), 57–69. https://doi.org/10.1111/cch.12809

13. Shean, M., & Mander, D. (2020). Building emotional safety for students in school environments: Challenges and opportunities. In R. Midford, G. Nutton, B. Hyndman, & S. Silburn (Eds.), *Health and education interdependence* (pp. 225–248). Springer.

14. There are three emergency hotlines to memorize if you live in the United States: 911 for physical safety and health emergencies; 988 for mental health and psychological safety emergencies; and 211 for getting connected to resources in a nonemergency situation.

15. Harlow, H. F. (1959). Love in infant monkeys. *Scientific American, 200*(6), 68–75.

16. Allen, K.-A., Gray, D. L., Baumeister, R. F., & Leary, M. R. (2022). The need to belong: A deep dive into the origins, implications, and future of a foundational construct. *Educational Psychology Review, 34*(2), 1133–1156. https://doi .org/10.1007/s10648-021-09633-6

17. Baumeister, R. F., & Leary, M. R. (1995). The need to belong: Desire for interpersonal attachments as a fundamental human motivation. *Psychological Bulletin, 117*(3), 497–529. https:// doi.org/10.1037/0033-2909.117.3.497

18. This advice was shared during an interview with Dr. Mark T. Greenberg, the founding director of the Edna Bennett Pierce Prevention Research Center at Penn State.

19. This advice was shared during an interview with David Martineau, a longtime colleague who has spent his academic and professional career in youth development, group facilitation, social services, and social justice education.

20. Malin, H. (2018). *Teaching for purpose: Preparing students for lives of meaning.* Harvard Education Press.

21. Park, C. L. (2016). Meaning making in the context of disasters. *Journal of Clinical Psychology, 72*(12), 1234–1246. https://doi.org/10.1002/ jclp.22270

22. Tavernier, R., & Willoughby, T. (2012). Adolescent turning points: The association between meaning-making and psychological well-being. *Developmental Psychology*, 48(4), 1058–1068. https://doi.org/10.1037/a0026326

23. Miller, L. (2015). *The spiritual child: The new science of parenting for health and lifelong thriving*. St. Martin's Press.

24. Although these needs fuel child and youth development, I find they also fuel me personally. While these may not be needed for adults to survive, they can dramatically improve our quality of life.

25. Schuman, M. (2017). *History of child labor in the United States—part 2: The reform movement: Monthly labor review: U.S. Bureau of Labor Statistics*. Retrieved August 2, 2022, from https://www.bls.gov/opub/mlr/2017/article/history-of-child-labor-in-the-united-states-part-2-the-reform-movement.htm

26. UNICEF. (n.d.). *History of child rights*. Retrieved August 2, 2022, from https://www.unicef.org/child-rights-convention/history-child-rights

27. I recommend reading *A Paradise Built in Hell: The Extraordinary Communities That Arise in Disaster*, which tells stories of how beauty can emerge from the brokenness of disasters.

Chapter 7

1. American Academy of Pediatrics, American Academy of Child and Adolescent Psychiatry, & Children's Hospital Association. (2021). *AAP-AACAP-CHA declaration of a national emergency in child and adolescent mental health*. Retrieved August 7, 2022, from http://www.aap.org/en/advocacy/child-and-adolescent-healthy-mental-development/aap-aacap-cha-declaration-of-a-national-emergency-in-child-and-adolescent-mental-health/

2. Office of the Surgeon General (OSG). (2021). *Protecting youth mental health: The U.S. Surgeon General's advisory*. U.S. Department of Health and Human Services. http://www.ncbi.nlm.nih.gov/books/NBK575984/

3. Ibid.

4. Anya, K. (2022). *The stolen year*. Hachette Books.

5. NAMI: National Alliance on Mental Illness. (n.d.). *Mental health in schools | NAMI: National Alliance on Mental Illness*. Retrieved August 13, 2022, from https://www.nami.org/Advocacy/Policy-Priorities/Improving-Health/Mental-Health-in-Schools

6. Office of the Surgeon General (OSG). (2021). *Protecting youth mental health: The U.S. Surgeon General's advisory*. U.S. Department of Health and Human Services. http://www.ncbi.nlm.nih.gov/books/NBK575984/

7. Sherman, R. F. (2022, April 5). *Social-emotional learning works. But it cannot replace mental illness care*. EdSurge. https://www.edsurge.com/news/2022-04-05-social-emotional-learning-works-but-it-cannot-replace-mental-illness-care

8. This is especially true for children in foster care. In 2021, the American Academy of Pediatrics reported that one in three children in foster care are put on psychotropic medications. My colleagues who work on foster care policy and advocacy name the mistreatment and overreliance on psychiatric medications as a major problem for children in the child welfare system.

9. I am a teacher and social worker who married a social worker, so our personal network is full of mental health professionals. Many friends and colleagues contributed to this list of common warning signs based on their collective years of experience working with young people.

10. An excellent book that explores how this impacts Black mental health care is Dr. Rheeda Walker's *The Unapologetic Guide to Black Mental Health: Navigate an Unequal System, Learn Tools for Emotional Wellness, and Get the Help You Deserve* (2020).

11. If you live in the United States, you can find a MHFA course at https://www.mentalhealthfirstaid.org/; if you live outside of the United States, check out https://mhfainternational.org/

12. Shatkin, J. P. (2015). *Child & adolescent mental health: A practical, all-in-one guide*. W. W. Norton & Company.

13. McKay, M., Wood, J. C., & Brantley, J. (2019). *The dialectical behavior therapy skills workbook* (2nd ed.). New Harbinger Publications.

14. EMDR Institute—Eye Movement Desensitization and Reprocessing Therapy. (2015, February 15). What is EMDR? https://www.emdr.com/what-is-emdr/

15. To find or become a licensed play therapist, check out the Association for Play Therapy: https://www.a4pt.org/

16. For more information on dance/movement therapy, check out the American Dance Therapy Association: https://www.adta.org/

17. Mullainathan, S., & Shafir, E. (2013). Freeing up intelligence. *Scientific American Mind*, *25*(1), 58–63. https://doi.org/10.1038/scientificamericanmind0114-58

18. American Academy of Child & Adolescent Psychiatry. (2017). *Panic disorder in children and adolescents*. Retrieved August 14, 2022, from https://www.aacap.org/AACAP/Families_and_Youth/Facts_for_Families/FFF-Guide/Panic-Disorder-In-Children-And-Adolescents-050.aspx

19. Blackburn, E., & Epel, E. (2017). *The telomere effect: A revolutionary approach to living younger, healthier, longer*. Grand Central Publishing, Hachette Book Group.

20. Menakem, R. (2017). *My grandmother's hands: Racialized trauma and the pathway to mending our hearts and bodies*. Central Recovery Press.

21. Kabat-Zinn, J. (1990). *Full catastrophe living: Using the wisdom of your body and mind to face stress, pain, and illness*. Dell Publishing.

22. This is a phrase I use with my own kids. We call my son's therapist his "coach" and their sessions are times to learn and practice "tips, tricks, and tools" that might help. When you talk to kids about mental health, pay attention to your language and what messages your words communicate about who they are and what they are experiencing.

23. To learn more about bullet journaling, check out *The Bullet Journal Method: Track the Past, Order the Present, Design the Future* by Ryder Carroll.

24. There isn't a strong empirical base for the benefits of mindfulness in young children. This may be because they do a better job than adults at being present.

25. Three books to read if you want to learn more about brain-and-body mental health connections: *The Healthy Brain Book* by Dr. William Sears and Dr. Vincent M. Fortanasce; *Brain Inflamed* by Dr. Kenneth Bock; and *The End of Mental Illness* by Dr. Daniel G. Amen.

26. Schiraldi, G. R. (2021). *The adverse childhood experiences recovery workbook: Heal the hidden wounds from childhood affecting your adult mental and physical health*. New Harbinger Publications.

27. This protocol has been modified for children and is adapted from *The Adverse Childhood Experience Recovery Workbook*.

28. Kabat-Zinn, J. (1990). *Full catastrophe living: Using the wisdom of your body and mind to face stress, pain, and illness*. Dell Publishing.

29. Ibid.

30. Ratey, J. J., & Hagerman, E. (2008). *Spark: The revolutionary new science of exercise and the brain: Supercharge your mental circuits to beat stress, sharpen your thinking, lift your mood, boost your memory, and much more*. Hachette Books.

31. Kindness is such an important part of supporting young people's mental health and wellness. Lady Gaga's foundation, Born This Way Foundation, has great resources and communications strategies to promote acts of kindness in your community and with kids.

32. Birdsong, M. (2020). *How we show up: Reclaiming family, friendship, and community*. Hachette Books.

Chapter 8

1. According to Bridget Adams, the goal of reduced and waived school fees is equitable access to all activities programming across the school district. Remaining fees are for clubs and sports that are nationally affiliated and require dues. In these cases, Bridget and her team work to subsidize or cover costs for students who need it.

2. While Blossom, Bloom, and Flourish are designed as girls' empowerment clubs; any student who is interested is welcome to participate.

3. McLaughlin, M. W. (2018). *You can't be what you can't see: The power of opportunity to change young lives.* Harvard Education Press.

4. Fisher, J. F., & Fisher, D. (2018). *Who you know: Unlocking innovations that expand students' networks.* Jossey-Bass.

5. Wolfe, R. E., Steinberg, A., & Hoffman, N. (Eds.). (2013). *Anytime anywhere: Students-centered learning for schools and teachers.* Harvard Education Press.

6. Intrator, S. M., & Siegel, D. (2014). *The quest for mastery: Positive youth development through out-of-school programs.* Harvard Education Press.

7. For more on purpose as a basic need, see Chapter 6.

8. Robinson, K. (2009). *The element: How finding your passion changed everything.* Penguin Books.

Chapter 9

1. MENTOR, formerly the National Mentoring Partnership, is a U.S.-based nonprofit started in the 1990s to build a youth mentoring field. MENTOR provides affiliates, communities, youth programs, schools, and individuals with expertise and resources on quality mentoring.

2. Personal interview with Richard Lerner on September 23, 2022.

3. In recent years, MENTOR and CERES Institute have partnered on a concept called *relationship-centered schools*, which centers social health and connections as a priority part of the school structure and educational experience.

4. Varga, S. M., & Zaff, J. F. (2017). *A new framework to advance understanding of relationships and youth development* (p. 14). America's Promise Alliance.

5. Ibid.

6. In my book, *Making It: What Today's Kids Need for Tomorrow's World*, I talk extensively about the importance of social capital and how vital it is

for young people to be ready for and do well in adult life. To further explore the importance of social capital for young people check out the research and writing of Julia Freeland Fisher.

7. Mineo, L. (2017, April 11). Over nearly 80 years, Harvard study has been showing how to live a healthy and happy life. *Harvard Gazette.* https://news.harvard.edu/gazette/story/2017/04/over-nearly-80-years-harvard-study-has-been-showing-how-to-live-a-healthy-and-happy-life/

8. Waldinger, R. (2015). *Robert Waldinger: What makes a good life? Lessons from the longest study on happiness | TED Talk.* https://www.ted.com/talks/robert_waldinger_what_makes_a_good_life_lessons_from_the_longest_study_on_happiness

9. Ibid.

10. Hari, J. (2018). *Lost connections: Why you're depressed and how to find hope.* Bloomsbury.

11. Ibid.

12. Zaraska, M. (2020). *Growing young: How friendship, optimism, and kindness can help you live to 100.* Appetite by Random House.

13. Asher, S. R., & Paquette, J. A. (2003). Loneliness and peer relations in childhood. *Current Directions in Psychological Science, 12*(3), 75–78. https://doi.org/10.1111/1467-8721.01233

14. Pinker, S. (2015). *The village effect: Why face-to-face contact matters* (2nd ed.). Atlantic Books.

15. There are many resources that make this connection clear. If you want dig deeper, I recommend *The Village Effect: Why Face-to-Face Contact Matters* by Susan Pinker.

16. Ginwright, S. A. (2022). *The four pivots: Reimagining justice, reimagining ourselves.* North Atlantic Books.

17. Krauss, S. M., Pittman, K. J., & Johnson, C. (2016). *Ready by design: The science (and art) of youth readiness.* The Forum for Youth Investment.

18. My thinking on this has been deeply influenced by Karen Pittman. Her unpublished paper,

"People, Places, and Possibilities," was instructive for this section.

19.   Search Institute. (2020). *Developmental relationships framework*. Search Institute.

20.   If you want to go deeper on family engagement practices, I recommend *Engage Every Family: Five Simple Principles* by Steve Constantino.

21.   Ripley, A. (2022). *High conflict: Why we get trapped and how we get out*. Simon and Schuster.

22.   Ibid.

23.   These four steps are sometimes described as an ancient Hawaiian practice, but I have not found research to back that up. Rather, this practice and process seem to be inspired by ho'oponopono, but not a historic practice of ho'oponopono.

24.   Krauss, S. M. (2021). *Making it: What today's kids need in tomorrow's world*. Jossey-Bass/Wiley.

Chapter 10

1.   Pinker, S. (2015). *The village effect: Why face-to-face contact matters* (2nd ed.). Atlantic Books.

2.   Krauss, S. M. (2021). *Making it: What today's kids need for tomorrow's world*. Jossey-Bass/Wiley.

3.   Tatum, B. D. (2017). *Why are all the Black kids sitting together in the cafeteria* (2nd ed.). Basic Books.

4.   Miller, C. C., Katz, J., Paris, F., & Bhatia, A. (2022, August 1). Vast new study shows a key to reducing poverty: More friendships between rich and poor. *The New York Times*. https://www.nytimes.com/interactive/2022/08/01/upshot/rich-poor-friendships.html

5.   Pinker, S. (2015). *The village effect: Why face-to-face contact matters* (2nd ed.). Atlantic Books.

6.   Brown, Brené. (2010). *The gifts of imperfection*. Minneapolis, MN: Hazelden Information & Educational Services.

7.   Brown, Brené. (2017). *Braving the wilderness*. London, UK: Vermilion.

8.   Personal interview with Dave Martineau on May 10, 2022.

9.   Ginwright, S. A. (2022). *The four pivots: Reimagining justice, reimagining ourselves*. North Atlantic Books.

10.   Ibid.; Turner, T. (2017). *Belonging: Remembering ourselves home*. Her Own Room Press.

11.   Russell, L. W., & Johnson, D. (2018). *The minority report: St. Louis* (p. 32). NAACP.

12.   Ginwright, S. A. (2022). *The four pivots: Reimagining justice, reimagining ourselves*. North Atlantic Books.

13.   Turner, T. (2017). *Belonging: Remembering ourselves home*. Her Own Room Press.

Chapter 11

1.   Interview and site visit to Kawailoa Youth and Family Wellness Campus on June 6, 2022.

2.   Goodyear-Ka'ōpua, N. (2013). *The seeds we planted: Portraits of a native Hawaiian Charter School*. University of Minnesota.

3.   Personal interview with Cheryl Lupenui on September 9, 2022.

4.   Velasquez-Manoff, M. (2019). Opinion | Want to be less racist? Move to Hawai'i. *The New York Times*. https://www.nytimes.com/2019/06/28/opinion/sunday/racism-Hawai'i.html

5.   Personal interview with Ka'anohiokalā Kalama-Macomber on September 9, 2022.

6.   Personal interview with Noelani Goodyear-Kaopua on September 9, 2022.

7.   Personal interview with Alice Wilson on September 23, 2022.

8.   Information from this section was informed by an interview with Ka'anohiokalā Kalama-Macomber on September 9, 2022.

9.   Brown Brené. (2021). *Atlas of the heart: Mapping meaningful connection and the language of human experience* (1st ed.) New York, NY: Random House.

10.   Interview with Professor Joanna Williams on September 16, 2022.

11. Hernández, L. E., & Darling-Hammond, L. (2022). *Creating identity-safe schools and classrooms* (Report). Learning Policy Institute.

12. The National Scientific Council on Adolescence. (2021). *The intersection of adolescent development and anti-Black racism* (Council Report No. 1). https://developingadolescent.org/

13. Ibid; Jackson, R. G., Coomer, M. N., Sanborn, E., Dagli, C., Hoy, Z. R. M., Skelton, S. M., & Thorius, K. K. (2018). *Teaching towards understandings of intersectionality*. Equity Dispatch. Midwest & Plains Equity Assistance Center (MAP EAC).

14. Ibid.; hooks, b., & powell, j. a. (2015, April 30). *Belonging through connection, connecting through love: Oneself, the other, and the earth*. Othering & Belonging Conference. https://www.youtube.com/watch?v=0sX7fqIU4gQ

15. National Academies of Sciences, Engineering, and Medicine. (2019). *The promise of adolescence: Realizing opportunity for all youth*. The National Academies Press.

16. Interview with Professor Joanna Williams on September 16, 2022.

17. Rivas-Drake, D., Syed, M., Umaña-Taylor, A., Markstrom, C., French, S., Schwartz, S. J., & Lee, R.; Ethnic and Racial Identity in the 21st Century Study Group. (2014). Feeling good, happy, and proud: A meta-analysis of positive ethnic–racial affect and adjustment. *Child Development*, 85(1), 77–102.

18. Tatum, B. D. (2017). *Why are all the Black kids sitting together in the cafeteria* (2nd ed.). Basic Books.

19. If you only have time to read one book on this huge and important topic, I recommend starting with *Why Are All the Black Kids Sitting Together in the Cafeteria? And Other Conversations About Race* by Beverly Daniel Tatum.

20. This is likely true for young people who experience rejection or feel the need to hide other aspects of their identities.

21. National Academies of Sciences, Engineering, and Medicine. (2019). *The promise of adolescence: Realizing opportunity for all youth*. The National Academies Press.

22. Ibid.

23. Interview with Professor Stephen Russell on July 22, 2022.

24. Friedman, J., & Young, J. (2022, August 17). America's censored classrooms. *PEN America*. https://pen.org/report/americas-censored-classrooms/

Chapter 12

1. Van Der Kolk, B. (2014). *The body keeps the score: Brain, mind, and body in the healing of trauma*. Penguin Books.

2. Flais, S. V. (Ed.). (2018). *Caring for your school age child: The complete and authoritative guide* (3rd ed.). Bantam Books Trade Paperback.

3. According to the evaluation, those who indicated being uncomfortable had experienced aggressive pets in the home.

4. Maplewood Richmond Heights School District. (2019). *MRH Home Visit Program: Program Evaluation*. Maplewood Richmond Heights School District.

5. For more on the practice and effectiveness of educator home visits, check out Parent Teacher Home Visits (PTHV), an evidence-based strategy to home visits that focuses on strengthening relationships, shifting mindsets, improving teaching, and bolstering student outcomes. Learn more at https://pthvp.org.

6. Personal interview with Richard Lerner on April 15, 2022.

7. Wolynn, M. (2017). *It didn't start with you: How inherited family trauma shapes who we are and how to end the cycle*. Penguin Random House.

8. To understand the known and possible impacts of COVID-19 and the intersecting racial uprisings and economic upheaval, I recommend Anya Kamenetz's book, *The Stolen Year*. This well-reported book tells the story of the first year of the COVID-19 pandemic and explores the historical context that shaped, framed, and inflamed it.

9. Personal interview with Dr. Pamela Cantor on August 19, 2022.

10. Ibid.

11. National Child Traumatic Stress Network Schools Committee. (2008). *Child trauma toolkit for educators*. National Center for Child Traumatic Stress.

12. Wolynn, M. (2017). *It didn't start with you: How inherited family trauma shapes who we are and how to end the cycle*. Penguin Random House.

13. Ibid.

Chapter 13

1. As of 2022, the oldest recorded person to have lived is Jeanne Calment. Her age at death is somewhat disputed and her life history is fascinating and worth researching. There is general agreement that she died around 120 years old (likely 122); Willingham, E. (2021, May 25). Humans could live up to 150 years, new research suggests. *Scientific American*. https://www.scientificamerican.com/article/humans-could-live-up-to-150-years-new-research-suggests/

2. Dizikes, P. (2016, April 11). *New study shows rich, poor have huge mortality gap in U.S.* MIT News | Massachusetts Institute of Technology. https://news.mit.edu/2016/study-rich-poor-huge-mortality-gap-us-0411

3. Blackburn, E., & Epel, E. (2017). *The telomere effect: A revolutionary approach to living younger, healthier, longer*. Grand Central Publishing, Hachette Book Group.

4. Zaraska, M. (2020). *Growing young: How friendship, optimism, and kindness can help you live to 100*. Appetite by Random House.

5. Krauss, S. M. (2023). Preparing for a 60-year career. In D. L. Blustein & L. Y. Flores (Eds.), *Rethinking work: Essays on building a better workplace*. Routledge.

6. Krauss, S. M. (2021). *Making it: What today's kids need for tomorrow's world*. Jossey-Bass/Wiley.

7. Gratton, L., & Scott, A. (2017). *The 100-year life: Living and working in an age of longevity*. Bloomsbury.

8. Buettner, D., & Skemp, S. (2016). Blue zones. *American Journal of Lifestyle Medicine*, *10*(5), 318–321. https://doi.org/10.1177/1559827616637066

9. Blackburn, E., & Epel, E. (2017). *The telomere effect: A revolutionary approach to living younger, healthier, longer*. Grand Central Publishing, Hachette Book Group.

10. Zaraska, M. (2020). *Growing young: How friendship, optimism, and kindness can help you live to 100*. Appetite by Random House; Levitin, D. J. (2020). *Successful aging: A neuroscientist explores the power and potential of our lives*. Dutton.

11. Krauss, S. M. (2021). *Making it: What today's kids need for tomorrow's world*. Jossey-Bass/Wiley.

12. Levitin, D. J. (2020). *Successful aging: A neuroscientist explores the power and potential of our lives*. Dutton.

13. Personal interview with Amanda Shabowich on October 14, 2022.

14. Personal interview with Peter Bishop on November 5, 2022.

Chapter 14

1. Della Volpe, J. (2021). *Fight: How Gen Z is channeling their fear and passion to save America*. St. Martin's Press.

2. Ginwright, S., & James, T. (2002). From assets to agents of change: Social justice, organizing, and youth development. *New Directions for Youth Development*, *96*, 27–46.

3. Personal interview with Kaʻanohiokalā Kalama-Macomber on September 9, 2022.

4. Weil, Z. (2021). *The world becomes what we teach: Educating a generation of solutionaries*. Lantern Publishing & Media.

5. The Week Junior. (2022, October 28). We hear you! *The Week Junior*, *3*(132), 12–13.

6. Ginwright, S., & James, T. (2002). From assets to agents of change: Social justice, organizing, and youth development. *New Directions for Youth Development*, *96*, 27–46.

7. Levine, P. (2013). *We are the ones we have been waiting for: The promise of civic renewal in America* (1st ed.). Oxford University Press; Personal interview with Robert Sherman on November 11, 2022.

8. Personal interview with Kei Kawashima-Ginsberg on October 14, 2022.

9. Ibid.

10. Personal interview with Alison Malmon on September 20, 2022.

11. Personal interview with Mia Stavarski on September 30, 2022.

12. Mesfin, S. (2022, May 21). Student mental health needs to be a priority in our lives and schools. *Northern Kentucky Tribune*, https://www.kentuckyteacher.org/leadership/guest-columns/2022/05/mental-health-needs-to-be-a-priority-in-our-lives-and-schools/; Personal interview with Rachel Belin on September 30, 2022.

13. Personal interview with Mia Stavarski on September 30, 2022.

14. Personal interview with Rachel Belin on September 30, 2022.

15. Ginwright, S. (2015). *Hope and healing in urban education: How urban activists and teachers are reclaiming matters of the heart*. Routledge.

16. Jimenez, E., Tokunaga, J., & Wolin, J. (2019). *Scan of the field of healing centered organizing: Lessons learned*. The Aspen Institute Forum for Community Solutions.

17. Personal interview with Albert Maldonado on October 21, 2022.

18. Personal interview with Amanda Shabowich on October 14, 2022.

Chapter 15

1. Personal interview with Whitney McNees Gershater on November 4, 2022.

2. Personal interview with Kit Danley on November 3, 2022.

3. Miller, L. (2015). *The spiritual child: The new science of parenting for health and lifelong thriving*. St. Martin's Press.

4. Ibid.

5. Isaacson, W. (2007). *Einstein: His life and universe*. Simon and Schuster; Miller, L. (2015). *The spiritual child: The new science of parenting for health and lifelong thriving*. St. Martin's Press.

6. Prade, C. (2022). Awe in childhood: Conjectures about a still unexplored research area. *Frontiers in Psychology*, *13*, 791534–791534; Bai, Y., Ocampo, J., Gening, J., Chen, S., Benet-Martinez, V., & Monroy, M. (2021). Awe, daily stress, and elevated life satisfaction. *Journal of Personality and Social Psychology: Attitudes and Social Cognition*, *120*(4), 837–860.

7. Paulson, S., Shiota, M. "Lani", Henderson, C., & Filippenko, A. V. (2021). Unpacking wonder: From curiosity to comprehension. *Annals of the New York Academy of Sciences*, *1501*(1): 10–29.

8. Personal interview with Marvin Berkowitz on March 4, 2022. Miller, L. (2015). *The spiritual child: The new science of parenting for health and lifelong thriving*. St. Martin's Press.

9. Ibid.

10. Miller, L. (2015). *The spiritual child: The new science of parenting for health and lifelong thriving*. St. Martin's Press.

11. Ibid.

12. Ibid.

Chapter 16

1. Thanks to Alex Briscoe for introducing me to this study.

2. Werner, E. E., & Smith, R. S. (1977, October 21). *An epidemiologic perspective on some antecedents and consequences of childhood mental health problems and learning disabilities: A report from the Kauai longitudinal study* [Paper presentation]. Modified from a paper presented at the Abramson Research Symposium on Epidemiologic Studies and Child Psychiatry, Annual Meeting of the American Academy of Child Psychiatry, Houston, TX. American Academy of Child Psychiatry.

3. Werner, E. E. (1993). Risk, resilience, and recovery: Perspectives from the Kauai longitudinal study. *Development and Psychopathology*, *5*(4), 503–515. https://doi.org/10.1017/S095457940000612X

4. Werner, E. E. (2005). Resilience and recovery: Findings from the Kauai longitudinal study. *Focal Point: Research, Policy, and Practice in Children's Mental Health, 19*(1), 11–14.

5. Werner, E. E., & Smith, R. S. (1977, October 21). *An epidemiologic perspective on some antecedents and consequences of childhood mental health problems and learning disabilities: A report from the Kauai longitudinal study* [Paper presentation]. Modified from a paper presented at the Abramson Research Symposium on Epidemiologic Studies and Child Psychiatry, Annual Meeting of the American Academy of Child Psychiatry, Houston, TX. American Academy of Child Psychiatry.

6. Ibid.

7. Ibid.

8. Graper, D. (2019). *Ferns: A classic shade garden plant.* South Dakota State University Extension. https://extension.sdstate.edu/ferns-classic-shade-garden-plant#:~:text=Ferns%20are%20a%20natural%20inhabitant,sun%20to%20grow%20their%20best

9. Personal interview with Elliot Washor on February 25, 2022.

10. Darling-Hammond, L., Hernández, L. E., Schachner, A., Plasencia, S., Cantor, P., Theokas, C., & Tijerina, E. (2022). *Design principles for schools: Putting the science of learning and development into action* (p. 182). https://soldalliance .org/design-principles/design-principles-for-schools-putting-the-science-of-learning-and-development-into-action/

11. Personal interview with Laura E. Hernández on November 1, 2022.

12. Darling-Hammond, L., Hernández, L. E., Schachner, A., Plasencia, S., Cantor, P., Theokas, C., & Tijerina, E. (2022). *Design principles for schools: Putting the science of learning and development into action* (p. 182). https://soldalliance .org/design-principles/design-principles-for-schools-putting-the-science-of-learning-and-development-into-action/

13. Social circus schools are an example of where you can find Whole Child, Whole Life principles and practices already in place. To learn more, check out Circus Harmony in St. Louis, Missouri, or the Social Circus Network, which is a part of the American Circus Educators.

Index

CORWIN

A SAGE Publishing Company

CORWIN HAS ONE MISSION: to enhance education through intentional professional learning.

We build long-term relationships with our authors, educators, clients, and associations who partner with us to develop and continuously improve the best evidence-based practices that establish and support lifelong learning.

SPEAKIN

Whole Child, Whole Life is for adults who are doing their best to care for kids at work, in the community, and at home. We want to join you on that journey and support you however we can. We are available to work with you and your team to put the whole child and the whole life principles and practices into action.

WANT TO WORK WITH STEPHANIE?

STEPHANIE MALIA

Through her consulting, Stephanie works "from school house to White House" to put the principles and practices of *Whole Child, Whole Life* into action.

Areas of experience and interest:
- Whole child approaches
- Youth mental health and student supports
- Child and youth well-being
- Youth farthest from opportunity
- Science of learning and development
- Personalized and competency-based learning
- Work-based and community-based learning
- School-community partnerships
- Coalitions, children's cabinets, and collective impact efforts
- State, district, and school policy
- Cross-system partnerships focused on children and education

To learn more, visit **stephaniemaliakrauss.com** or contact **info@stephaniemaliakrauss.com**.

WANT TO WORK WITH MANUEL?

MANUEL S. HERRERA

Manuel offers a variety of workshops and talks on visual thinking, creativity, and sketchnoting. He is available to capture your ideas, professional journey, or presentation in his unique and playful illustration style.

For more information and examples of his work, visit **manueldraws.com** or contact **manuelherrera33@gmail.com**.